EARTH'S MIGHTI

THE AVENGERS

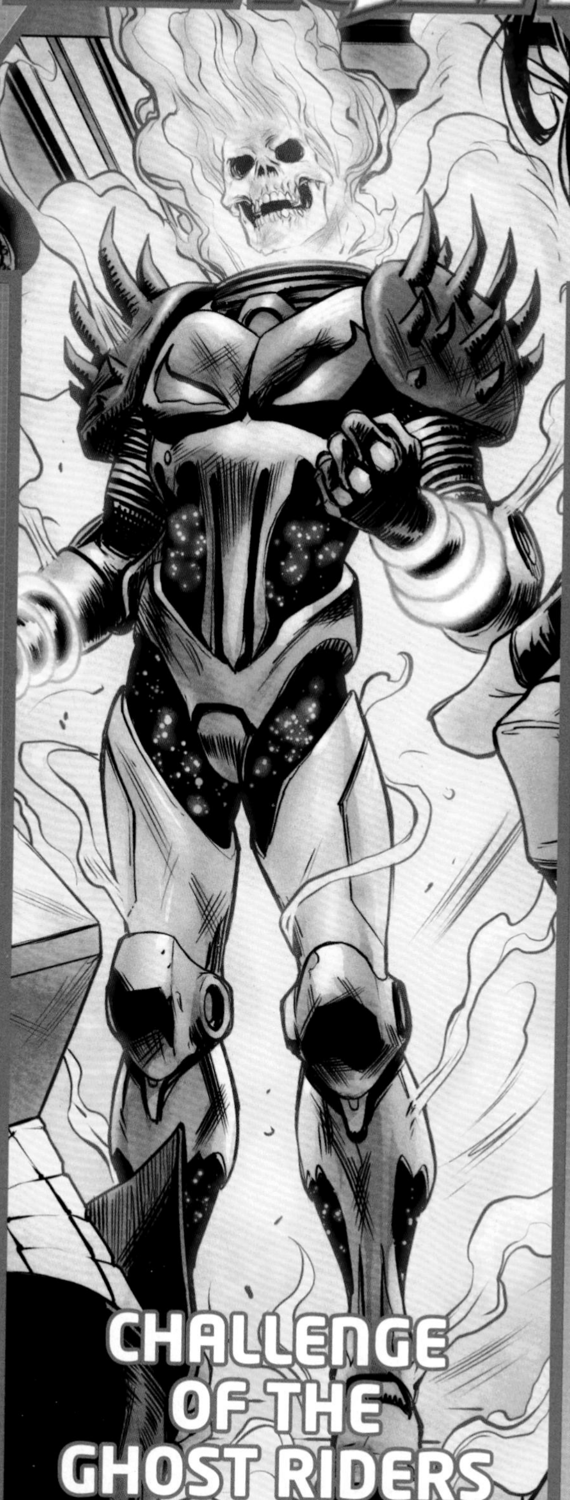

CHALLENGE OF THE GHOST RIDERS

ON A DAY UNLIKE ANY OTHER, A DARK CELESTIAL INVASION LED IRON MAN, THOR AND CAPTAIN AMERICA TO RE-FORM THE AVENGERS, ADDING BLACK PANTHER, CAPTAIN MARVEL, SHE-HULK AND GHOST RIDER TO THEIR RANKS.

THE AVENGERS HAVE BEEN STRUGGLING TO KEEP THE PEACE BETWEEN SEVERAL AGGRESSIVE FACTIONS, INCLUDING RUSSIA'S WINTER GUARD, NAMOR'S DEFENDERS OF THE DEEP AND EVEN THE ARMIES OF THE DARK ELF KING, MALEKITH.

DESPITE T'CHALLA'S GROWING SUSPICIONS OF PHILLIP COULSON AND HIS MORALLY GRAY SQUADRON SUPREME, IT SEEMED THINGS WERE QUIETING DOWN AT AVENGERS MOUNTAIN — WITH THE EXCEPTION OF ROBBIE REYES' DEMONIC CAR, WHICH SEEMS TO HAVE A DANGEROUS MIND OF ITS OWN…

EARTH'S MIGHTIEST HEROES
THE AVENGERS

CHALLENGE OF THE GHOST RIDERS

JASON AARON
WRITER

STEFANO CASELLI
WITH **LUCIANO VECCHIO** (#24)
ARTISTS

JASON KEITH
WITH **ERICK ARCINIEGA** (#25)
COLOR ARTISTS

VC's CORY PETIT
LETTERER

STEFANO CASELLI & **FRANK MARTIN**
COVER ART

SHANNON ANDREWS BALLESTEROS
ASSISTANT EDITOR

ALANNA SMITH
ASSOCIATE EDITOR

TOM BREVOORT
EDITOR

AVENGERS CREATED BY **STAN LEE** & **JACK KIRBY**

COLLECTION EDITOR **JENNIFER GRÜNWALD**
ASSISTANT MANAGING EDITOR **MAIA LOY**
ASSISTANT EDITOR **CAITLIN O'CONNELL**
EDITOR, SPECIAL PROJECTS **MARK D. BEAZLEY**

VP PRODUCTION & SPECIAL PROJECTS **JEFF YOUNGQUIST**
BOOK DESIGNER **ADAM DEL RE**
SVP PRINT, SALES & MARKETING **DAVID GABRIEL**
EDITOR IN CHIEF **C.B. CEBULSKI**

AVENGERS BY JASON AARON VOL. 5: CHALLENGE OF THE GHOST RIDERS. Contains material originally published in magazine form as AVENGERS (2018) #22-25 and ALL-NEW GHOST RIDER (2014) #1. First printing 2019. ISBN 978-1-302-92093-7. Published by MARVEL WORLDWIDE, INC., a subsidiary of MARVEL ENTERTAINMENT, LLC. OFFICE OF PUBLICATION: 1290 Avenue of the Americas, New York, NY 10104. © 2019 MARVEL No similarity between any of the names, characters, persons, and/or institutions in this magazine with those of any living or dead person or institution is intended, and any such similarity which may exist is purely coincidental. Printed in Canada. KEVIN FEIGE, Chief Creative Officer; DAN BUCKLEY, President, Marvel Entertainment; JOHN NEE, Publisher; JOE QUESADA, EVP & Creative Director; TOM BREVOORT, SVP of Publishing; DAVID BOGART, Associate Publisher & SVP of Talent Affairs; Publishing Partnership; DAVID GABRIEL, VP of Print & Digital Publishing; JEFF YOUNGQUIST, VP of Production & Special Projects; DAN CARR, Executive Director of Publishing Technology; ALEX MORALES, Director of Publishing Operations; DAN EDINGTON, Managing Editor; SUSAN CRESPI, Production Manager; STAN LEE, Chairman Emeritus. For information regarding advertising in Marvel Comics or on Marvel.com, please contact Vit DeBellis, Custom Solutions & Integrated Advertising Manager, at vdebellis@marvel.com. For Marvel subscription inquiries, please call 888-511-5480. Manufactured between 12/6/2019 and 1/7/2020 by SOLISCO PRINTERS, SCOTT, QC, CANADA.

9 8 7 6 5 4 3 2 1

22 CHALLENGE OF THE GHOST RIDERS PART 1

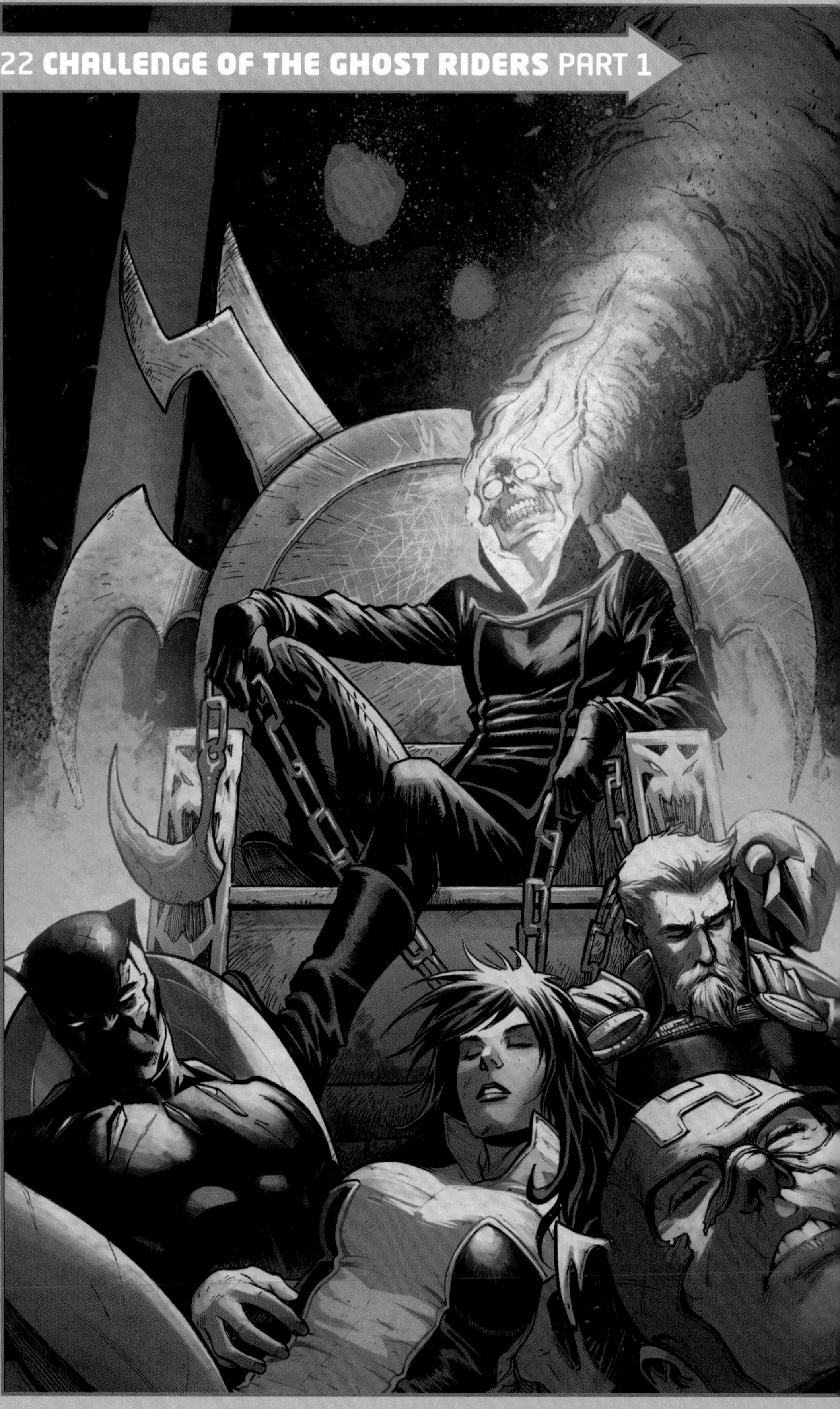

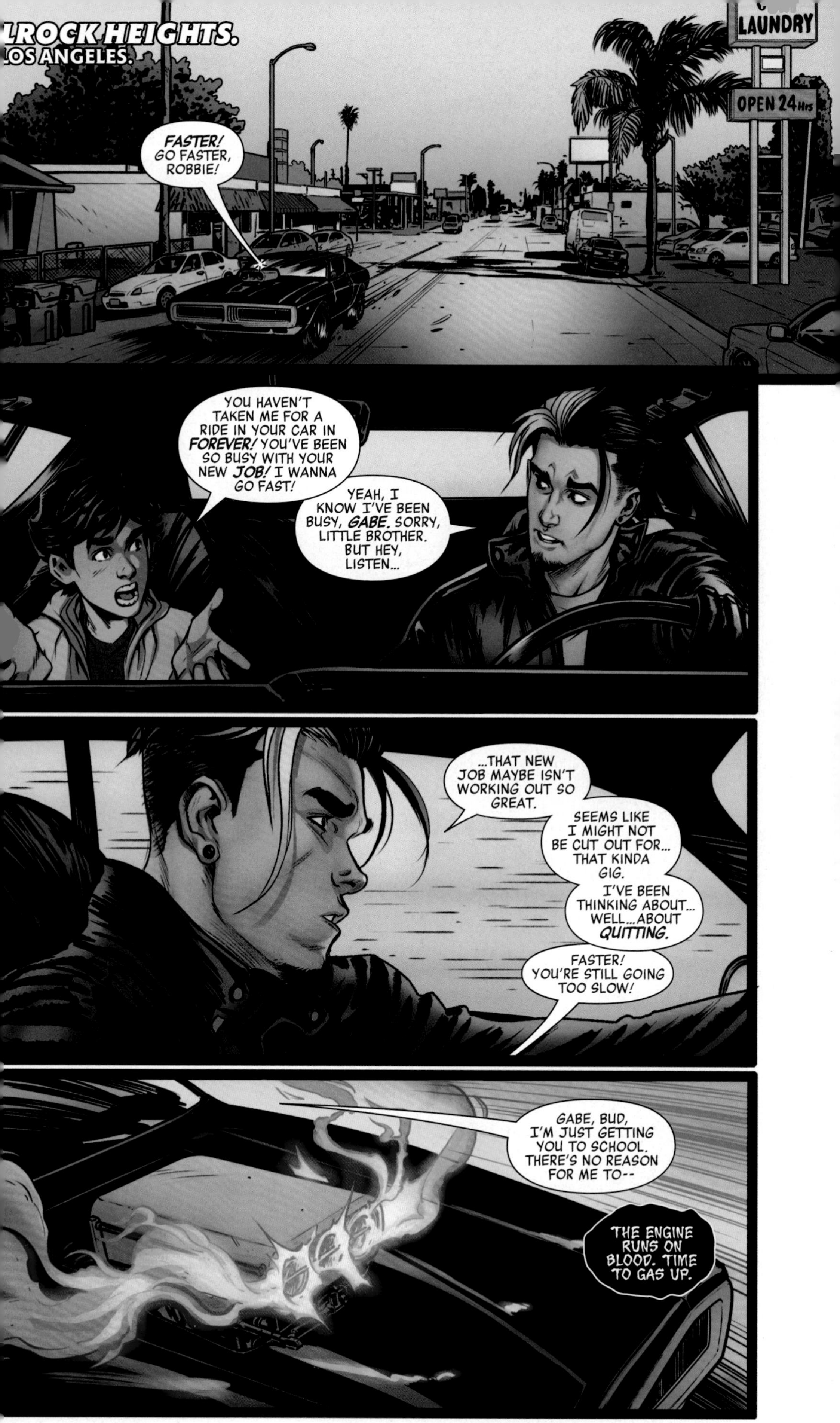

LROCK HEIGHTS.
LOS ANGELES.
LAUNDRY
OPEN 24 HRS
FASTER! GO FASTER, ROBBIE!
YOU HAVEN'T TAKEN ME FOR A RIDE IN YOUR CAR IN FOREVER! YOU'VE BEEN SO BUSY WITH YOUR NEW JOB! I WANNA GO FAST!
YEAH, I KNOW I'VE BEEN BUSY, GABE. SORRY, LITTLE BROTHER. BUT HEY, LISTEN...
...THAT NEW JOB MAYBE ISN'T WORKING OUT SO GREAT.
SEEMS LIKE I MIGHT NOT BE CUT OUT FOR... THAT KINDA GIG.
I'VE BEEN THINKING ABOUT... WELL...ABOUT QUITTING.
FASTER! YOU'RE STILL GOING TOO SLOW!
GABE, BUD, I'M JUST GETTING YOU TO SCHOOL. THERE'S NO REASON FOR ME TO--
THE ENGINE RUNS ON BLOOD. TIME TO GAS UP.

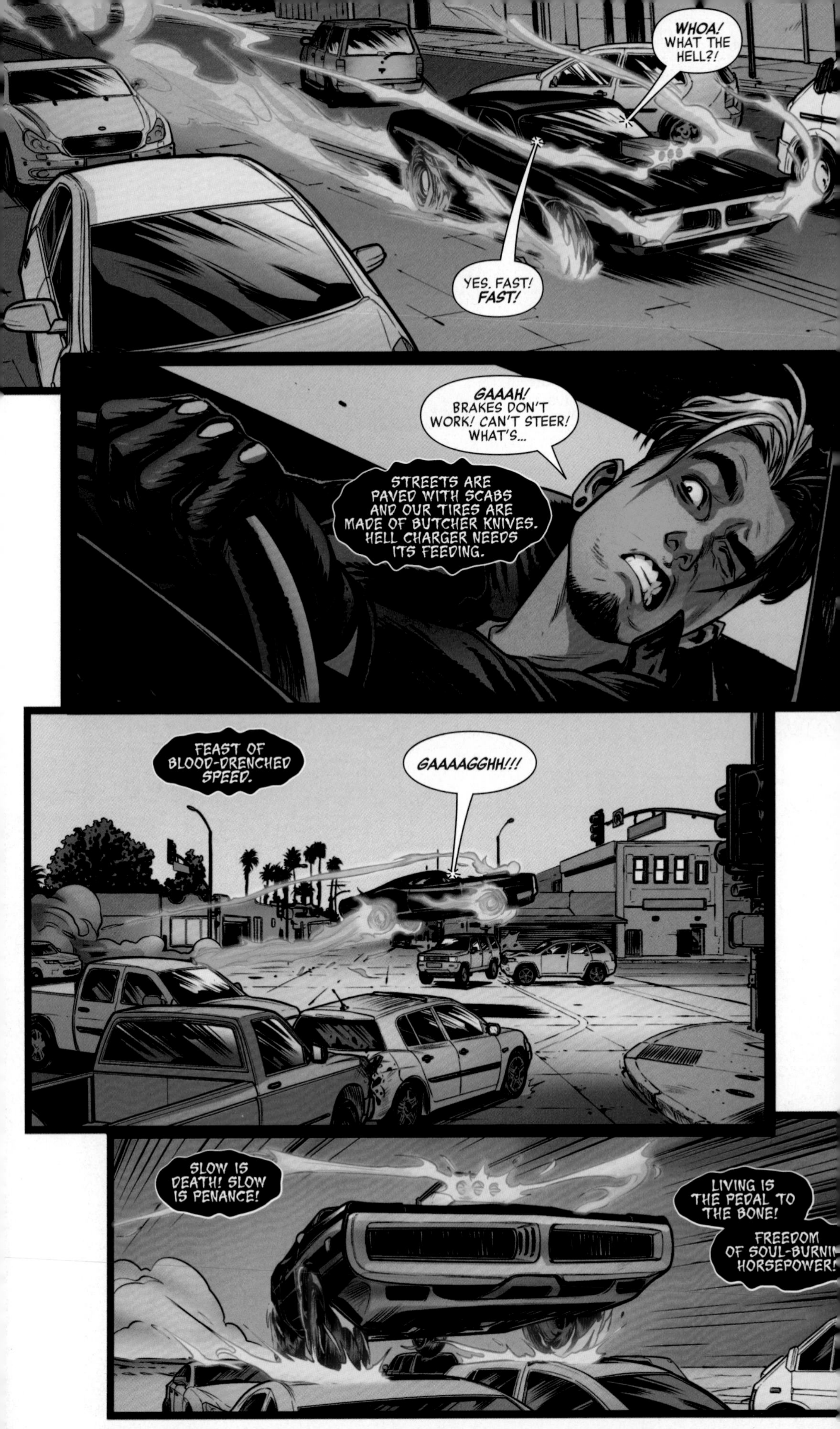
WHOA! WHAT THE HELL?!
YES. FAST! FAST!
GAAAH! BRAKES DON'T WORK! CAN'T STEER! WHAT'S...
STREETS ARE PAVED WITH SCABS AND OUR TIRES ARE MADE OF BUTCHER KNIVES. HELL CHARGER NEEDS ITS FEEDING.
FEAST OF BLOOD-DRENCHED SPEED.
GAAAAGGHH!!!
SLOW IS DEATH! SLOW IS PENANCE!
LIVING IS THE PEDAL TO THE BONE!
FREEDOM OF SOUL-BURNI HORSEPOWER!

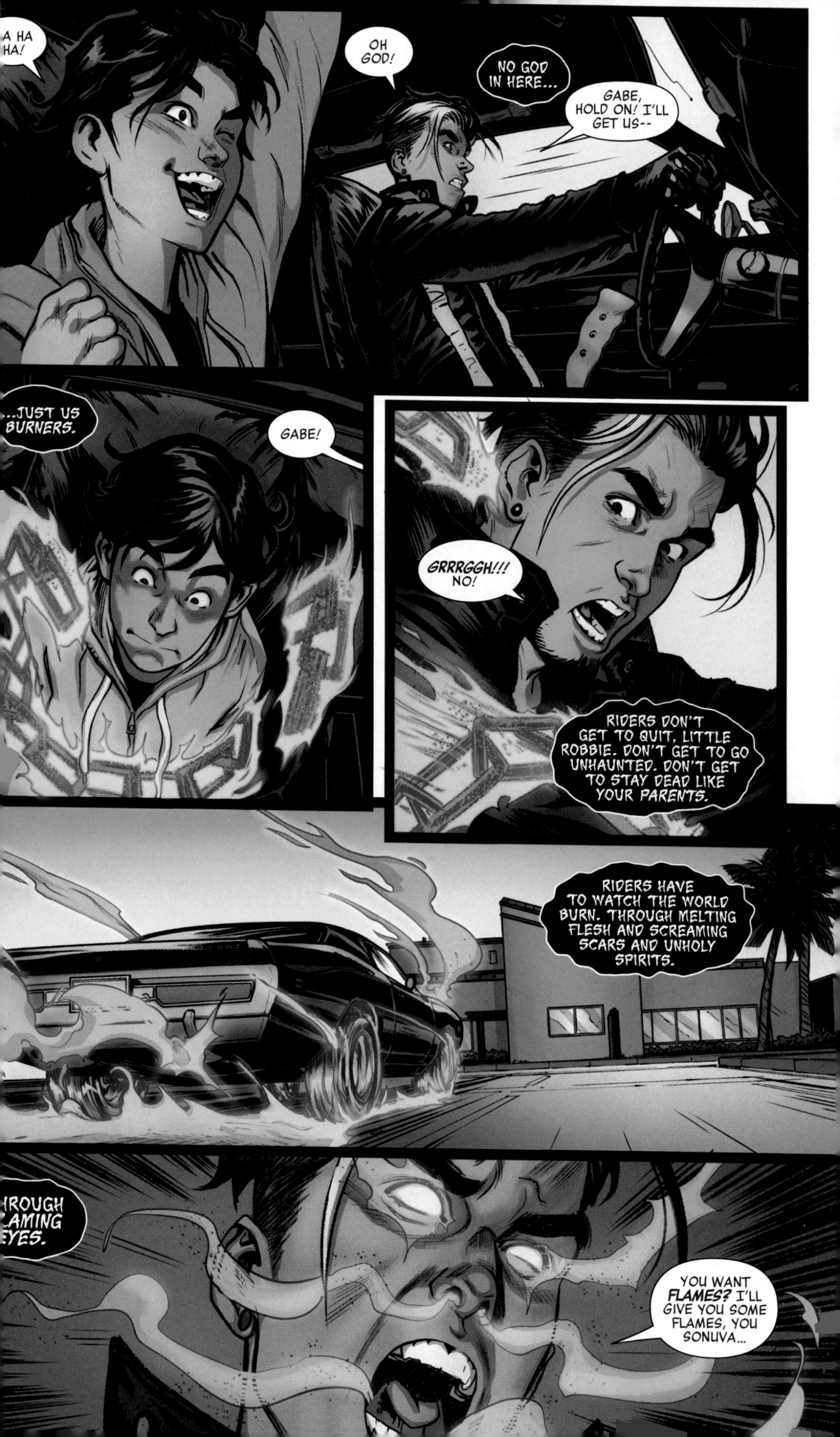
A HA
HA!
OH
GOD!
NO GOD
IN HERE...
GABE,
HOLD ON! I'LL
GET US--
...JUST US
BURNERS.
GABE!
GRRRGGH!!!
NO!
RIDERS DON'T
GET TO QUIT, LITTLE
ROBBIE. DON'T GET TO GO
UNHAUNTED. DON'T GET
TO STAY DEAD LIKE
YOUR PARENTS.
RIDERS HAVE
TO WATCH THE WORLD
BURN. THROUGH MELTING
FLESH AND SCREAMING
SCARS AND UNHOLY
SPIRITS.
HROUGH
LAMING
EYES.
YOU WANT
FLAMES? I'LL
GIVE YOU SOME
FLAMES, YOU
SONUVA...

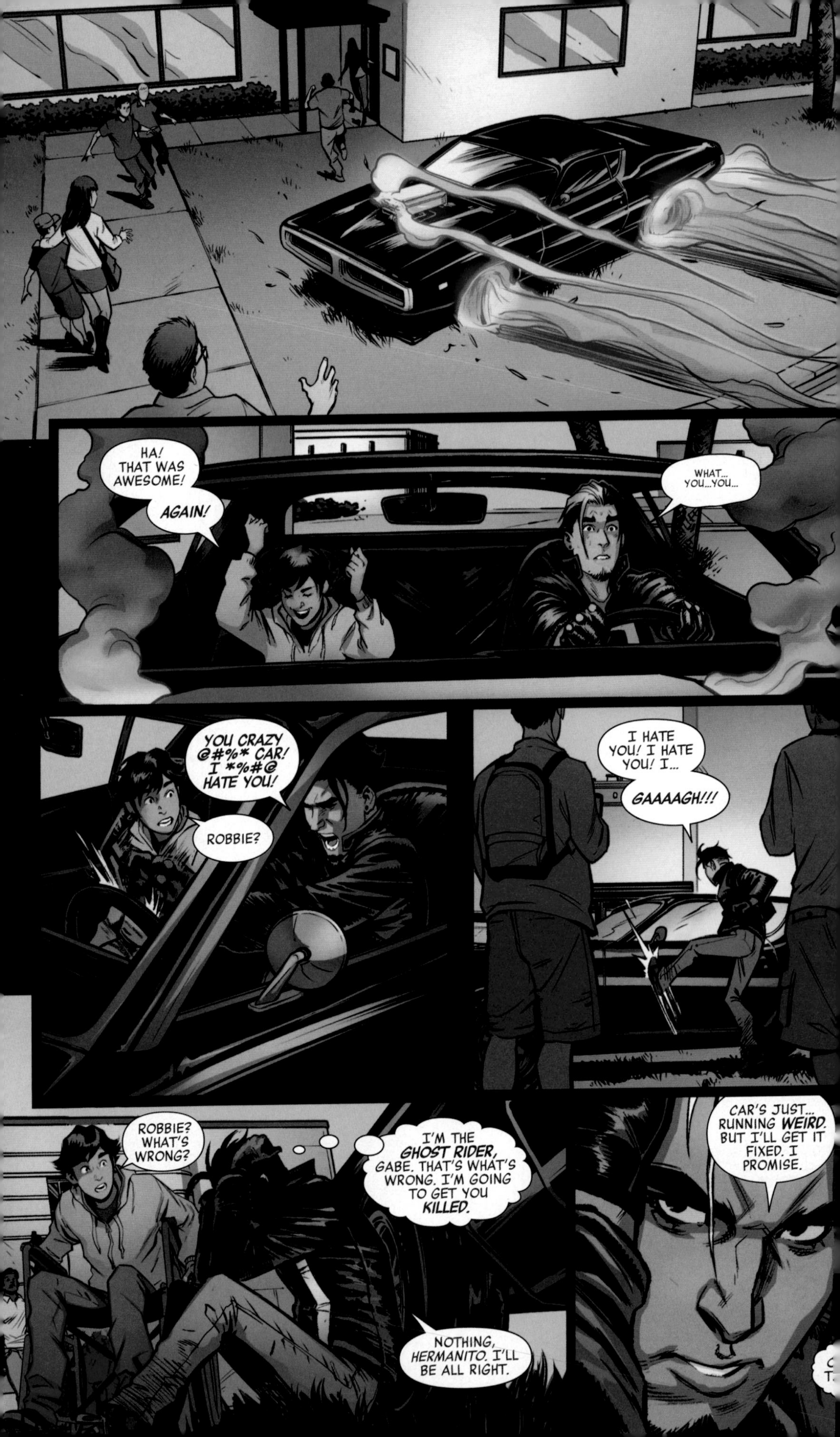
HA! THAT WAS AWESOME!
AGAIN!
WHAT... YOU...YOU...
YOU CRAZY @#%* CAR! I *%#@ HATE YOU!
ROBBIE?
I HATE YOU! I HATE YOU! I...
GAAAAGH!!!
ROBBIE? WHAT'S WRONG?
I'M THE GHOST RIDER, GABE. THAT'S WHAT'S WRONG. I'M GOING TO GET YOU KILLED.
NOTHING, HERMANITO. I'LL BE ALL RIGHT.
CAR'S JUST... RUNNING WEIRD. BUT I'LL GET IT FIXED. I PROMISE.

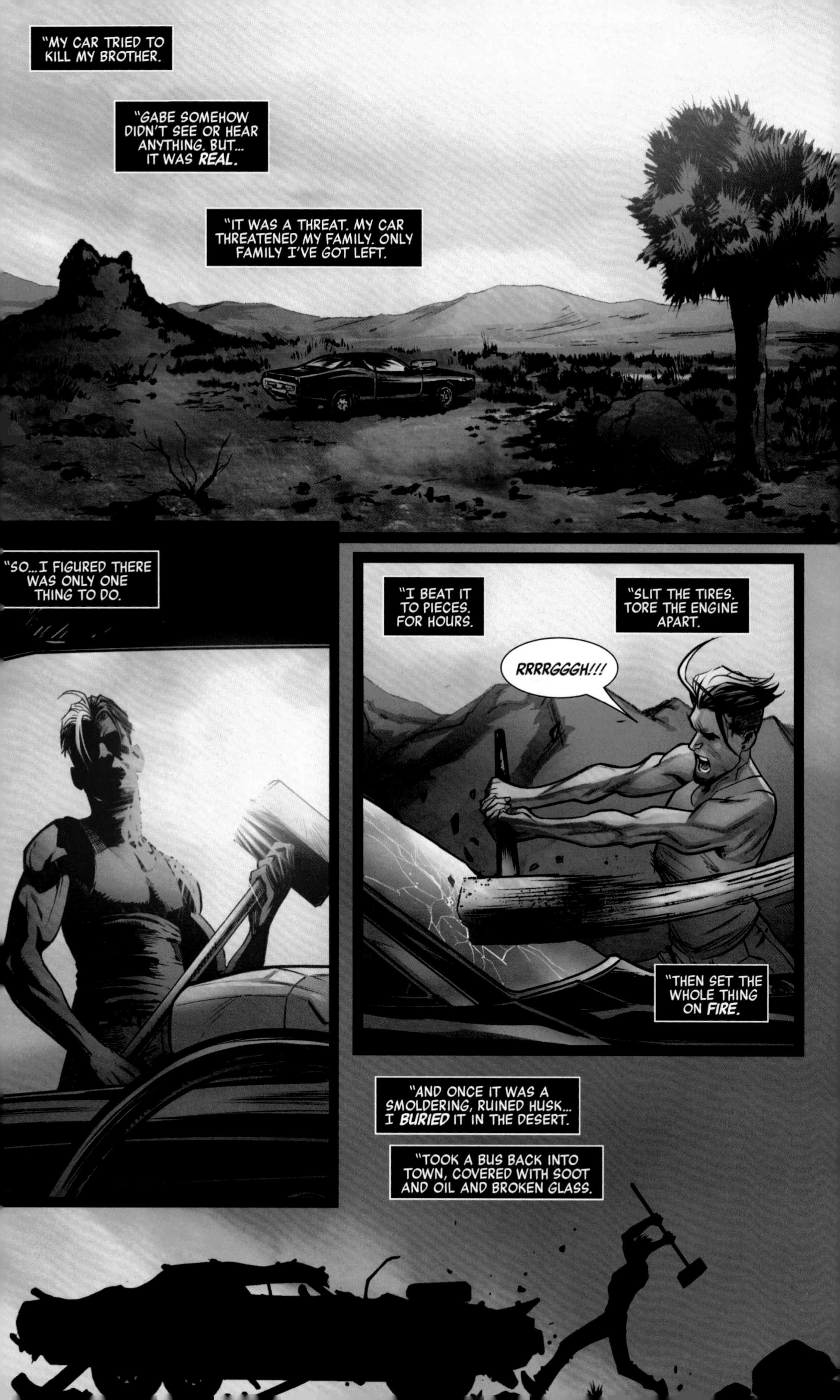
"MY CAR TRIED TO KILL MY BROTHER.
"GABE SOMEHOW DIDN'T SEE OR HEAR ANYTHING. BUT... IT WAS **REAL.**
"IT WAS A THREAT. MY CAR THREATENED MY FAMILY. ONLY FAMILY I'VE GOT LEFT.
"SO...I FIGURED THERE WAS ONLY ONE THING TO DO.
"I BEAT IT TO PIECES. FOR HOURS.
"SLIT THE TIRES. TORE THE ENGINE APART.
RRRRGGGH!!!
"THEN SET THE WHOLE THING ON **FIRE.**
"AND ONCE IT WAS A SMOLDERING, RUINED HUSK... I **BURIED** IT IN THE DESERT.
"TOOK A BUS BACK INTO TOWN, COVERED WITH SOOT AND OIL AND BROKEN GLASS.

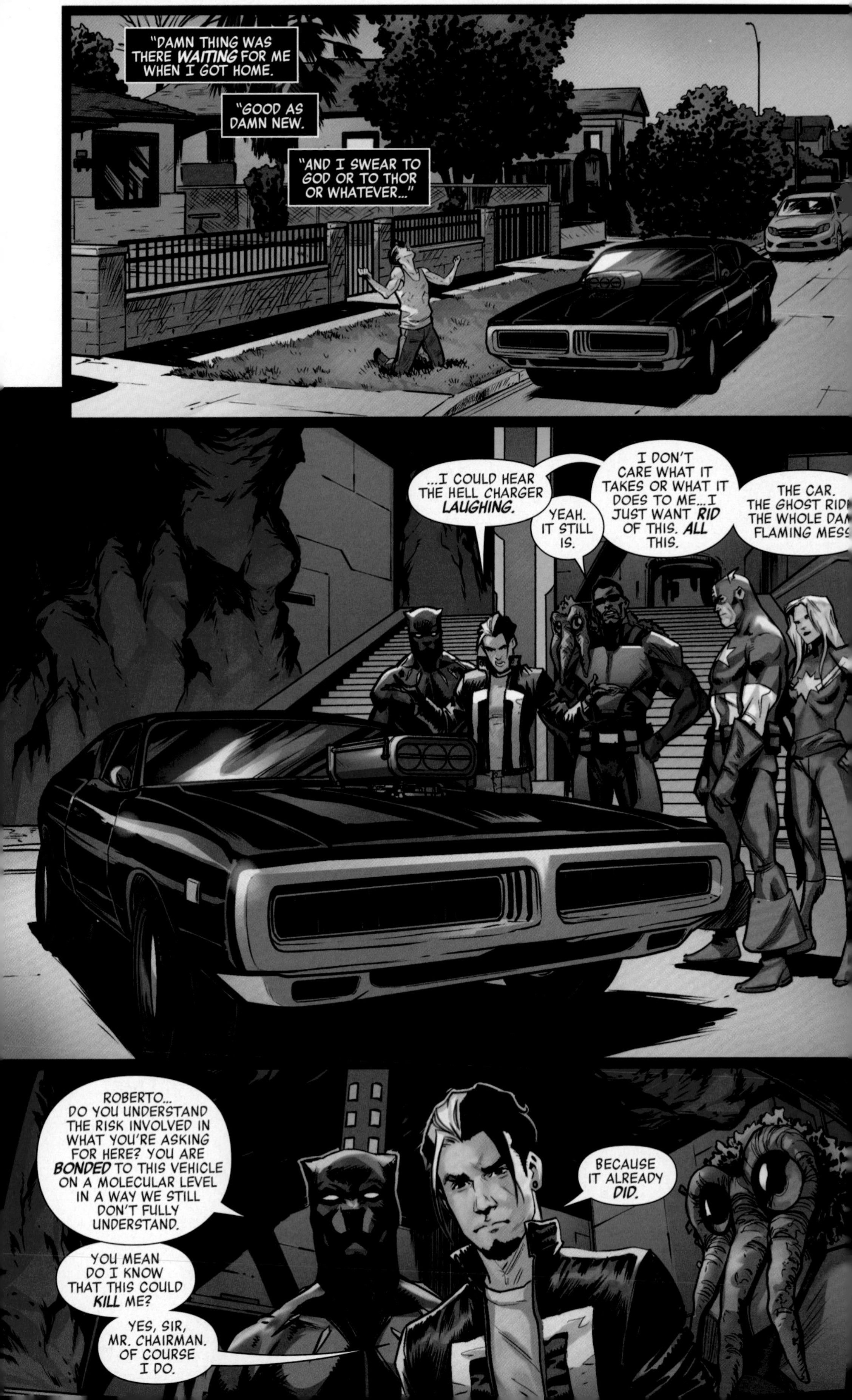
"DAMN THING WAS THERE *WAITING* FOR ME WHEN I GOT HOME.
"GOOD AS DAMN NEW.
"AND I SWEAR TO GOD OR TO THOR OR WHATEVER..."
...I COULD HEAR THE HELL CHARGER *LAUGHING.*
YEAH. IT STILL IS.
I DON'T CARE WHAT IT TAKES OR WHAT IT DOES TO ME...I JUST WANT *RID* OF THIS. *ALL* THIS.
THE CAR. THE GHOST RID THE WHOLE DAM FLAMING MESS
ROBERTO... DO YOU UNDERSTAND THE RISK INVOLVED IN WHAT YOU'RE ASKING FOR HERE? YOU ARE *BONDED* TO THIS VEHICLE ON A MOLECULAR LEVEL IN A WAY WE STILL DON'T FULLY UNDERSTAND.
YOU MEAN DO I KNOW THAT THIS COULD *KILL* ME?
YES, SIR, MR. CHAIRMAN. OF COURSE I DO.
BECAUSE IT ALREADY *DID.*

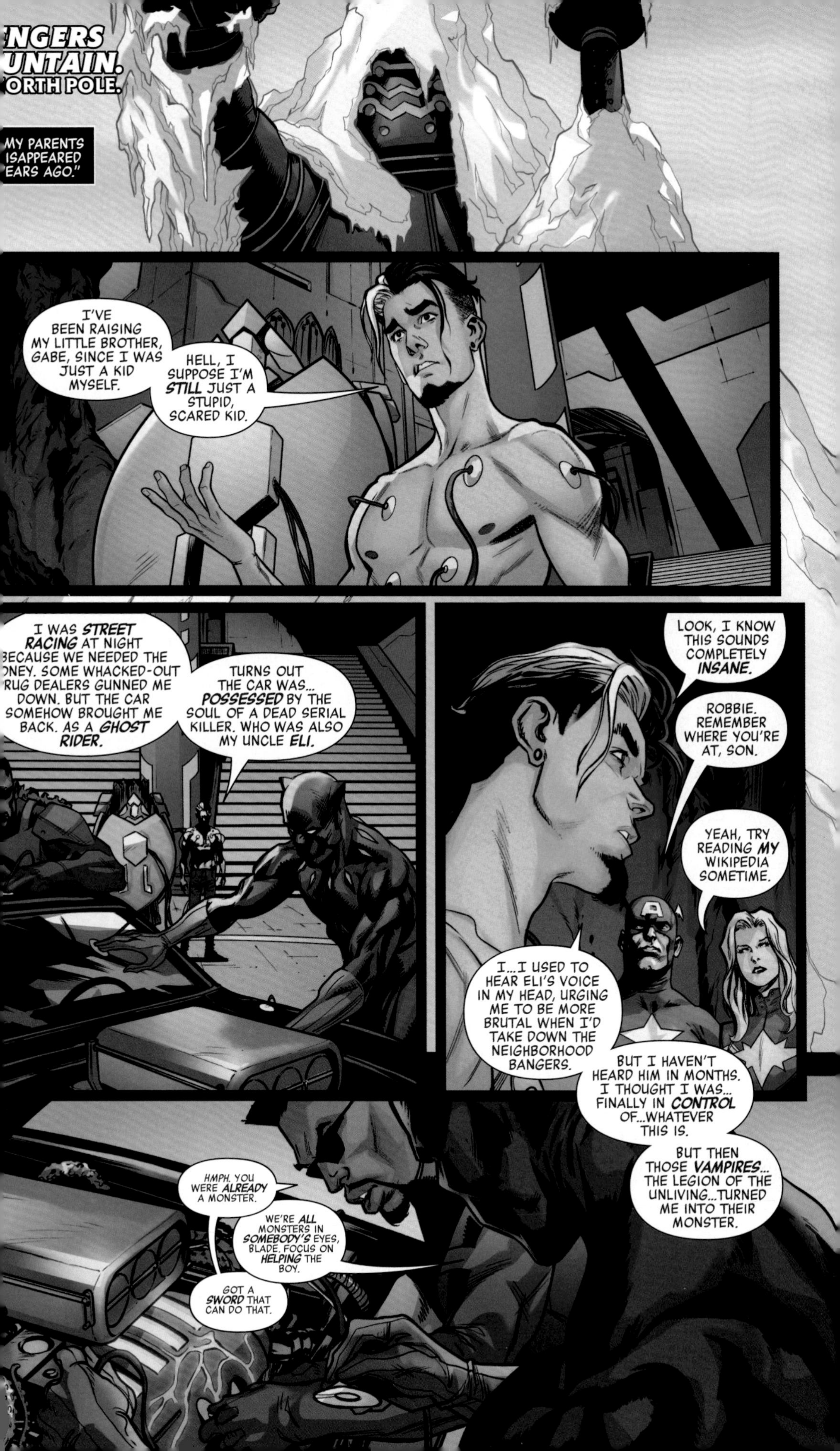

NGERS
UNTAIN.
ORTH POLE.
MY PARENTS
ISAPPEARED
EARS AGO."
I'VE BEEN RAISING MY LITTLE BROTHER, GABE, SINCE I WAS JUST A KID MYSELF.
HELL, I SUPPOSE I'M STILL JUST A STUPID, SCARED KID.
I WAS STREET RACING AT NIGHT BECAUSE WE NEEDED THE ONEY. SOME WHACKED-OUT RUG DEALERS GUNNED ME DOWN. BUT THE CAR SOMEHOW BROUGHT ME BACK. AS A GHOST RIDER.
TURNS OUT THE CAR WAS... POSSESSED BY THE SOUL OF A DEAD SERIAL KILLER. WHO WAS ALSO MY UNCLE ELI.
LOOK, I KNOW THIS SOUNDS COMPLETELY INSANE.
ROBBIE. REMEMBER WHERE YOU'RE AT, SON.
YEAH, TRY READING MY WIKIPEDIA SOMETIME.
I...I USED TO HEAR ELI'S VOICE IN MY HEAD, URGING ME TO BE MORE BRUTAL WHEN I'D TAKE DOWN THE NEIGHBORHOOD BANGERS.
BUT I HAVEN'T HEARD HIM IN MONTHS. I THOUGHT I WAS... FINALLY IN CONTROL OF...WHATEVER THIS IS.
BUT THEN THOSE VAMPIRES... THE LEGION OF THE UNLIVING...TURNED ME INTO THEIR MONSTER.
HMPH. YOU WERE ALREADY A MONSTER.
WE'RE ALL MONSTERS IN SOMEBODY'S EYES, BLADE. FOCUS ON HELPING THE BOY.
GOT A SWORD THAT CAN DO THAT.

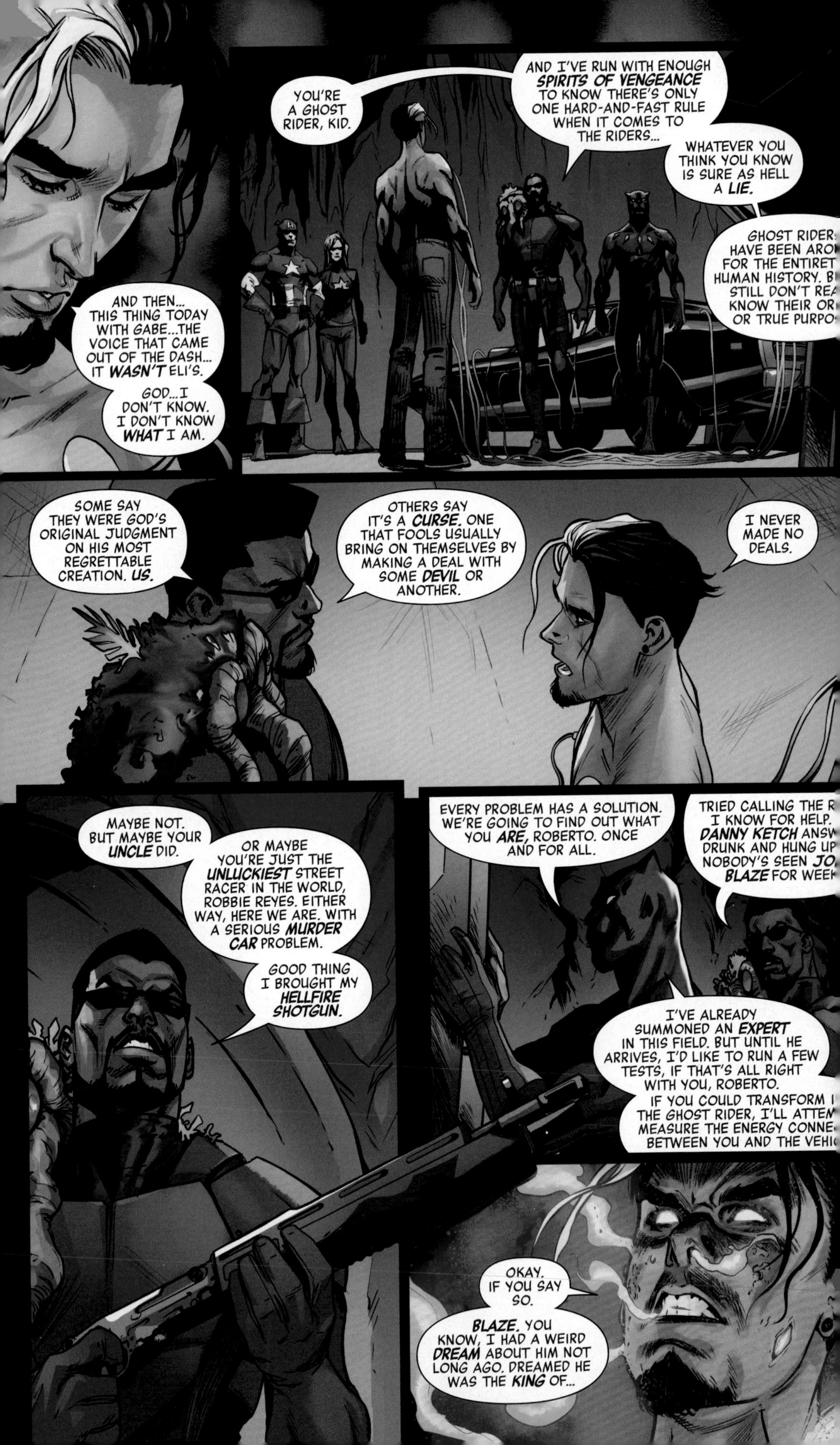
YOU'RE A GHOST RIDER, KID.
AND I'VE RUN WITH ENOUGH SPIRITS OF VENGEANCE TO KNOW THERE'S ONLY ONE HARD-AND-FAST RULE WHEN IT COMES TO THE RIDERS...
WHATEVER YOU THINK YOU KNOW IS SURE AS HELL A LIE.
GHOST RIDERS HAVE BEEN ARO FOR THE ENTIRET HUMAN HISTORY. B STILL DON'T REA KNOW THEIR OR OR TRUE PURPO
AND THEN... THIS THING TODAY WITH GABE...THE VOICE THAT CAME OUT OF THE DASH... IT WASN'T ELI'S.
GOD...I DON'T KNOW. I DON'T KNOW WHAT I AM.
SOME SAY THEY WERE GOD'S ORIGINAL JUDGMENT ON HIS MOST REGRETTABLE CREATION. US.
OTHERS SAY IT'S A CURSE. ONE THAT FOOLS USUALLY BRING ON THEMSELVES BY MAKING A DEAL WITH SOME DEVIL OR ANOTHER.
I NEVER MADE NO DEALS.
MAYBE NOT. BUT MAYBE YOUR UNCLE DID.
OR MAYBE YOU'RE JUST THE UNLUCKIEST STREET RACER IN THE WORLD, ROBBIE REYES. EITHER WAY, HERE WE ARE. WITH A SERIOUS MURDER CAR PROBLEM.
GOOD THING I BROUGHT MY HELLFIRE SHOTGUN.
EVERY PROBLEM HAS A SOLUTION. WE'RE GOING TO FIND OUT WHAT YOU ARE, ROBERTO. ONCE AND FOR ALL.
TRIED CALLING THE R I KNOW FOR HELP. DANNY KETCH ANSW DRUNK AND HUNG UP NOBODY'S SEEN JO BLAZE FOR WEEK
I'VE ALREADY SUMMONED AN EXPERT IN THIS FIELD. BUT UNTIL HE ARRIVES, I'D LIKE TO RUN A FEW TESTS, IF THAT'S ALL RIGHT WITH YOU, ROBERTO.
IF YOU COULD TRANSFORM I THE GHOST RIDER, I'LL ATTEM MEASURE THE ENERGY CONNE BETWEEN YOU AND THE VEHI
OKAY. IF YOU SAY SO.
BLAZE. YOU KNOW, I HAD A WEIRD DREAM ABOUT HIM NOT LONG AGO. DREAMED HE WAS THE KING OF...

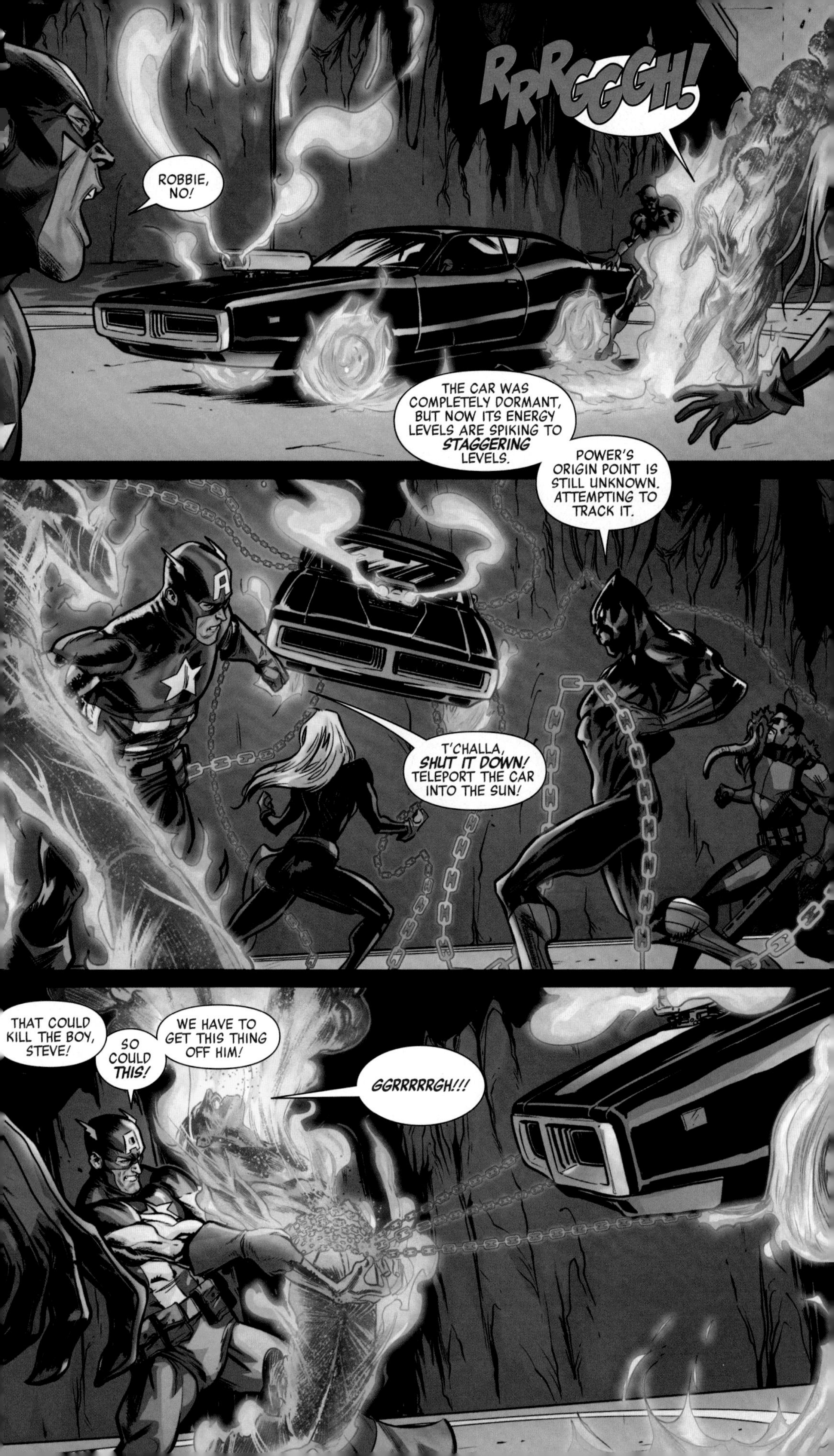
RRRGGGH!
ROBBIE, NO!
THE CAR WAS COMPLETELY DORMANT, BUT NOW ITS ENERGY LEVELS ARE SPIKING TO STAGGERING LEVELS.
POWER'S ORIGIN POINT IS STILL UNKNOWN. ATTEMPTING TO TRACK IT.
T'CHALLA, SHUT IT DOWN! TELEPORT THE CAR INTO THE SUN!
THAT COULD KILL THE BOY, STEVE!
SO COULD THIS!
WE HAVE TO GET THIS THING OFF HIM!
GGRRRRRGH!!!

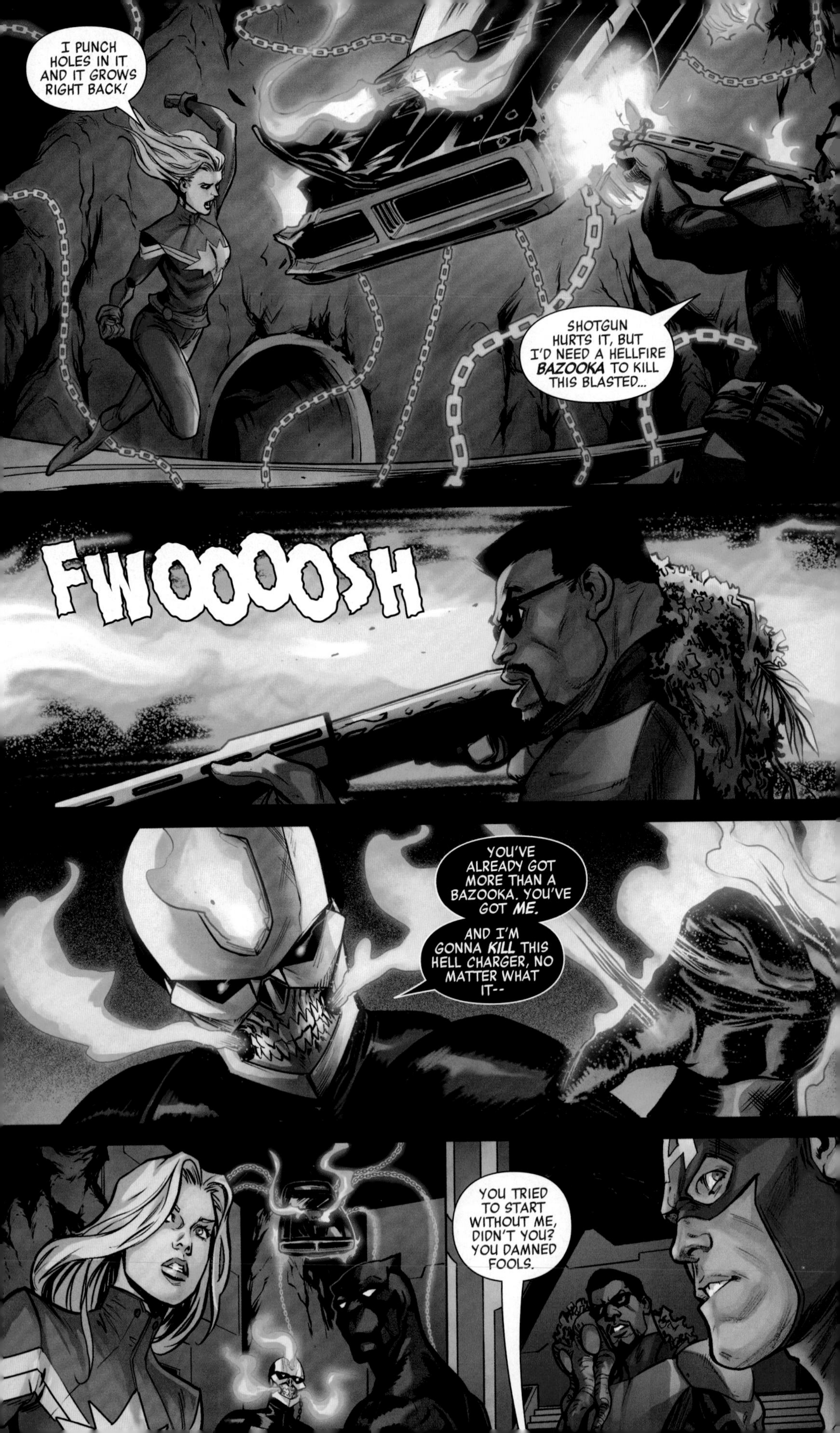
I PUNCH HOLES IN IT AND IT GROWS RIGHT BACK!
SHOTGUN HURTS IT, BUT I'D NEED A HELLFIRE BAZOOKA TO KILL THIS BLASTED...
FWOOOOSH
YOU'VE ALREADY GOT MORE THAN A BAZOOKA. YOU'VE GOT ME.
AND I'M GONNA KILL THIS HELL CHARGER, NO MATTER WHAT IT--
YOU TRIED TO START WITHOUT ME, DIDN'T YOU? YOU DAMNED FOOLS.

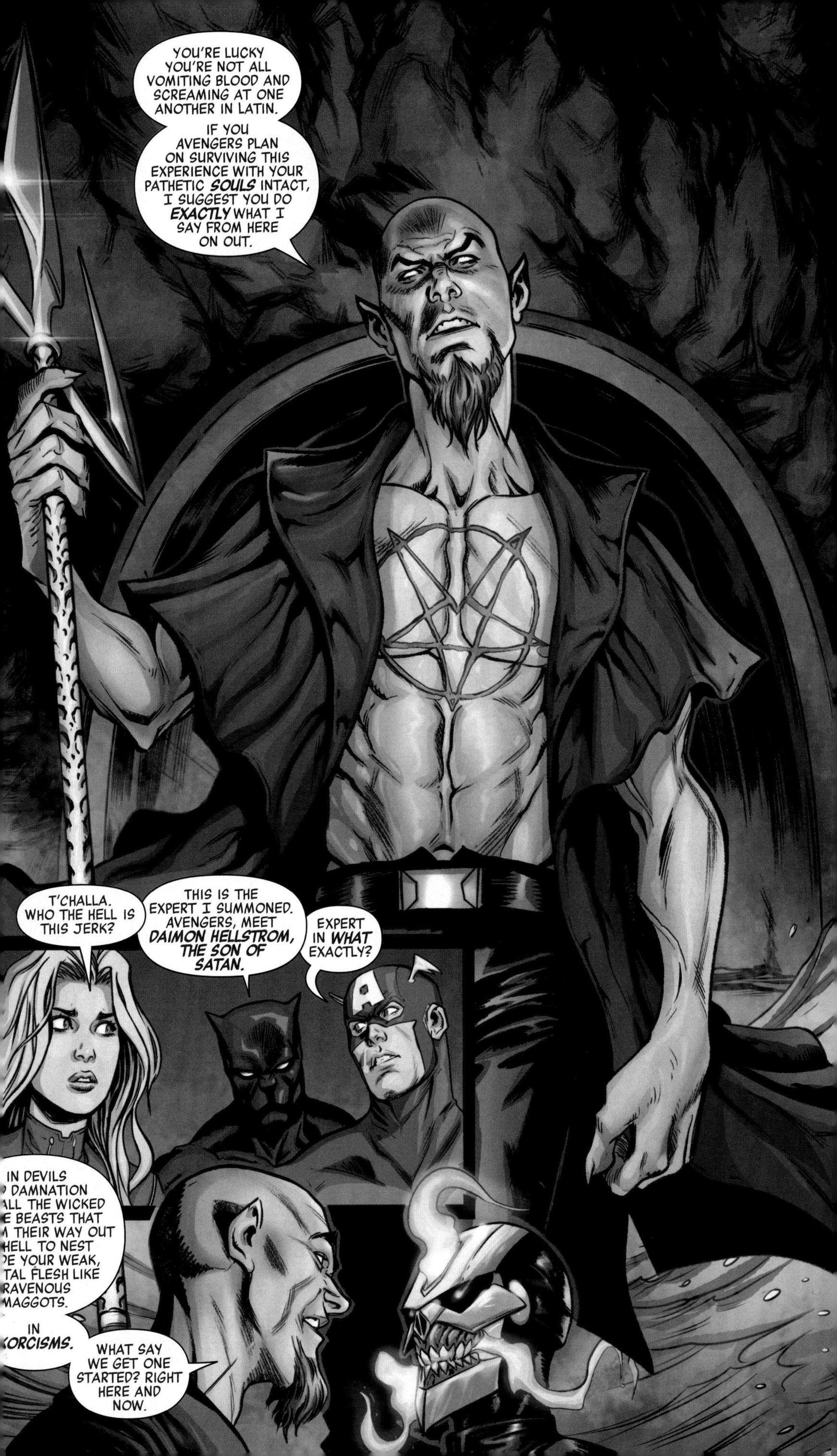
YOU'RE LUCKY YOU'RE NOT ALL VOMITING BLOOD AND SCREAMING AT ONE ANOTHER IN LATIN.
IF YOU AVENGERS PLAN ON SURVIVING THIS EXPERIENCE WITH YOUR PATHETIC SOULS INTACT, I SUGGEST YOU DO EXACTLY WHAT I SAY FROM HERE ON OUT.
T'CHALLA. WHO THE HELL IS THIS JERK?
THIS IS THE EXPERT I SUMMONED. AVENGERS, MEET DAIMON HELLSTROM, THE SON OF SATAN.
EXPERT IN WHAT EXACTLY?
IN DEVILS DAMNATION THE WICKED BEASTS THAT THEIR WAY OUT HELL TO NEST YOUR WEAK, FLESH LIKE RAVENOUS MAGGOTS.
IN
WHAT SAY WE GET ONE STARTED? RIGHT HERE AND NOW.

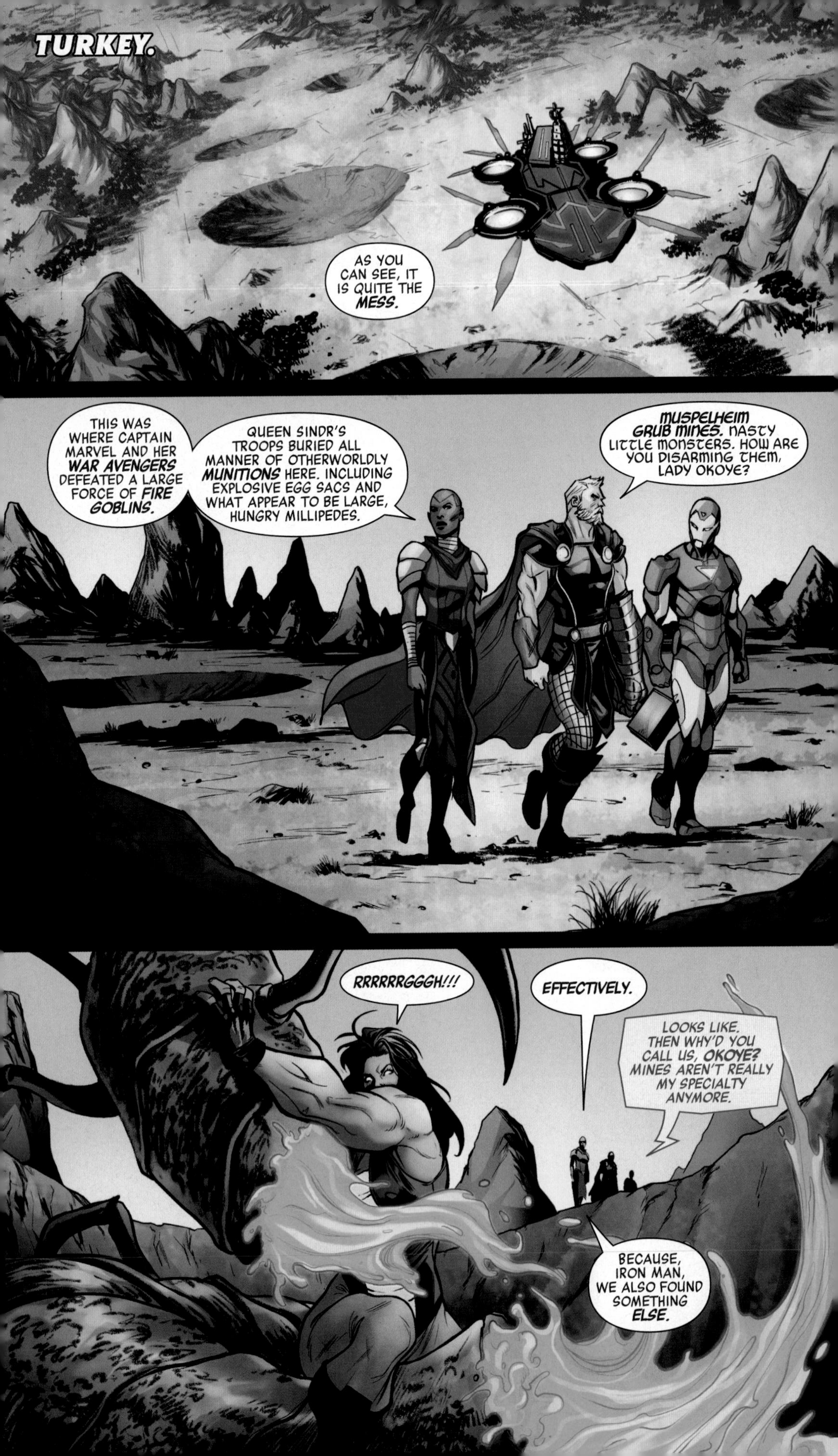
TURKEY.
AS YOU CAN SEE, IT IS QUITE THE MESS.
THIS WAS WHERE CAPTAIN MARVEL AND HER WAR AVENGERS DEFEATED A LARGE FORCE OF FIRE GOBLINS.
QUEEN SINDR'S TROOPS BURIED ALL MANNER OF OTHERWORLDLY MUNITIONS HERE. INCLUDING EXPLOSIVE EGG SACS AND WHAT APPEAR TO BE LARGE, HUNGRY MILLIPEDES.
MUSPELHEIM GRUB MINES. NASTY LITTLE MONSTERS. HOW ARE YOU DISARMING THEM, LADY OKOYE?
RRRRRRGGGH!!!
EFFECTIVELY.
LOOKS LIKE. THEN WHY'D YOU CALL US, OKOYE? MINES AREN'T REALLY MY SPECIALTY ANYMORE.
BECAUSE, IRON MAN, WE ALSO FOUND SOMETHING ELSE.

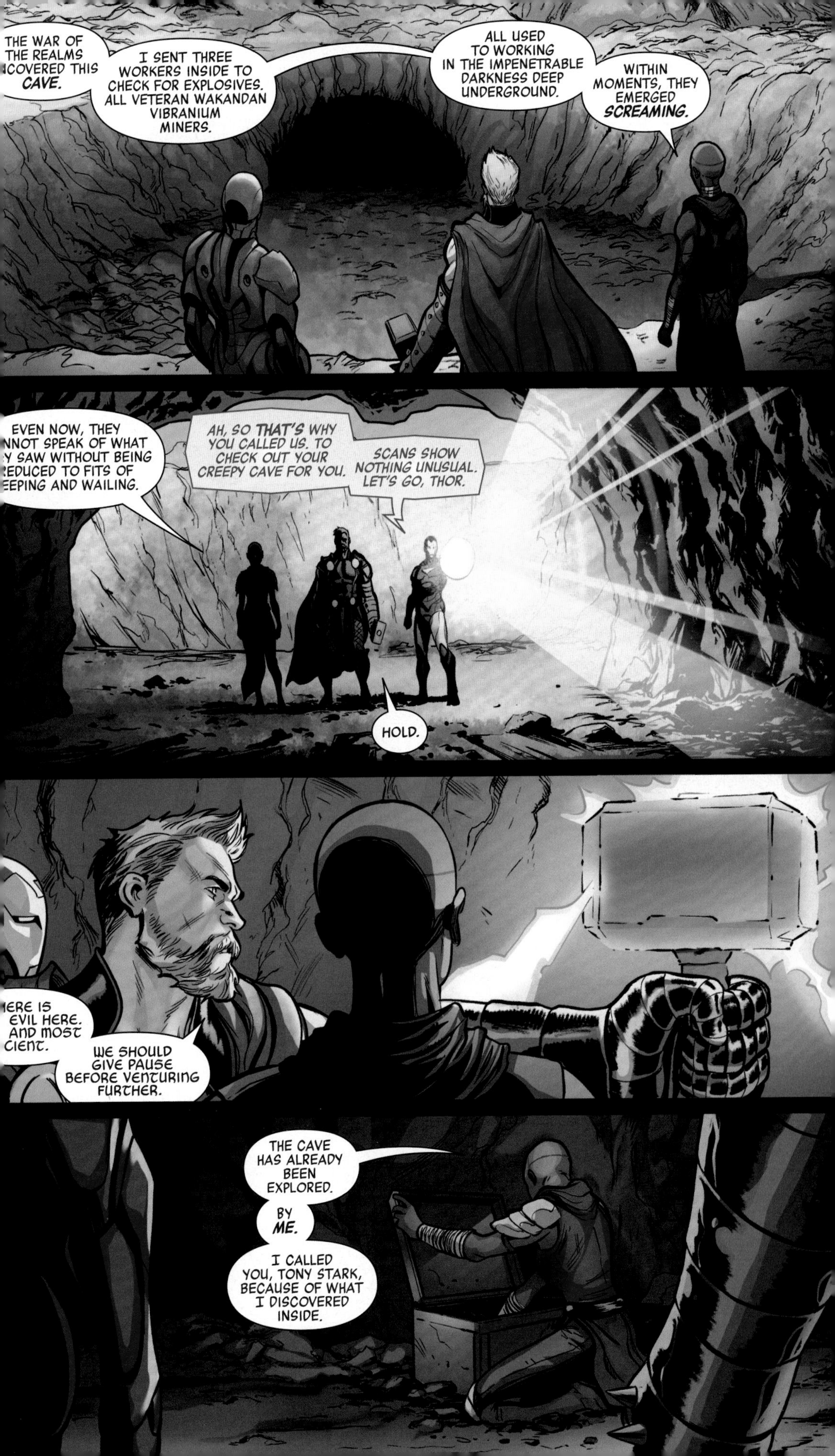
THE WAR OF THE REALMS COVERED THIS CAVE.
I SENT THREE WORKERS INSIDE TO CHECK FOR EXPLOSIVES. ALL VETERAN WAKANDAN VIBRANIUM MINERS.
ALL USED TO WORKING IN THE IMPENETRABLE DARKNESS DEEP UNDERGROUND.
WITHIN MOMENTS, THEY EMERGED SCREAMING.
EVEN NOW, THEY NNOT SPEAK OF WHAT Y SAW WITHOUT BEING REDUCED TO FITS OF EEPING AND WAILING.
AH, SO THAT'S WHY YOU CALLED US. TO CHECK OUT YOUR CREEPY CAVE FOR YOU.
SCANS SHOW NOTHING UNUSUAL. LET'S GO, THOR.
HOLD.
IERE IS EVIL HERE. AND MOST CIENT.
WE SHOULD GIVE PAUSE BEFORE VENTURING FURTHER.
THE CAVE HAS ALREADY BEEN EXPLORED.
BY ME.
I CALLED YOU, TONY STARK, BECAUSE OF WHAT I DISCOVERED INSIDE.

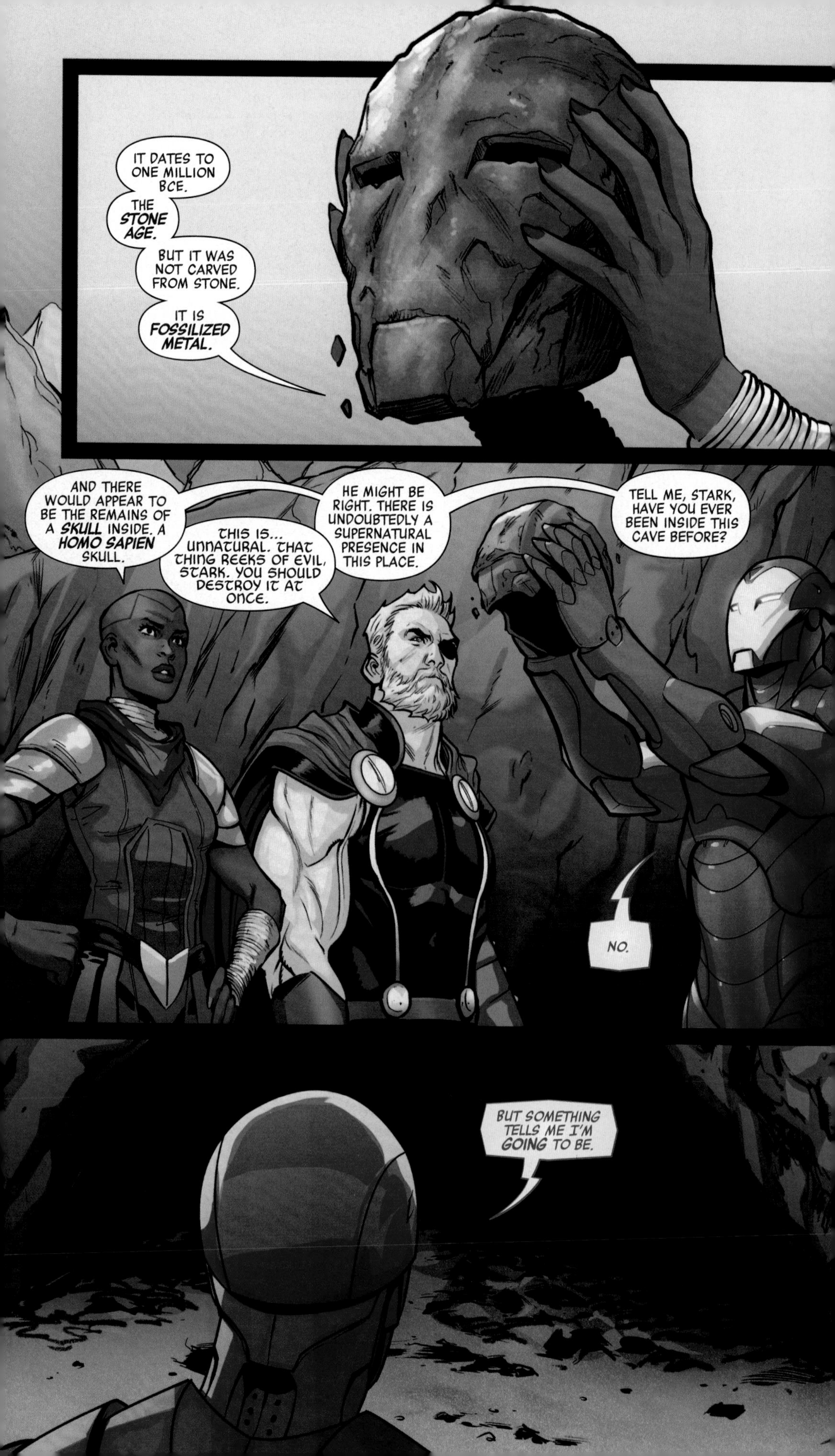
IT DATES TO ONE MILLION BCE.
THE STONE AGE.
BUT IT WAS NOT CARVED FROM STONE.
IT IS FOSSILIZED METAL.
AND THERE WOULD APPEAR TO BE THE REMAINS OF A SKULL INSIDE. A HOMO SAPIEN SKULL.
THIS IS... UNNATURAL. THAT THING REEKS OF EVIL, STARK. YOU SHOULD DESTROY IT AT ONCE.
HE MIGHT BE RIGHT. THERE IS UNDOUBTEDLY A SUPERNATURAL PRESENCE IN THIS PLACE.
TELL ME, STARK, HAVE YOU EVER BEEN INSIDE THIS CAVE BEFORE?
NO.
BUT SOMETHING TELLS ME I'M GOING TO BE.

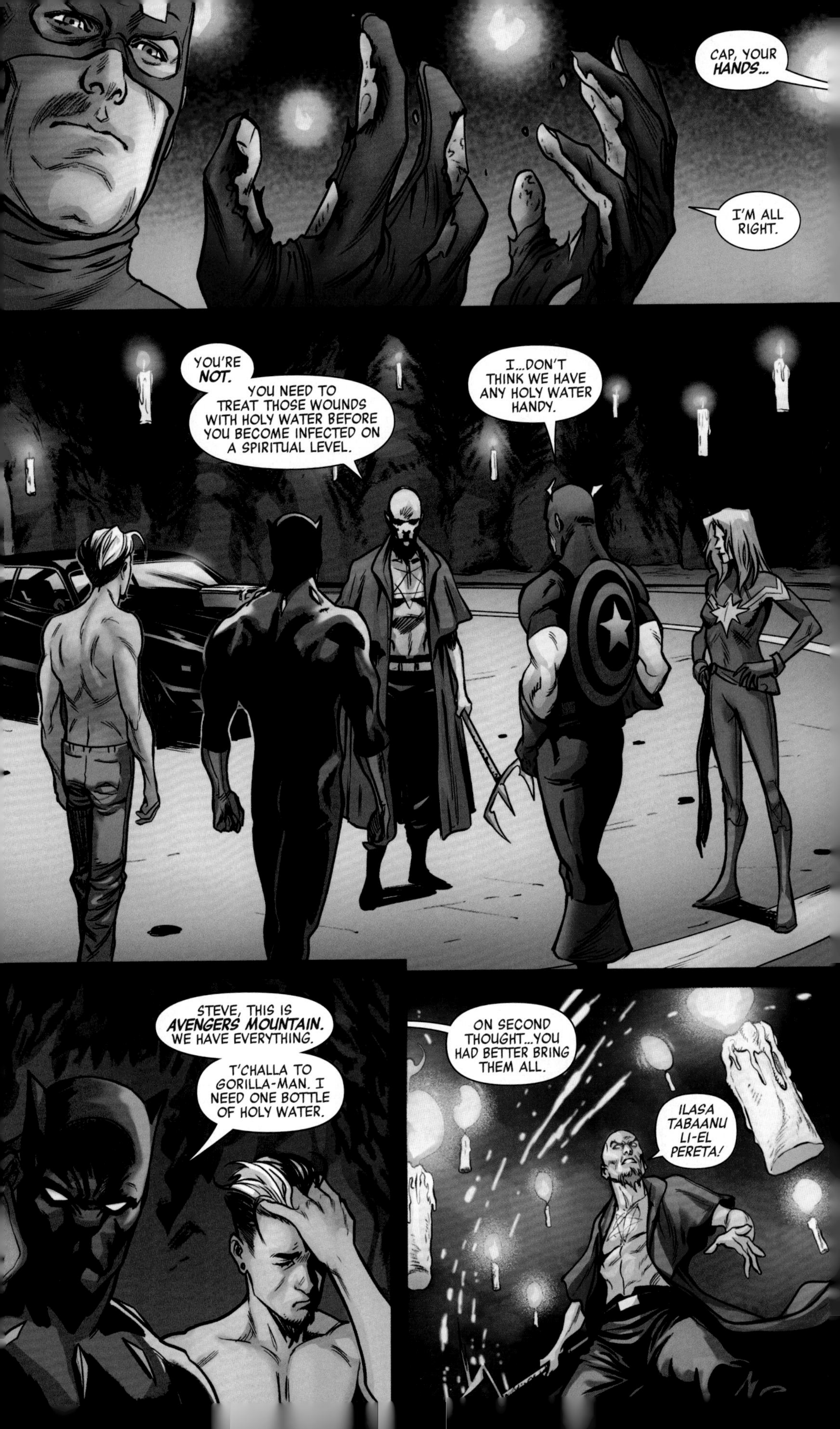
CAP, YOUR HANDS...
I'M ALL RIGHT.
YOU'RE NOT.
YOU NEED TO TREAT THOSE WOUNDS WITH HOLY WATER BEFORE YOU BECOME INFECTED ON A SPIRITUAL LEVEL.
I...DON'T THINK WE HAVE ANY HOLY WATER HANDY.
STEVE, THIS IS AVENGERS MOUNTAIN. WE HAVE EVERYTHING.
T'CHALLA TO GORILLA-MAN. I NEED ONE BOTTLE OF HOLY WATER.
ON SECOND THOUGHT...YOU HAD BETTER BRING THEM ALL.
ILASA TABAANU LI-EL PERETA!

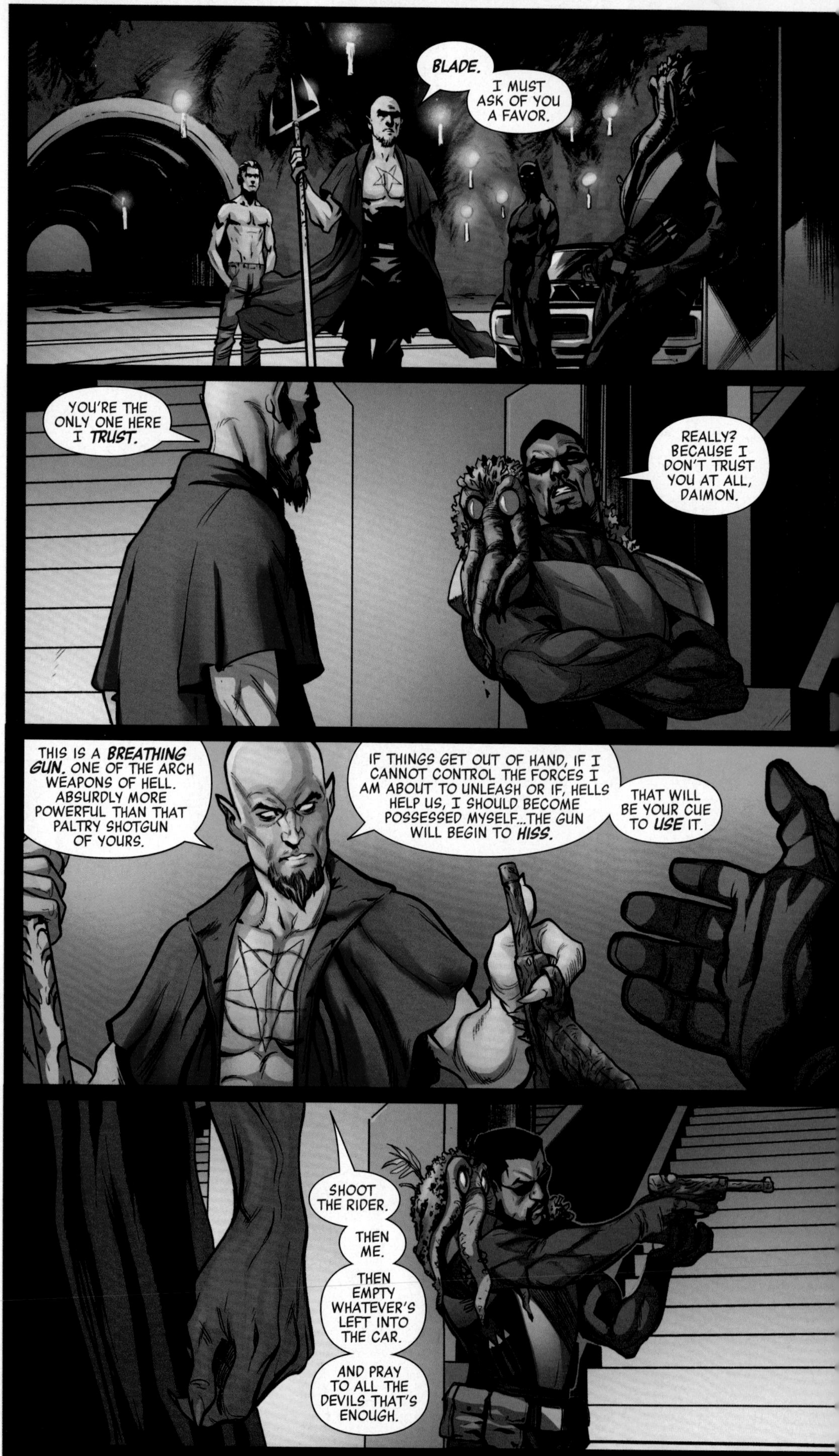
BLADE.
I MUST ASK OF YOU A FAVOR.
YOU'RE THE ONLY ONE HERE I TRUST.
REALLY? BECAUSE I DON'T TRUST YOU AT ALL, DAIMON.
THIS IS A BREATHING GUN. ONE OF THE ARCH WEAPONS OF HELL. ABSURDLY MORE POWERFUL THAN THAT PALTRY SHOTGUN OF YOURS.
IF THINGS GET OUT OF HAND, IF I CANNOT CONTROL THE FORCES I AM ABOUT TO UNLEASH OR IF, HELLS HELP US, I SHOULD BECOME POSSESSED MYSELF...THE GUN WILL BEGIN TO HISS.
THAT WILL BE YOUR CUE TO USE IT.
SHOOT THE RIDER.
THEN ME.
THEN EMPTY WHATEVER'S LEFT INTO THE CAR.
AND PRAY TO ALL THE DEVILS THAT'S ENOUGH.

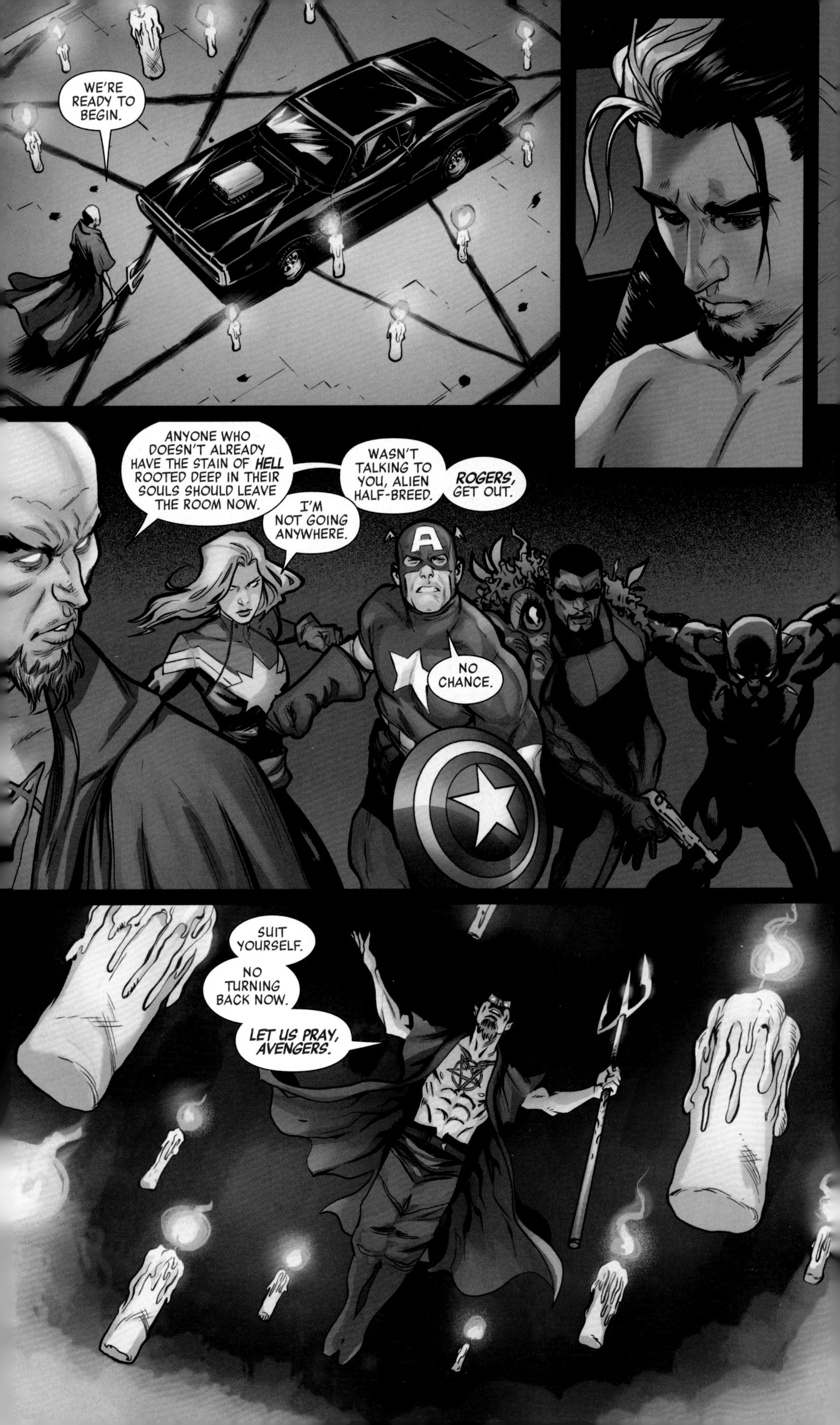
WE'RE READY TO BEGIN.
ANYONE WHO DOESN'T ALREADY HAVE THE STAIN OF HELL ROOTED DEEP IN THEIR SOULS SHOULD LEAVE THE ROOM NOW.
I'M NOT GOING ANYWHERE.
WASN'T TALKING TO YOU, ALIEN HALF-BREED.
ROGERS, GET OUT.
NO CHANCE.
SUIT YOURSELF.
NO TURNING BACK NOW.
LET US PRAY, AVENGERS.

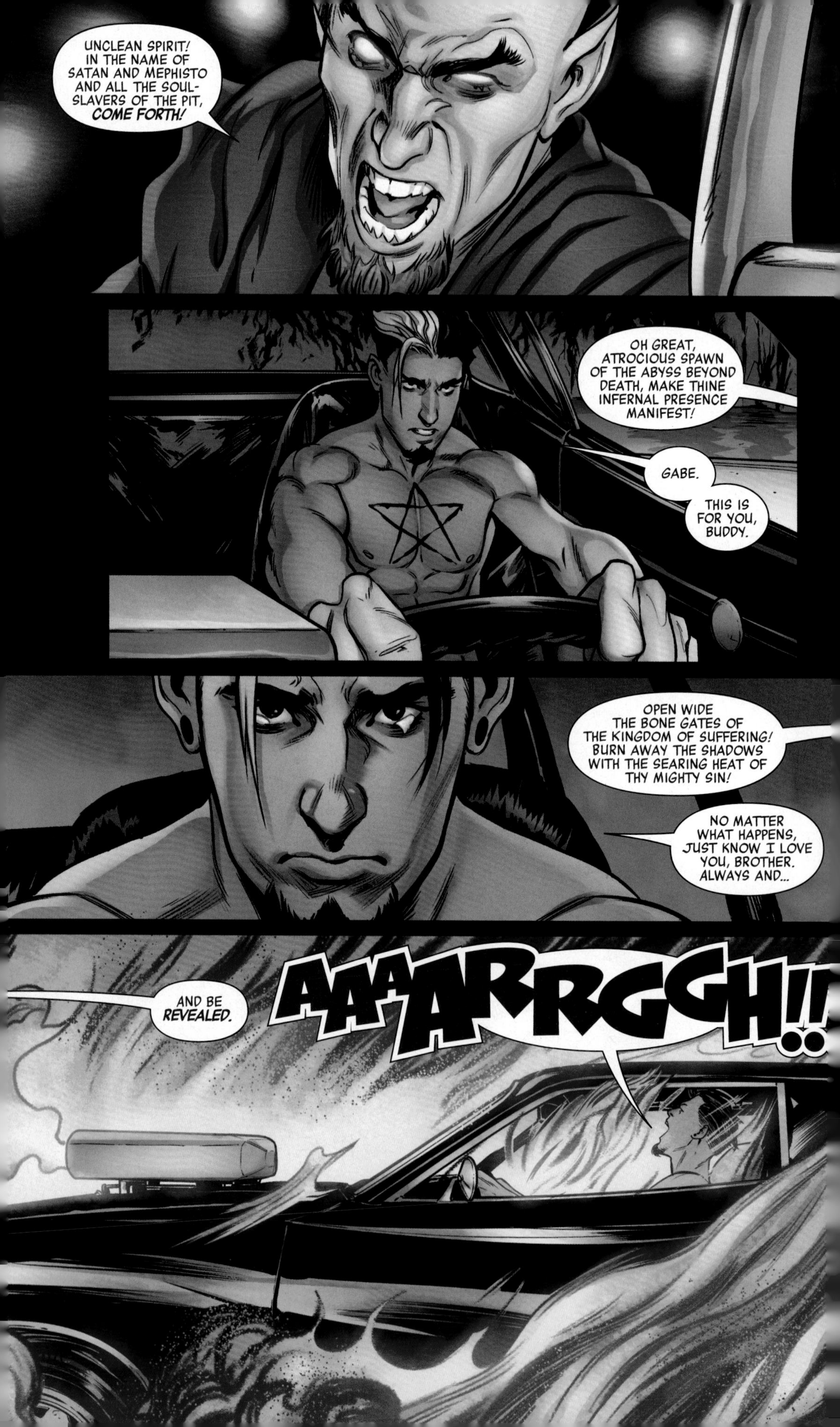

UNCLEAN SPIRIT! IN THE NAME OF SATAN AND MEPHISTO AND ALL THE SOUL-SLAVERS OF THE PIT, COME FORTH!
OH GREAT, ATROCIOUS SPAWN OF THE ABYSS BEYOND DEATH, MAKE THINE INFERNAL PRESENCE MANIFEST!
GABE.
THIS IS FOR YOU, BUDDY.
OPEN WIDE THE BONE GATES OF THE KINGDOM OF SUFFERING! BURN AWAY THE SHADOWS WITH THE SEARING HEAT OF THY MIGHTY SIN!
NO MATTER WHAT HAPPENS, JUST KNOW I LOVE YOU, BROTHER. ALWAYS AND...
AND BE REVEALED.
AAAARRGGH!!

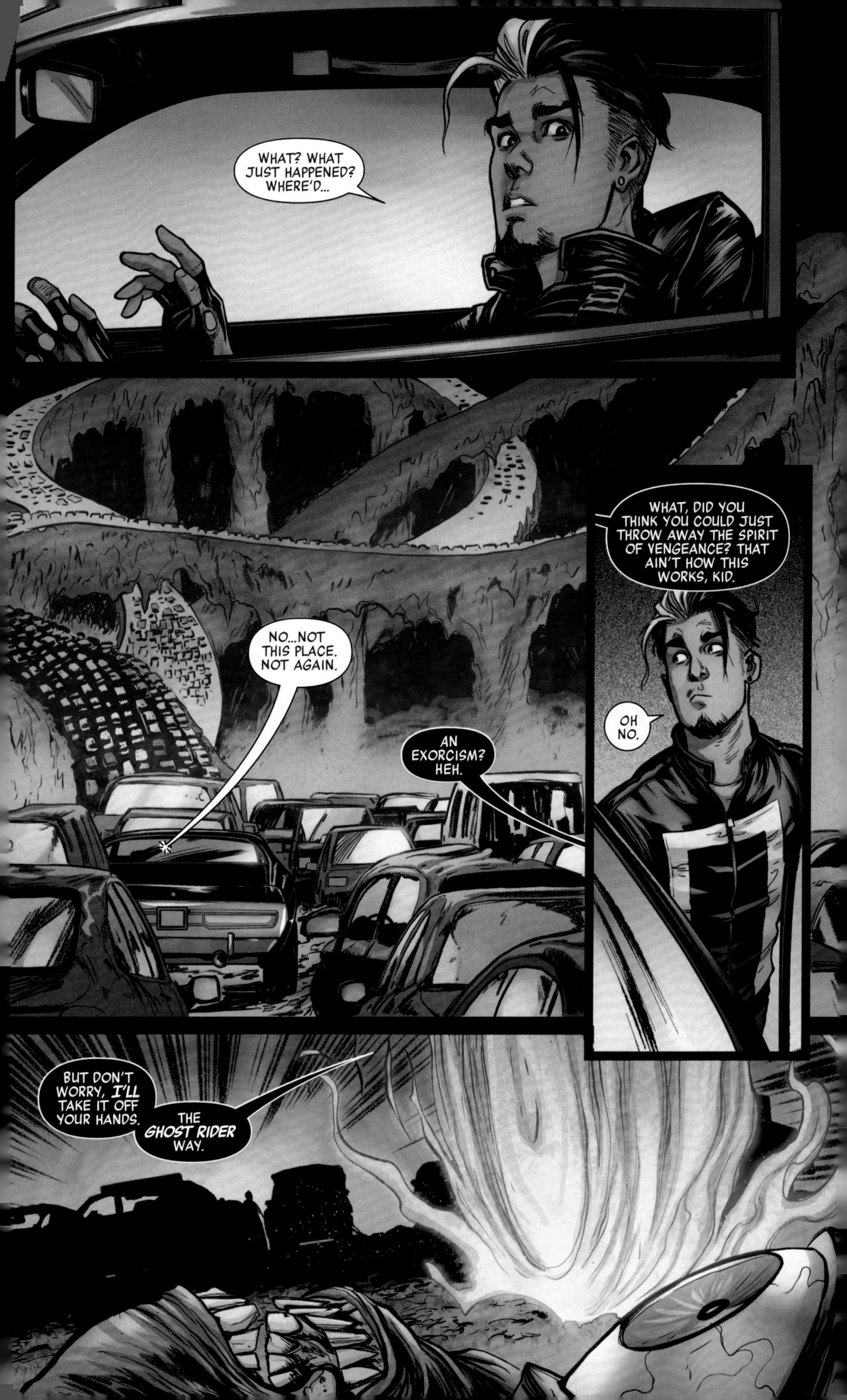
WHAT? WHAT JUST HAPPENED? WHERE'D...
NO...NOT THIS PLACE. NOT AGAIN.
AN EXORCISM? HEH.
WHAT, DID YOU THINK YOU COULD JUST THROW AWAY THE SPIRIT OF VENGEANCE? THAT AIN'T HOW THIS WORKS, KID.
OH NO.
BUT DON'T WORRY, I'LL TAKE IT OFF YOUR HANDS.
THE GHOST RIDER WAY.

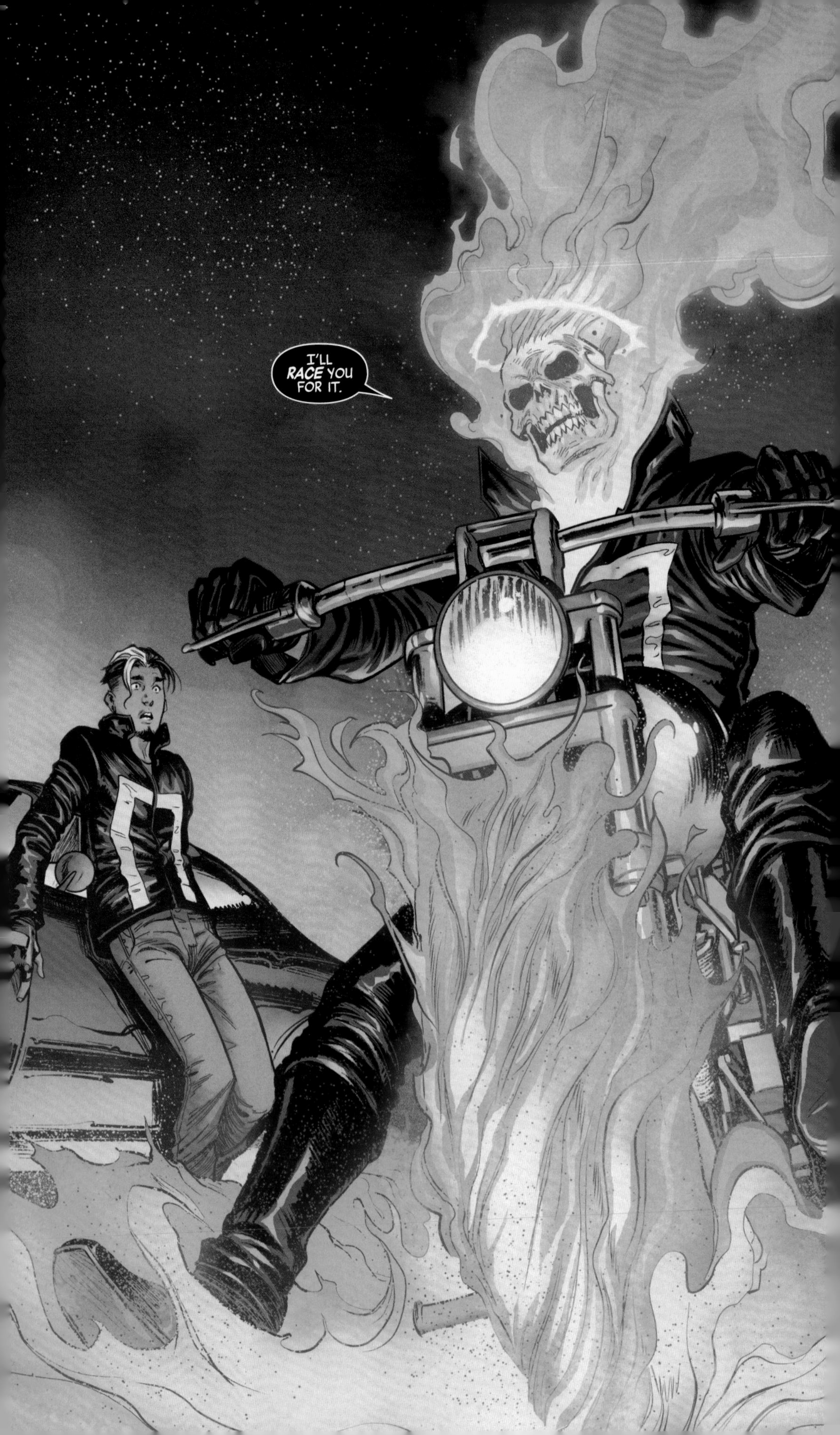
I'LL RACE YOU FOR IT.

23 **CHALLENGE OF THE GHOST RIDERS** PART 2

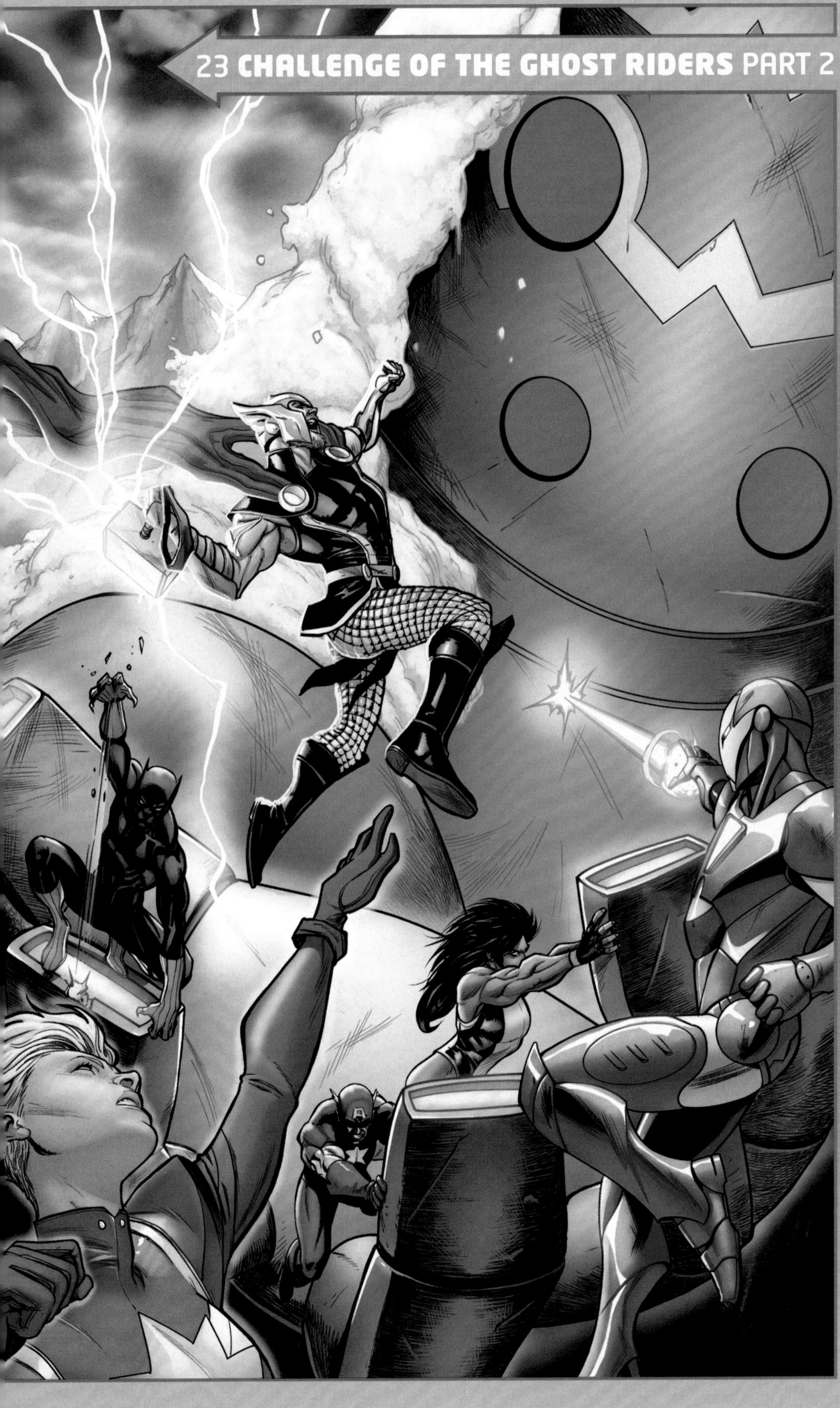

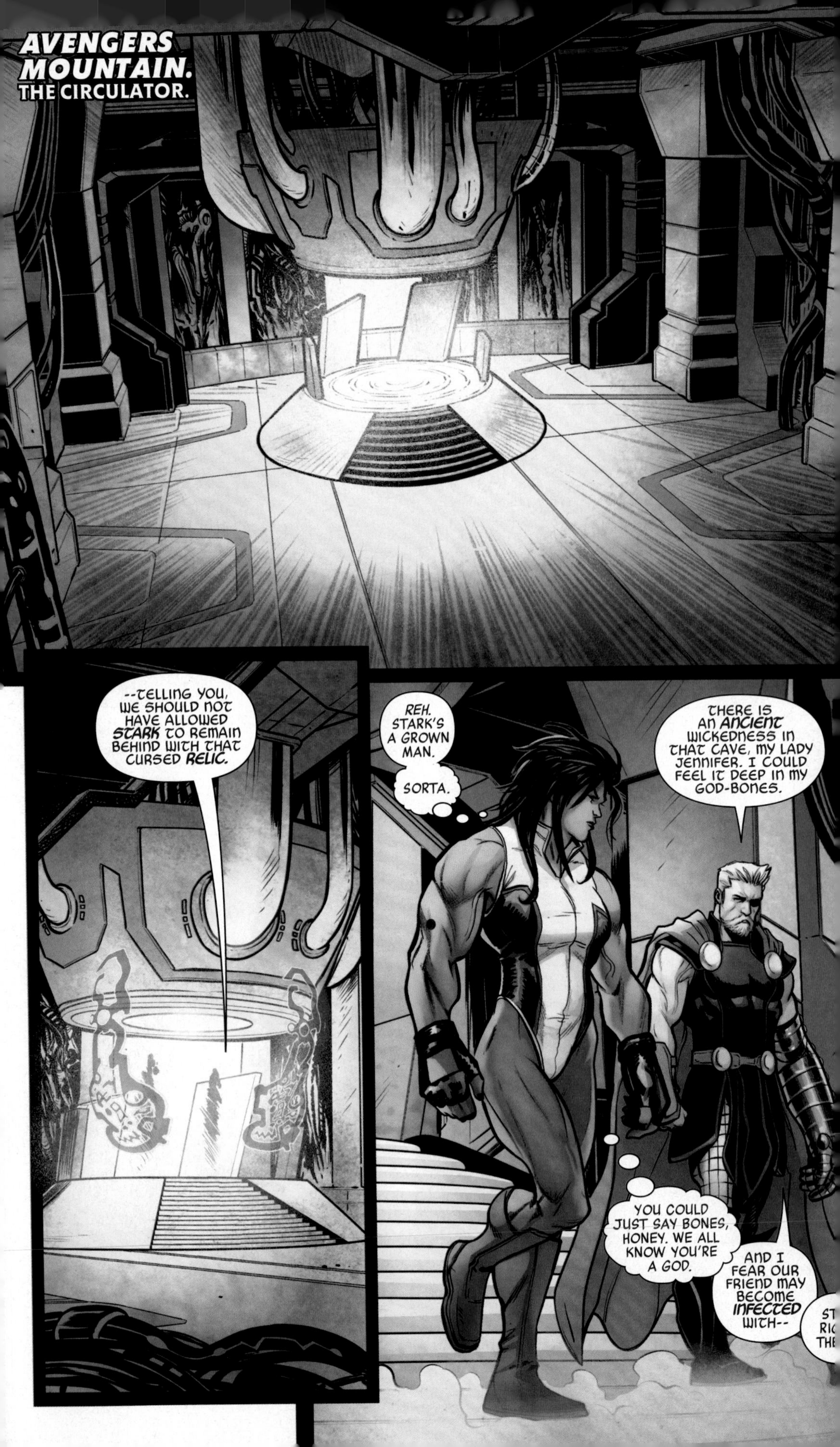
AVENGERS MOUNTAIN. THE CIRCULATOR.
--TELLING YOU, WE SHOULD NOT HAVE ALLOWED STARK TO REMAIN BEHIND WITH THAT CURSED RELIC.
REH. STARK'S A GROWN MAN.
SORTA.
THERE IS AN ANCIENT WICKEDNESS IN THAT CAVE, MY LADY JENNIFER. I COULD FEEL IT DEEP IN MY GOD-BONES.
YOU COULD JUST SAY BONES, HONEY. WE ALL KNOW YOU'RE A GOD.
AND I FEAR OUR FRIEND MAY BECOME INFECTED WITH--

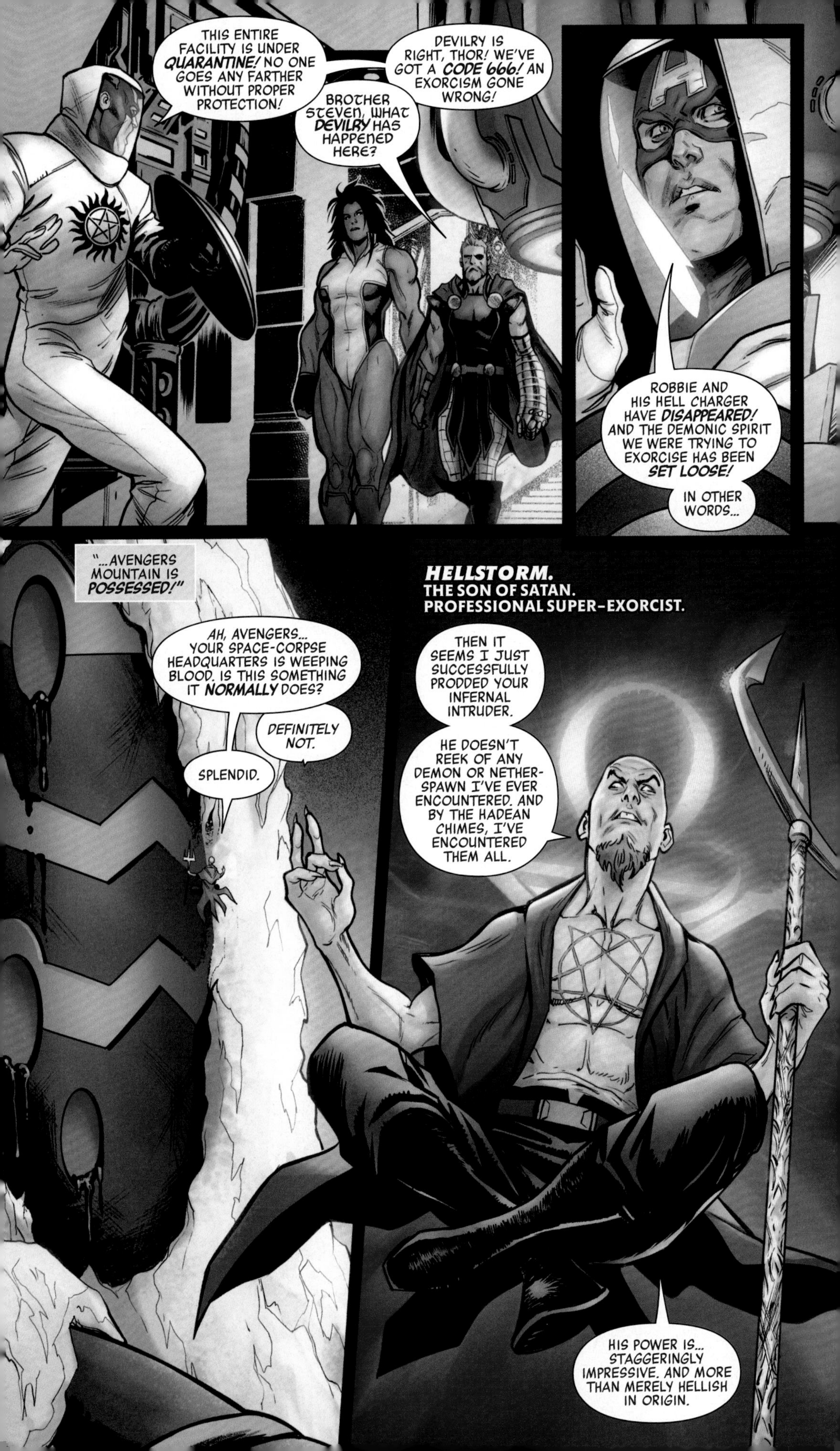
THIS ENTIRE FACILITY IS UNDER QUARANTINE! NO ONE GOES ANY FARTHER WITHOUT PROPER PROTECTION!
BROTHER STEVEN, WHAT DEVILRY HAS HAPPENED HERE?
DEVILRY IS RIGHT, THOR! WE'VE GOT A CODE 666! AN EXORCISM GONE WRONG!
ROBBIE AND HIS HELL CHARGER HAVE DISAPPEARED! AND THE DEMONIC SPIRIT WE WERE TRYING TO EXORCISE HAS BEEN SET LOOSE!
IN OTHER WORDS...
"...AVENGERS MOUNTAIN IS POSSESSED!"
HELLSTORM.
THE SON OF SATAN.
PROFESSIONAL SUPER-EXORCIST.
AH, AVENGERS... YOUR SPACE-CORPSE HEADQUARTERS IS WEEPING BLOOD. IS THIS SOMETHING IT NORMALLY DOES?
DEFINITELY NOT.
SPLENDID.
THEN IT SEEMS I JUST SUCCESSFULLY PRODDED YOUR INFERNAL INTRUDER.
HE DOESN'T REEK OF ANY DEMON OR NETHER-SPAWN I'VE EVER ENCOUNTERED. AND BY THE HADEAN CHIMES, I'VE ENCOUNTERED THEM ALL.
HIS POWER IS... STAGGERINGLY IMPRESSIVE. AND MORE THAN MERELY HELLISH IN ORIGIN.

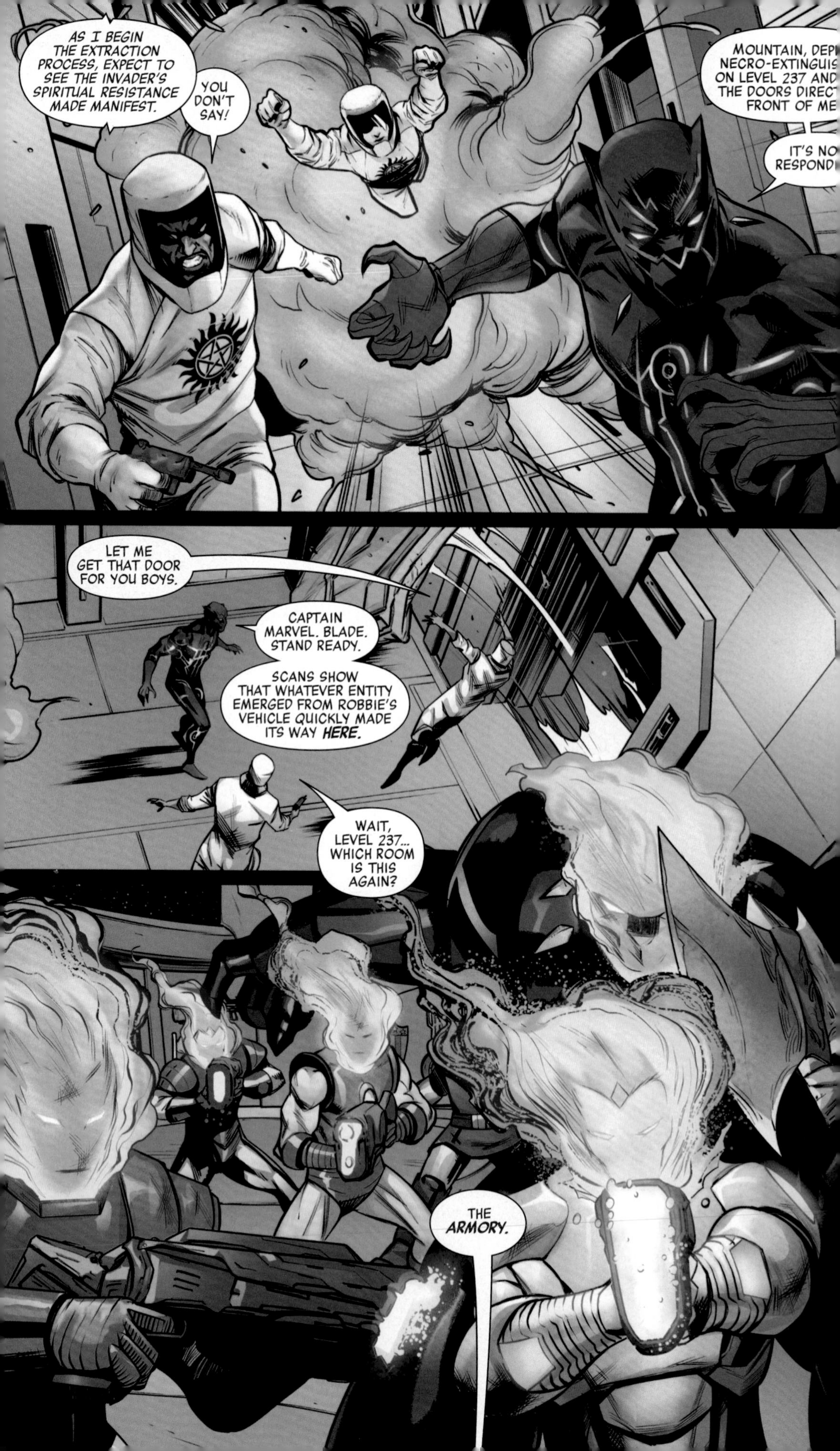
AS I BEGIN THE EXTRACTION PROCESS, EXPECT TO SEE THE INVADER'S SPIRITUAL RESISTANCE MADE MANIFEST.
YOU DON'T SAY!
MOUNTAIN, DEP NECRO-EXTINGUIS ON LEVEL 237 AND THE DOORS DIRECT FRONT OF ME
IT'S NO RESPOND
LET ME GET THAT DOOR FOR YOU BOYS.
CAPTAIN MARVEL. BLADE. STAND READY.
SCANS SHOW THAT WHATEVER ENTITY EMERGED FROM ROBBIE'S VEHICLE QUICKLY MADE ITS WAY HERE.
WAIT, LEVEL 237... WHICH ROOM IS THIS AGAIN?
THE ARMORY.

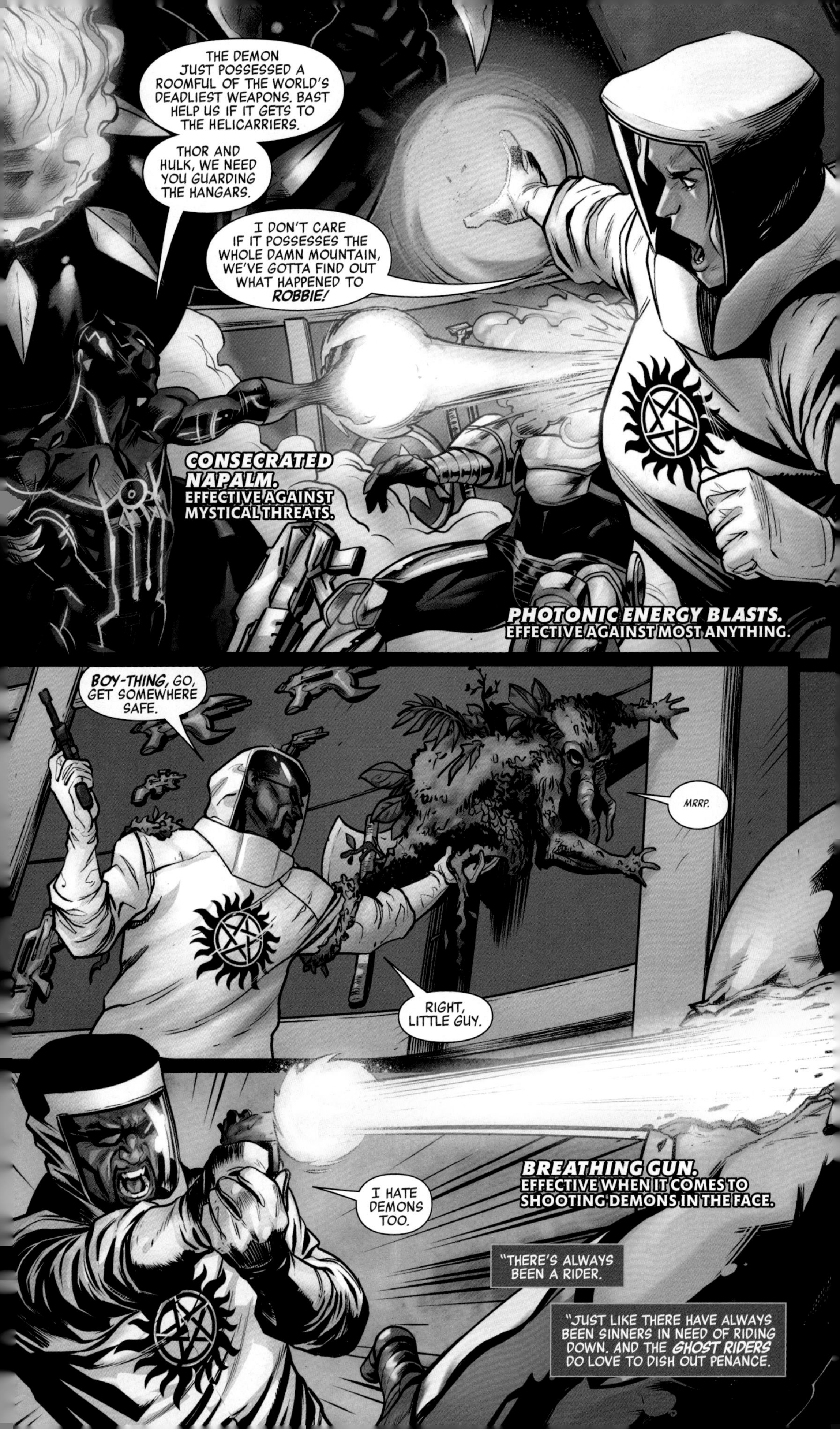
THE DEMON JUST POSSESSED A ROOMFUL OF THE WORLD'S DEADLIEST WEAPONS. BAST HELP US IF IT GETS TO THE HELICARRIERS.
THOR AND HULK, WE NEED YOU GUARDING THE HANGARS.
I DON'T CARE IF IT POSSESSES THE WHOLE DAMN MOUNTAIN, WE'VE GOTTA FIND OUT WHAT HAPPENED TO ROBBIE!
CONSECRATED NAPALM. EFFECTIVE AGAINST MYSTICAL THREATS.
PHOTONIC ENERGY BLASTS. EFFECTIVE AGAINST MOST ANYTHING.
BOY-THING, GO, GET SOMEWHERE SAFE.
MRRP.
RIGHT, LITTLE GUY.
I HATE DEMONS TOO.
BREATHING GUN. EFFECTIVE WHEN IT COMES TO SHOOTING DEMONS IN THE FACE.
"THERE'S ALWAYS BEEN A RIDER.
"JUST LIKE THERE HAVE ALWAYS BEEN SINNERS IN NEED OF RIDING DOWN. AND THE GHOST RIDERS DO LOVE TO DISH OUT PENANCE.

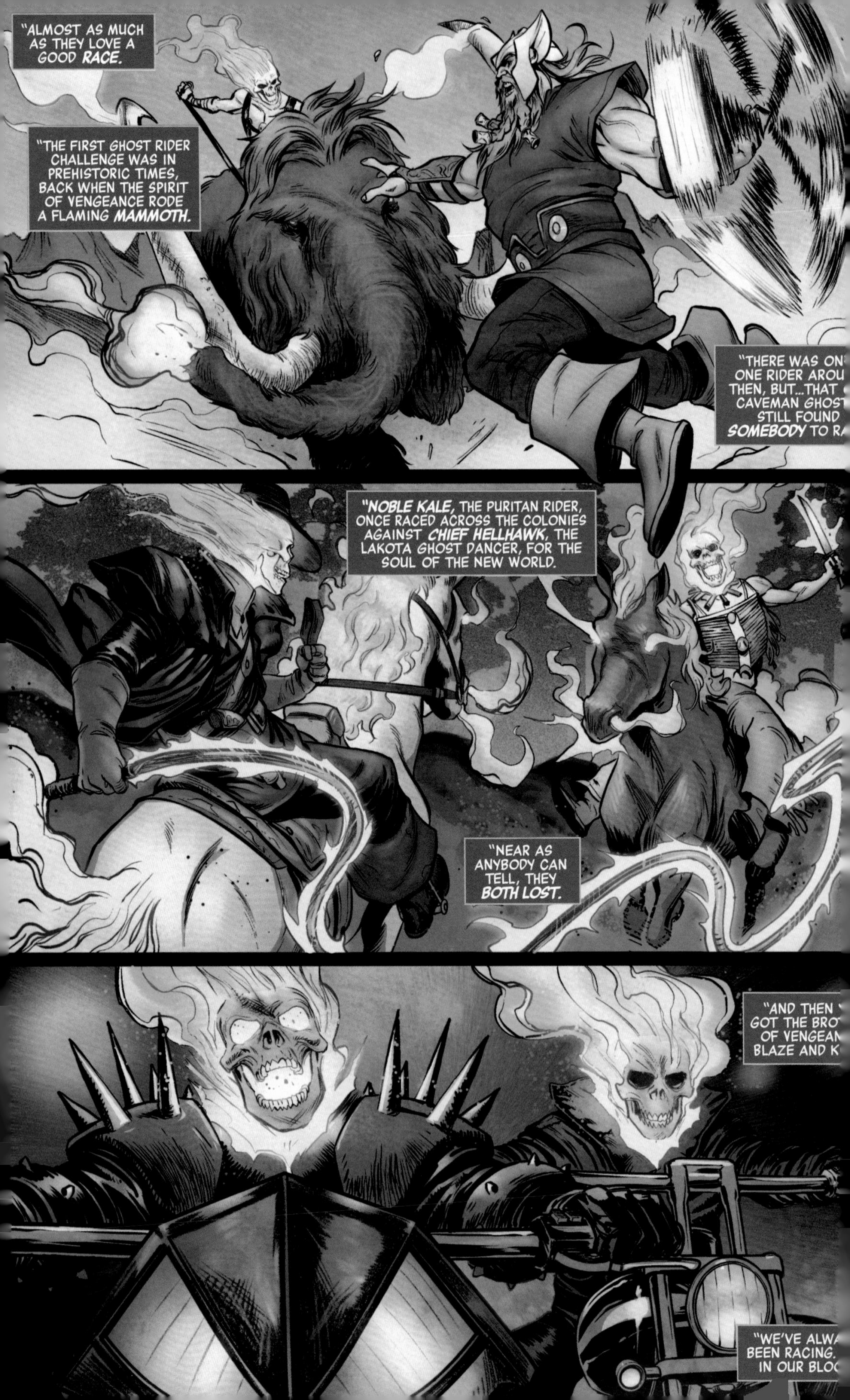
"ALMOST AS MUCH AS THEY LOVE A GOOD RACE.
"THE FIRST GHOST RIDER CHALLENGE WAS IN PREHISTORIC TIMES, BACK WHEN THE SPIRIT OF VENGEANCE RODE A FLAMING MAMMOTH.
"THERE WAS ON ONE RIDER AROU THEN, BUT...THAT CAVEMAN GHOST STILL FOUND SOMEBODY TO R
"NOBLE KALE, THE PURITAN RIDER, ONCE RACED ACROSS THE COLONIES AGAINST CHIEF HELLHAWK, THE LAKOTA GHOST DANCER, FOR THE SOUL OF THE NEW WORLD.
"NEAR AS ANYBODY CAN TELL, THEY BOTH LOST.
"AND THEN GOT THE BRO OF VENGEAN BLAZE AND K
"WE'VE ALWA BEEN RACING. IN OUR BLO

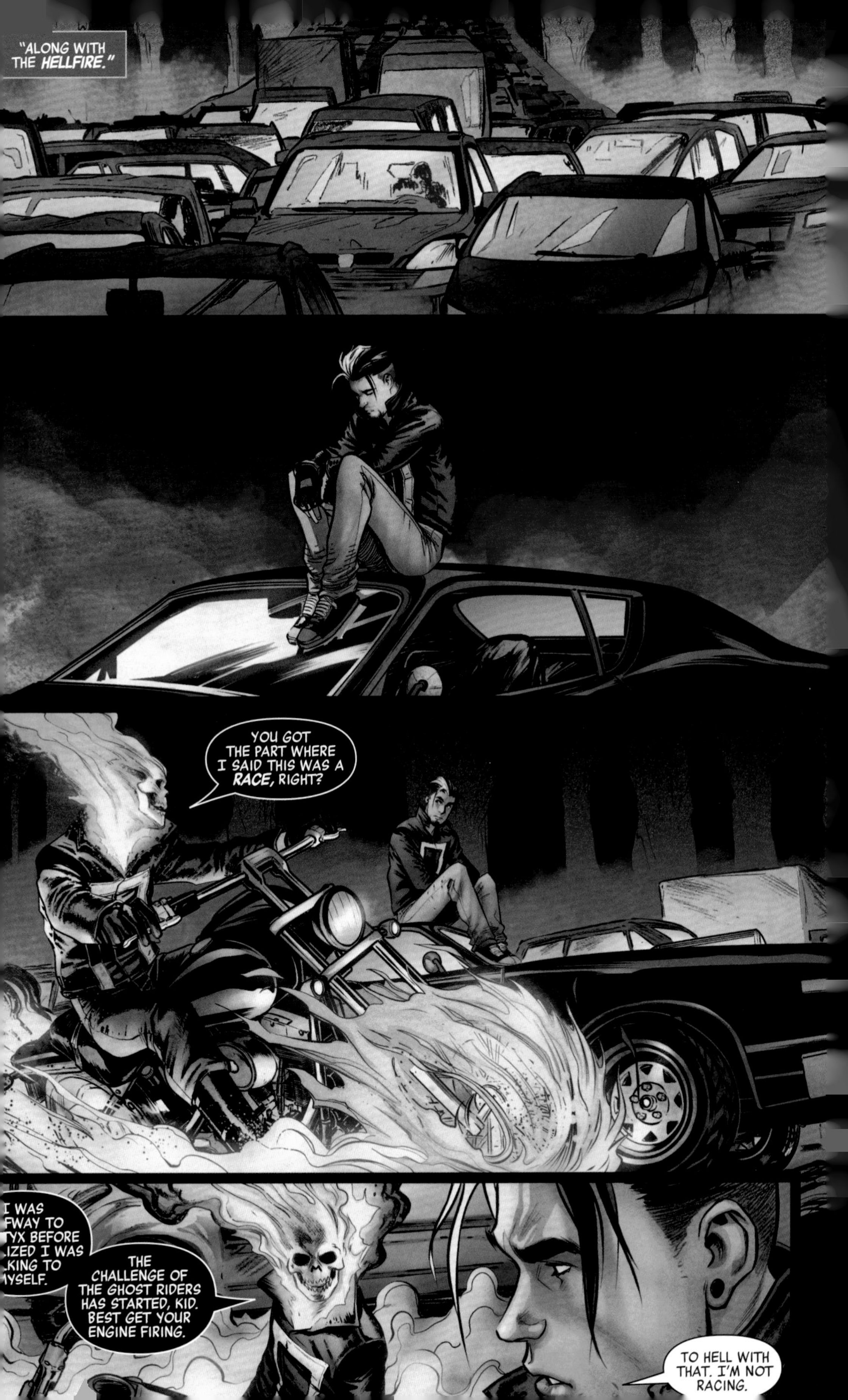
"ALONG WITH THE HELLFIRE."
YOU GOT THE PART WHERE I SAID THIS WAS A RACE, RIGHT?
I WAS FWAY TO TYX BEFORE IZED I WAS KING TO YSELF.
THE CHALLENGE OF THE GHOST RIDERS HAS STARTED, KID. BEST GET YOUR ENGINE FIRING.
TO HELL WITH THAT. I'M NOT RACING.

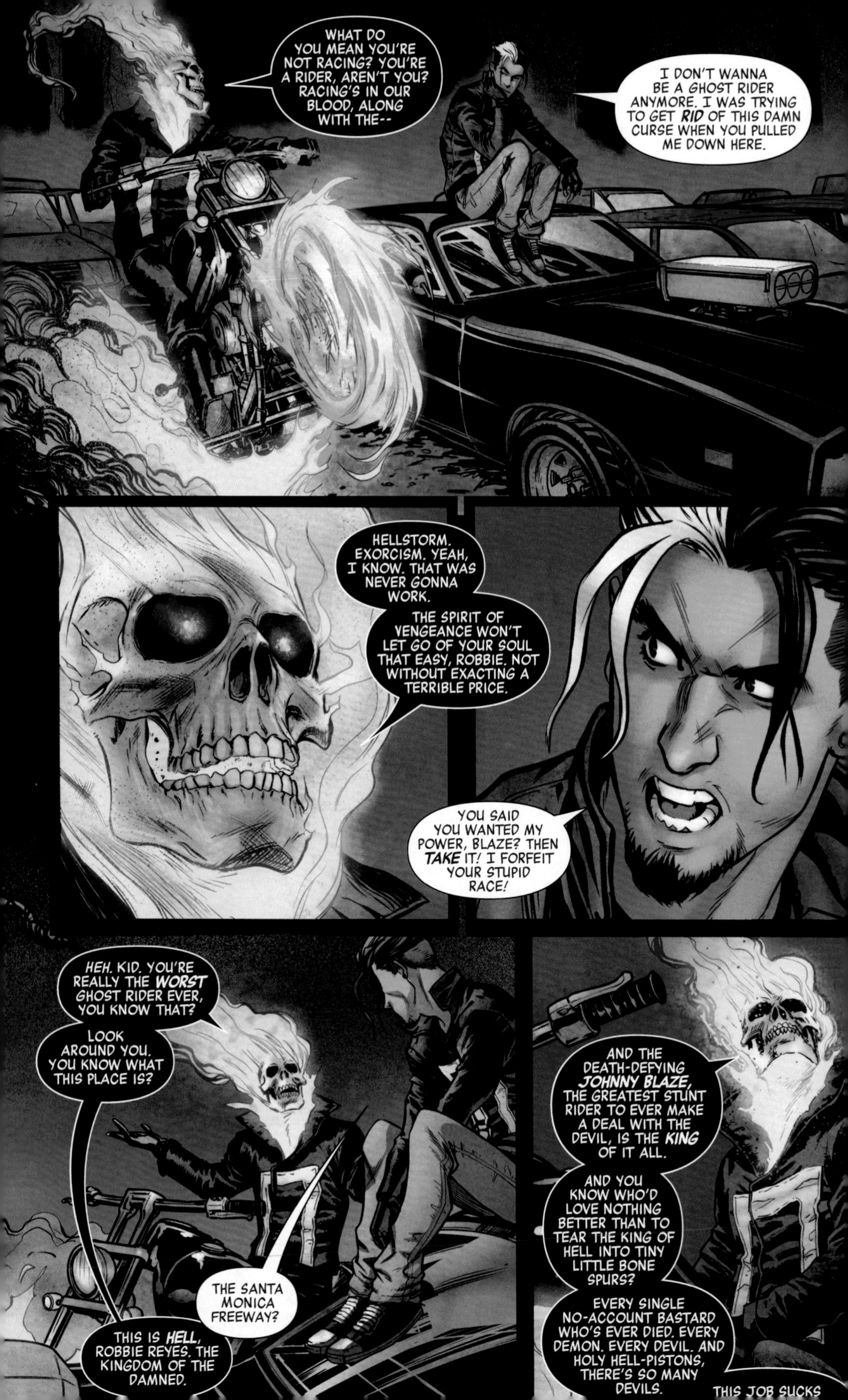
WHAT DO YOU MEAN YOU'RE NOT RACING? YOU'RE A RIDER, AREN'T YOU? RACING'S IN OUR BLOOD, ALONG WITH THE--
I DON'T WANNA BE A GHOST RIDER ANYMORE. I WAS TRYING TO GET RID OF THIS DAMN CURSE WHEN YOU PULLED ME DOWN HERE.
HELLSTORM. EXORCISM. YEAH, I KNOW. THAT WAS NEVER GONNA WORK.
THE SPIRIT OF VENGEANCE WON'T LET GO OF YOUR SOUL THAT EASY, ROBBIE. NOT WITHOUT EXACTING A TERRIBLE PRICE.
YOU SAID YOU WANTED MY POWER, BLAZE? THEN TAKE IT! I FORFEIT YOUR STUPID RACE!
HEH. KID. YOU'RE REALLY THE WORST GHOST RIDER EVER, YOU KNOW THAT?
LOOK AROUND YOU. YOU KNOW WHAT THIS PLACE IS?
THE SANTA MONICA FREEWAY?
THIS IS HELL, ROBBIE REYES. THE KINGDOM OF THE DAMNED.
AND THE DEATH-DEFYING JOHNNY BLAZE, THE GREATEST STUNT RIDER TO EVER MAKE A DEAL WITH THE DEVIL, IS THE KING OF IT ALL.
AND YOU KNOW WHO'D LOVE NOTHING BETTER THAN TO TEAR THE KING OF HELL INTO TINY LITTLE BONE SPURS?
EVERY SINGLE NO-ACCOUNT BASTARD WHO'S EVER DIED. EVERY DEMON. EVERY DEVIL. AND HOLY HELL-PISTONS, THERE'S SO MANY DEVILS.
THIS JOB SUCKS

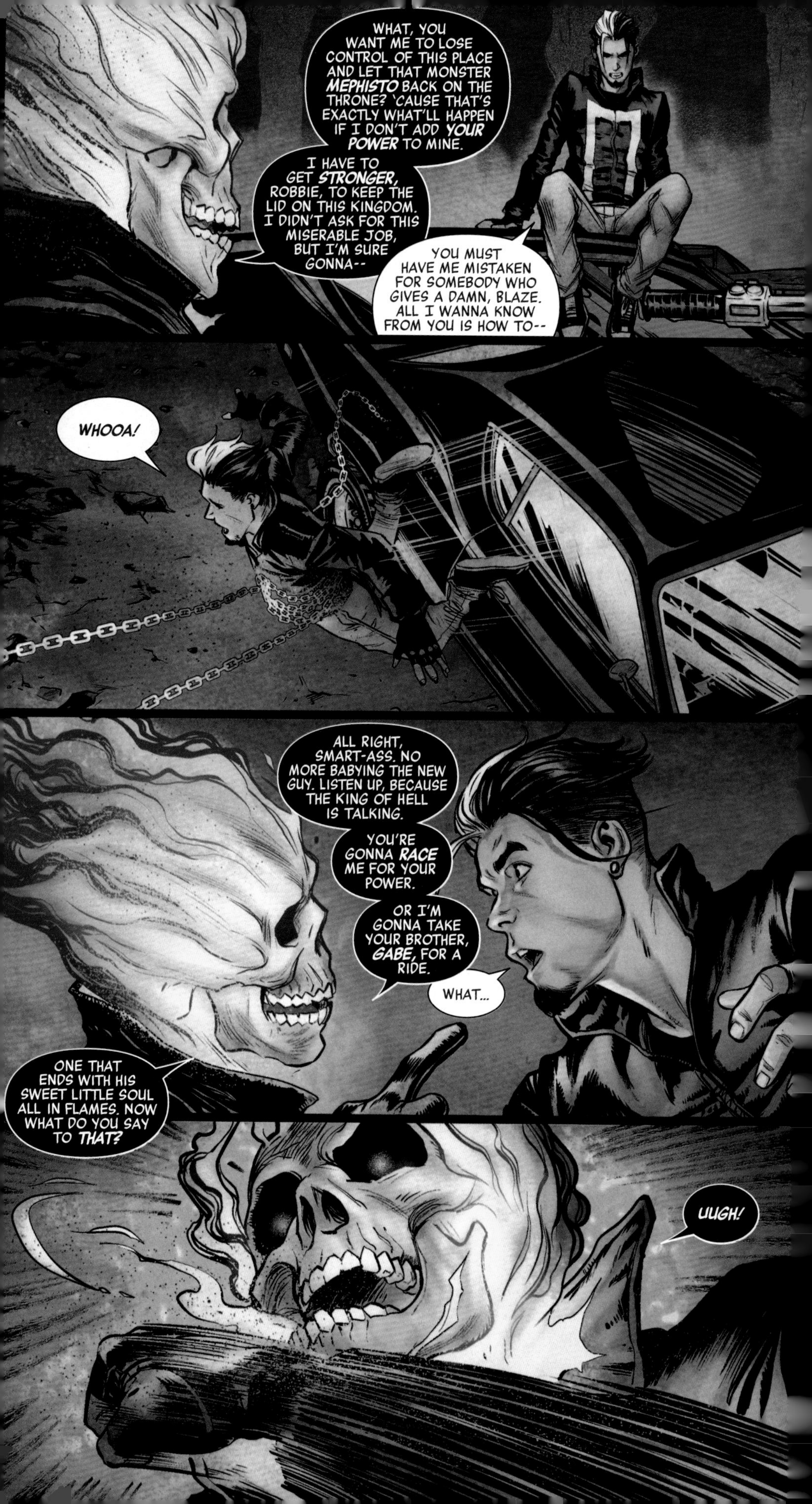
WHAT, YOU WANT ME TO LOSE CONTROL OF THIS PLACE AND LET THAT MONSTER MEPHISTO BACK ON THE THRONE? 'CAUSE THAT'S EXACTLY WHAT'LL HAPPEN IF I DON'T ADD YOUR POWER TO MINE.
I HAVE TO GET STRONGER, ROBBIE, TO KEEP THE LID ON THIS KINGDOM. I DIDN'T ASK FOR THIS MISERABLE JOB, BUT I'M SURE GONNA--
YOU MUST HAVE ME MISTAKEN FOR SOMEBODY WHO GIVES A DAMN, BLAZE. ALL I WANNA KNOW FROM YOU IS HOW TO--
WHOOA!
ALL RIGHT, SMART-ASS. NO MORE BABYING THE NEW GUY. LISTEN UP, BECAUSE THE KING OF HELL IS TALKING.
YOU'RE GONNA RACE ME FOR YOUR POWER.
OR I'M GONNA TAKE YOUR BROTHER, GABE, FOR A RIDE.
WHAT...
ONE THAT ENDS WITH HIS SWEET LITTLE SOUL ALL IN FLAMES. NOW WHAT DO YOU SAY TO THAT?
UUGH!

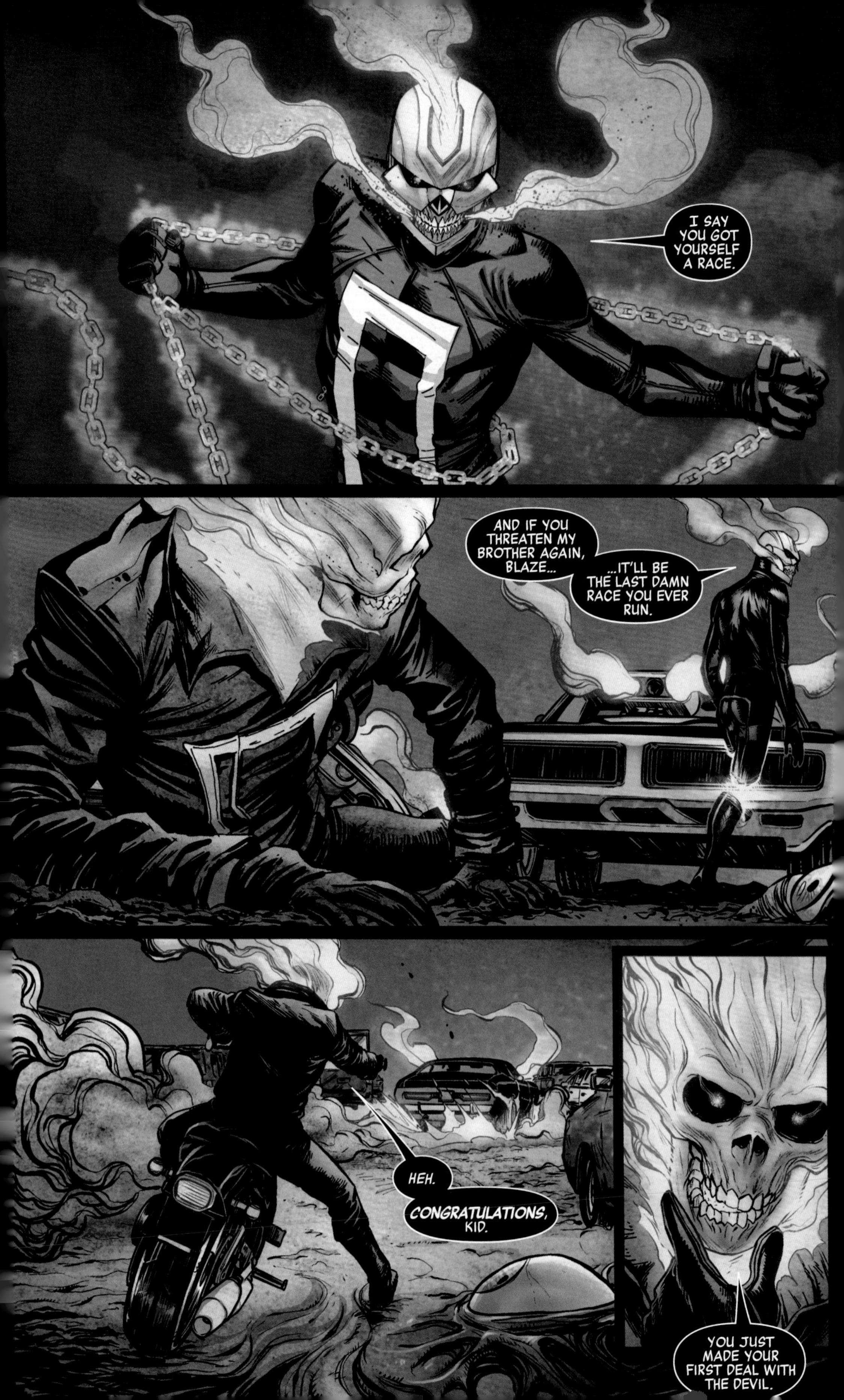
I SAY YOU GOT YOURSELF A RACE.
AND IF YOU THREATEN MY BROTHER AGAIN, BLAZE...
...IT'LL BE THE LAST DAMN RACE YOU EVER RUN.
HEH.
CONGRATULATIONS, KID.
YOU JUST MADE YOUR FIRST DEAL WITH THE DEVIL.

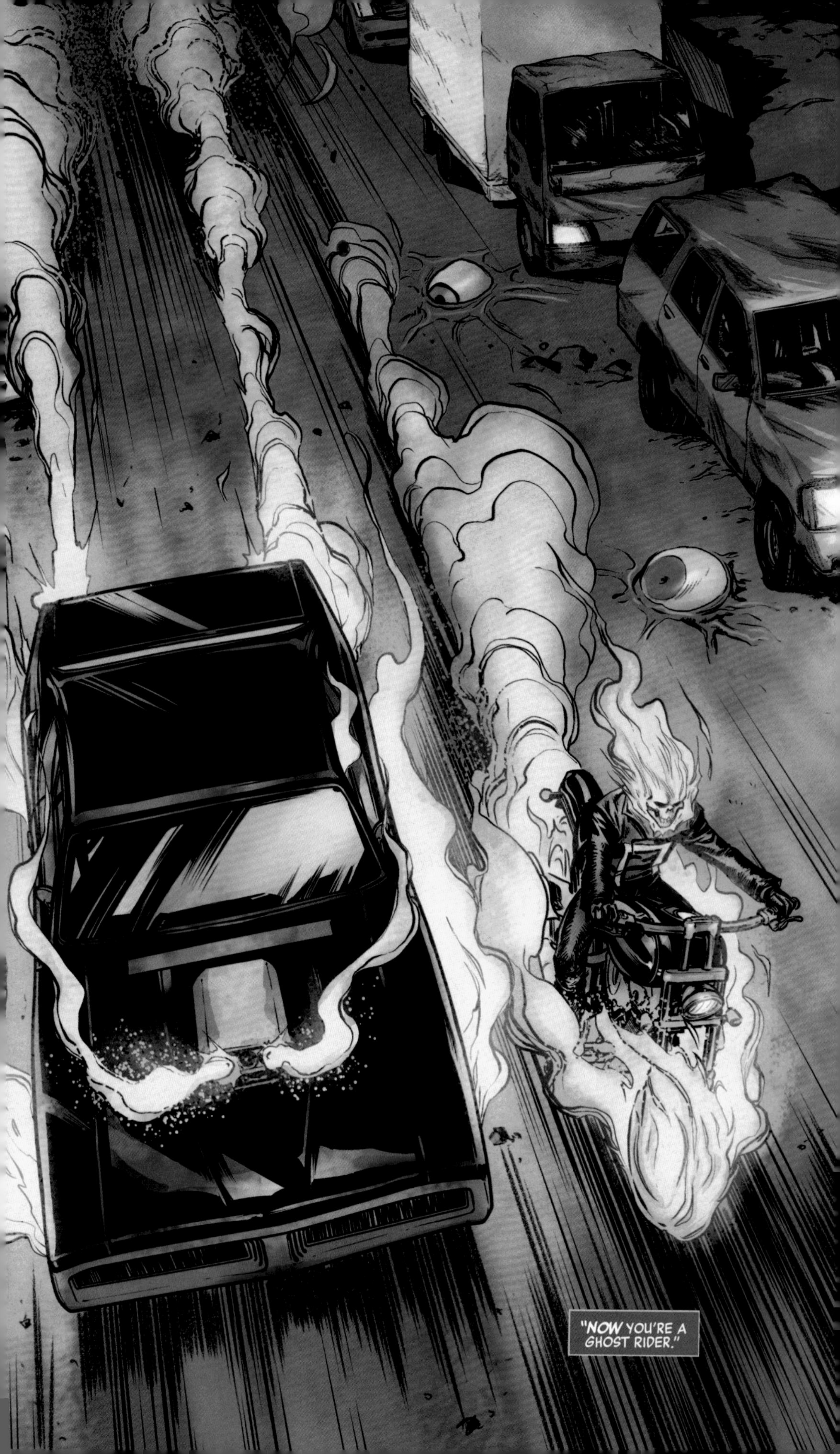
"NOW YOU'RE A GHOST RIDER."

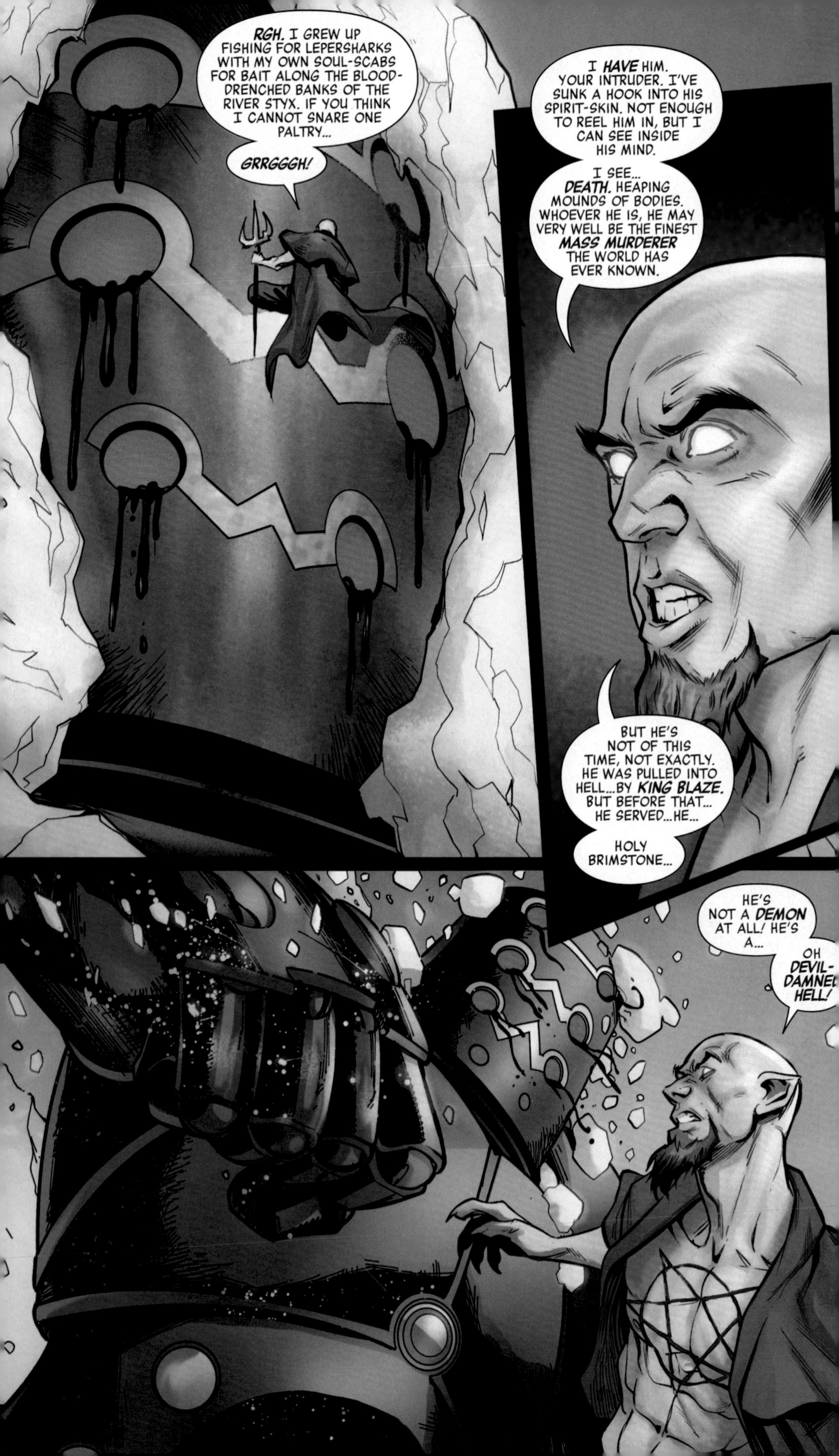
RGH. I GREW UP FISHING FOR LEPERSHARKS WITH MY OWN SOUL-SCABS FOR BAIT ALONG THE BLOOD-DRENCHED BANKS OF THE RIVER STYX. IF YOU THINK I CANNOT SNARE ONE PALTRY...
GRRGGGH!
I HAVE HIM. YOUR INTRUDER. I'VE SUNK A HOOK INTO HIS SPIRIT-SKIN. NOT ENOUGH TO REEL HIM IN, BUT I CAN SEE INSIDE HIS MIND.
I SEE... DEATH. HEAPING MOUNDS OF BODIES. WHOEVER HE IS, HE MAY VERY WELL BE THE FINEST MASS MURDERER THE WORLD HAS EVER KNOWN.
BUT HE'S NOT OF THIS TIME, NOT EXACTLY. HE WAS PULLED INTO HELL...BY KING BLAZE. BUT BEFORE THAT... HE SERVED...HE...
HOLY BRIMSTONE...
HE'S NOT A DEMON AT ALL! HE'S A...
OH DEVIL-DAMNED HELL!

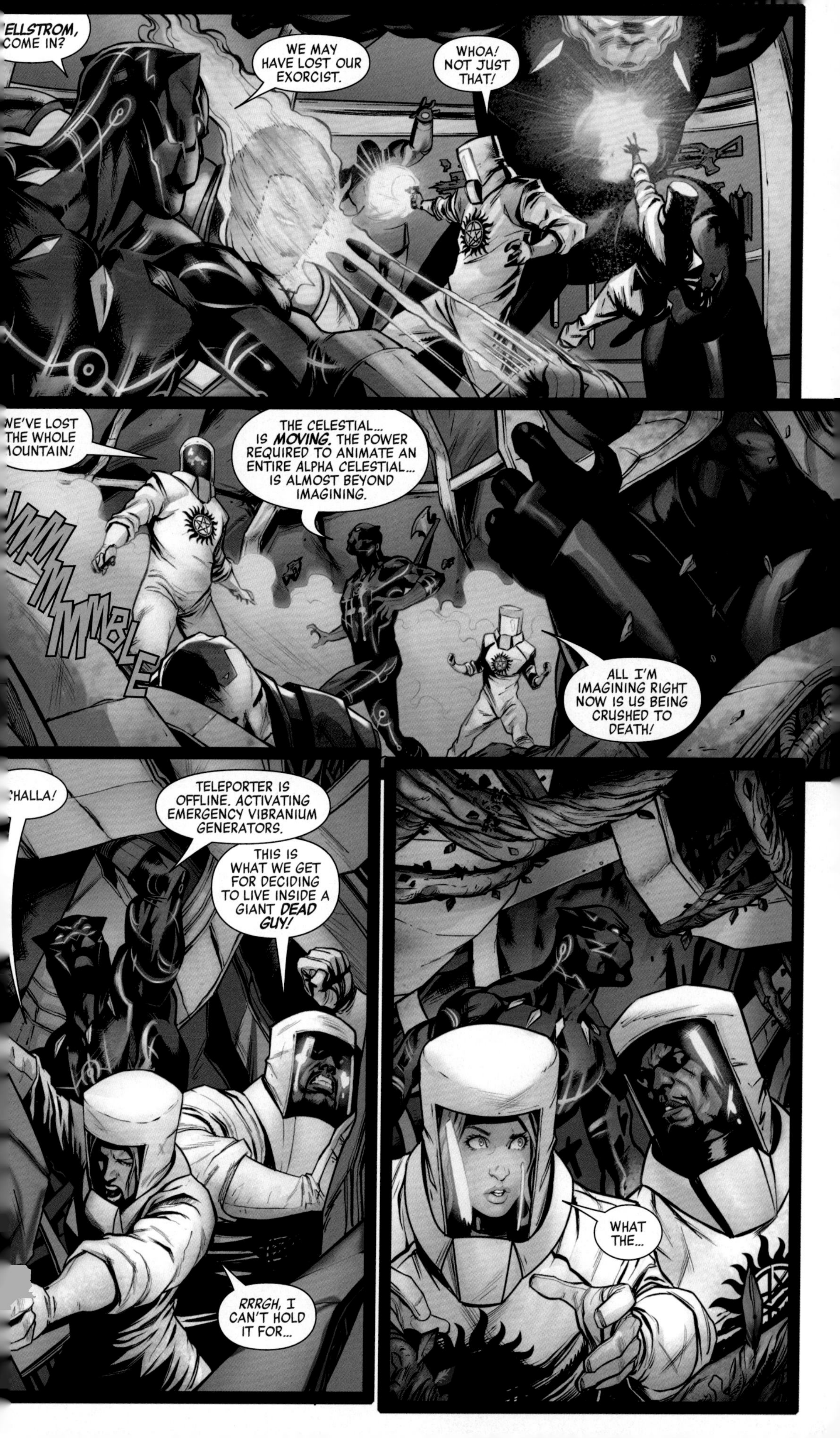
ELLSTROM, COME IN?
WE MAY HAVE LOST OUR EXORCIST.
WHOA! NOT JUST THAT!
WE'VE LOST THE WHOLE MOUNTAIN!
THE CELESTIAL... IS MOVING. THE POWER REQUIRED TO ANIMATE AN ENTIRE ALPHA CELESTIAL... IS ALMOST BEYOND IMAGINING.
MMMMMBLE
ALL I'M IMAGINING RIGHT NOW IS US BEING CRUSHED TO DEATH!
CHALLA!
TELEPORTER IS OFFLINE. ACTIVATING EMERGENCY VIBRANIUM GENERATORS.
THIS IS WHAT WE GET FOR DECIDING TO LIVE INSIDE A GIANT DEAD GUY!
RRRGH, I CAN'T HOLD IT FOR...
WHAT THE...

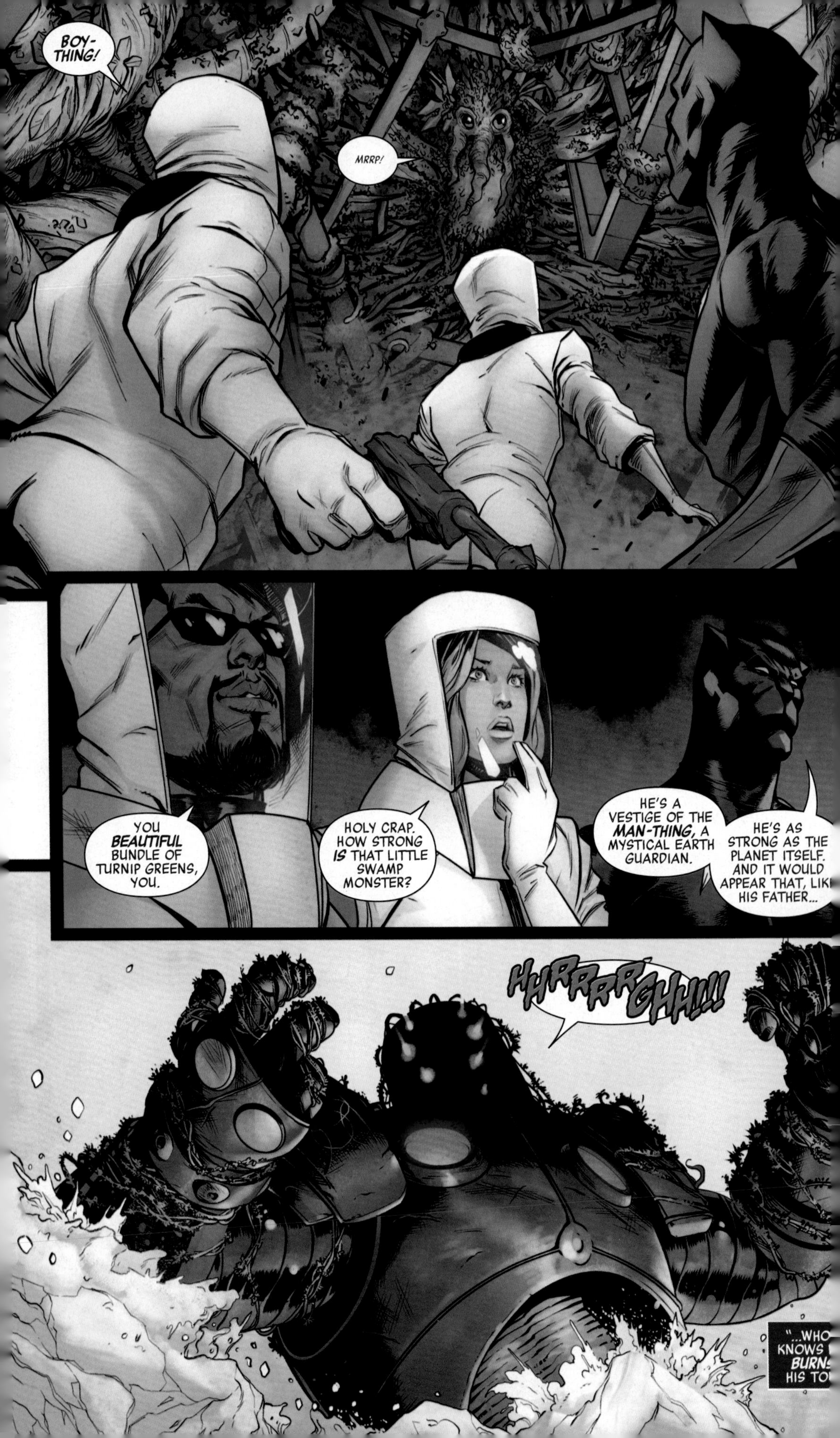
BOY-THING!
MRRP!
YOU BEAUTIFUL BUNDLE OF TURNIP GREENS, YOU.
HOLY CRAP. HOW STRONG IS THAT LITTLE SWAMP MONSTER?
HE'S A VESTIGE OF THE MAN-THING, A MYSTICAL EARTH GUARDIAN.
HE'S AS STRONG AS THE PLANET ITSELF. AND IT WOULD APPEAR THAT, LIK HIS FATHER...
HURRRRRGHH!!!
"...WHO KNOWS BURNS HIS TO

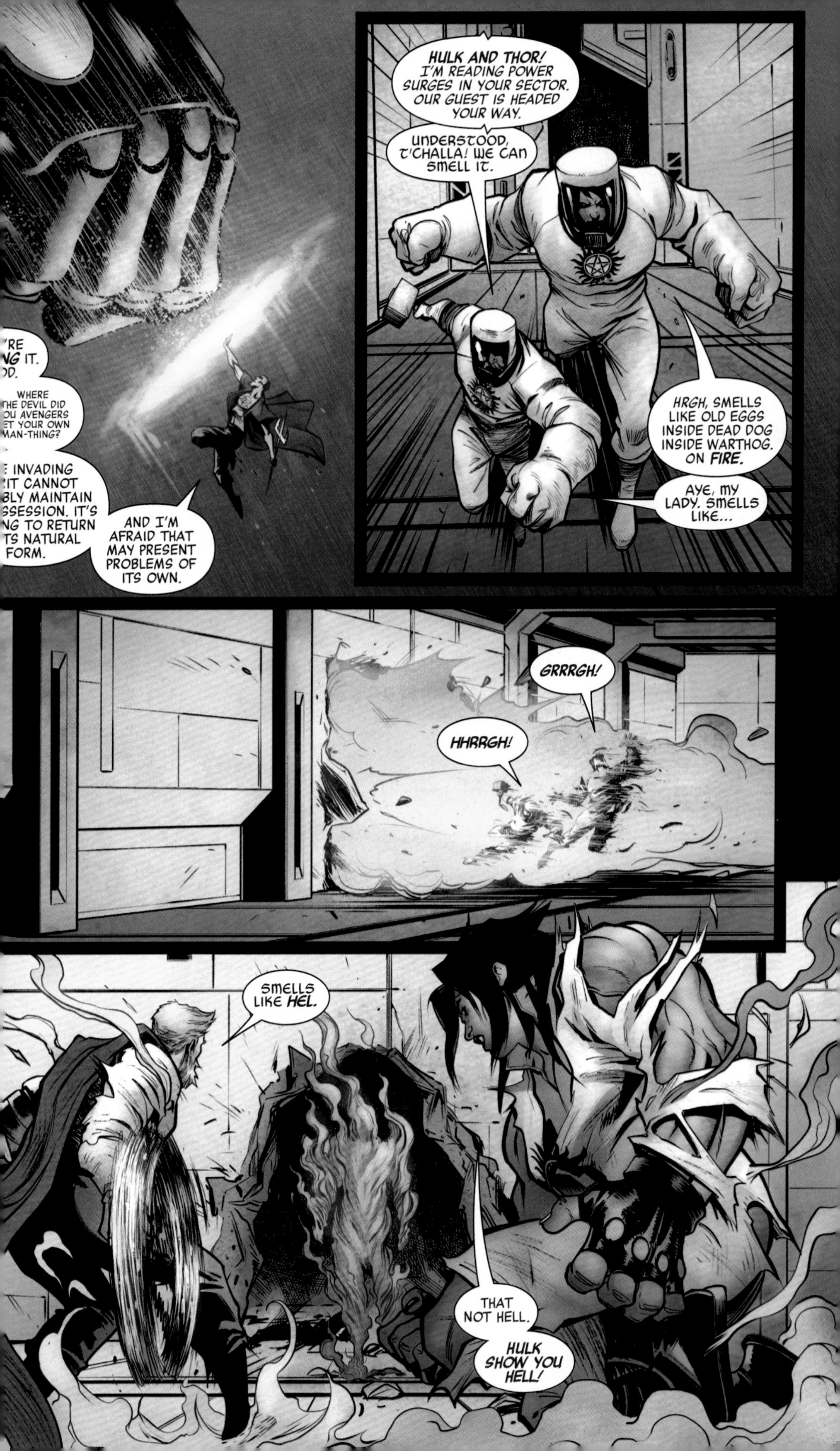
'RE
NG IT.
OD.
WHERE THE DEVIL DID
OU AVENGERS
ET YOUR OWN
MAN-THING?
E INVADING
RIT CANNOT
BLY MAINTAIN
SSESSION. IT'S
NG TO RETURN
TS NATURAL
FORM.
AND I'M AFRAID THAT MAY PRESENT PROBLEMS OF ITS OWN.
HULK AND THOR! I'M READING POWER SURGES IN YOUR SECTOR. OUR GUEST IS HEADED YOUR WAY.
UNDERSTOOD, T'CHALLA! WE CAN SMELL IT.
HRGH, SMELLS LIKE OLD EGGS INSIDE DEAD DOG INSIDE WARTHOG. ON FIRE.
AYE, MY LADY. SMELLS LIKE...
GRRRGH!
HHRRGH!
SMELLS LIKE HEL.
THAT NOT HELL.
HULK SHOW YOU HELL!

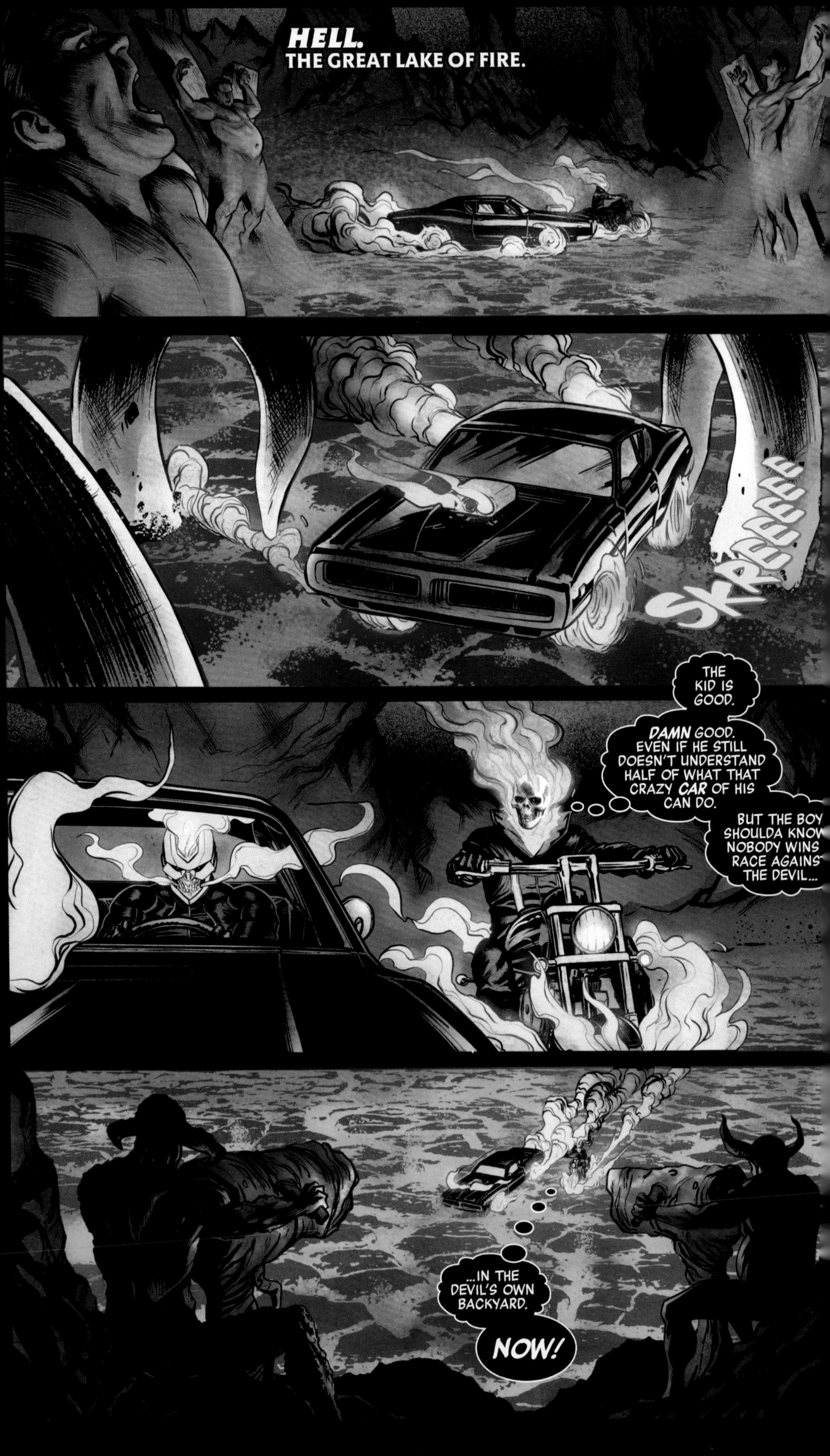
HELL.
THE GREAT LAKE OF FIRE.
SKREEEEEE
THE KID IS GOOD.
DAMN GOOD. EVEN IF HE STILL DOESN'T UNDERSTAND HALF OF WHAT THAT CRAZY CAR OF HIS CAN DO.
BUT THE BOY SHOULDA KNOW NOBODY WINS RACE AGAINST THE DEVIL...
...IN THE DEVIL'S OWN BACKYARD.
NOW!

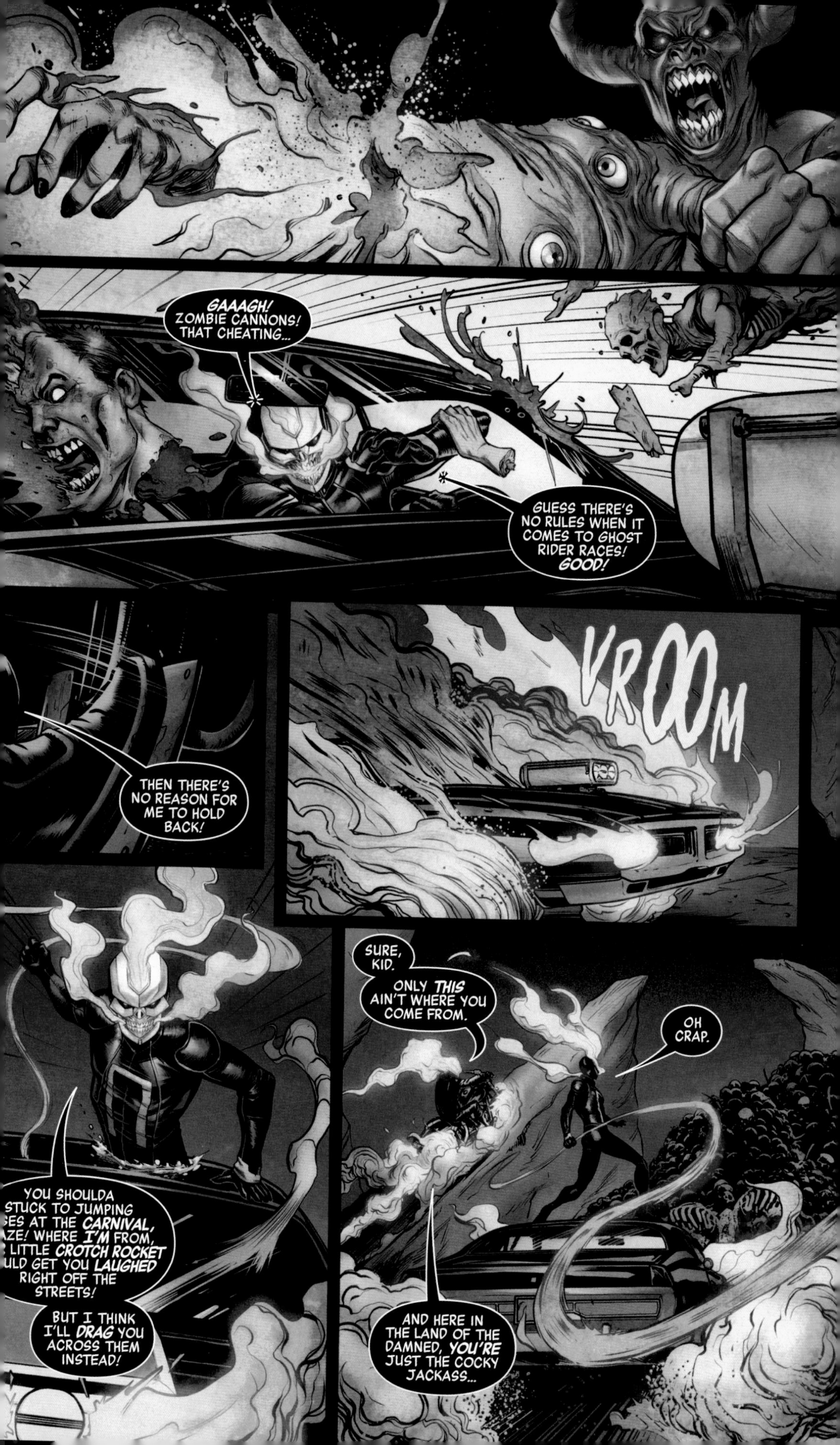

GAAAGH! ZOMBIE CANNONS! THAT CHEATING...
GUESS THERE'S NO RULES WHEN IT COMES TO GHOST RIDER RACES! GOOD!
THEN THERE'S NO REASON FOR ME TO HOLD BACK!
VROOM
YOU SHOULDA STUCK TO JUMPING ...ES AT THE CARNIVAL, ...ZE! WHERE I'M FROM, ... LITTLE CROTCH ROCKET ...ULD GET YOU LAUGHED RIGHT OFF THE STREETS!
BUT I THINK I'LL DRAG YOU ACROSS THEM INSTEAD!
SURE, KID.
ONLY THIS AIN'T WHERE YOU COME FROM.
OH CRAP.
AND HERE IN THE LAND OF THE DAMNED, YOU'RE JUST THE COCKY JACKASS...

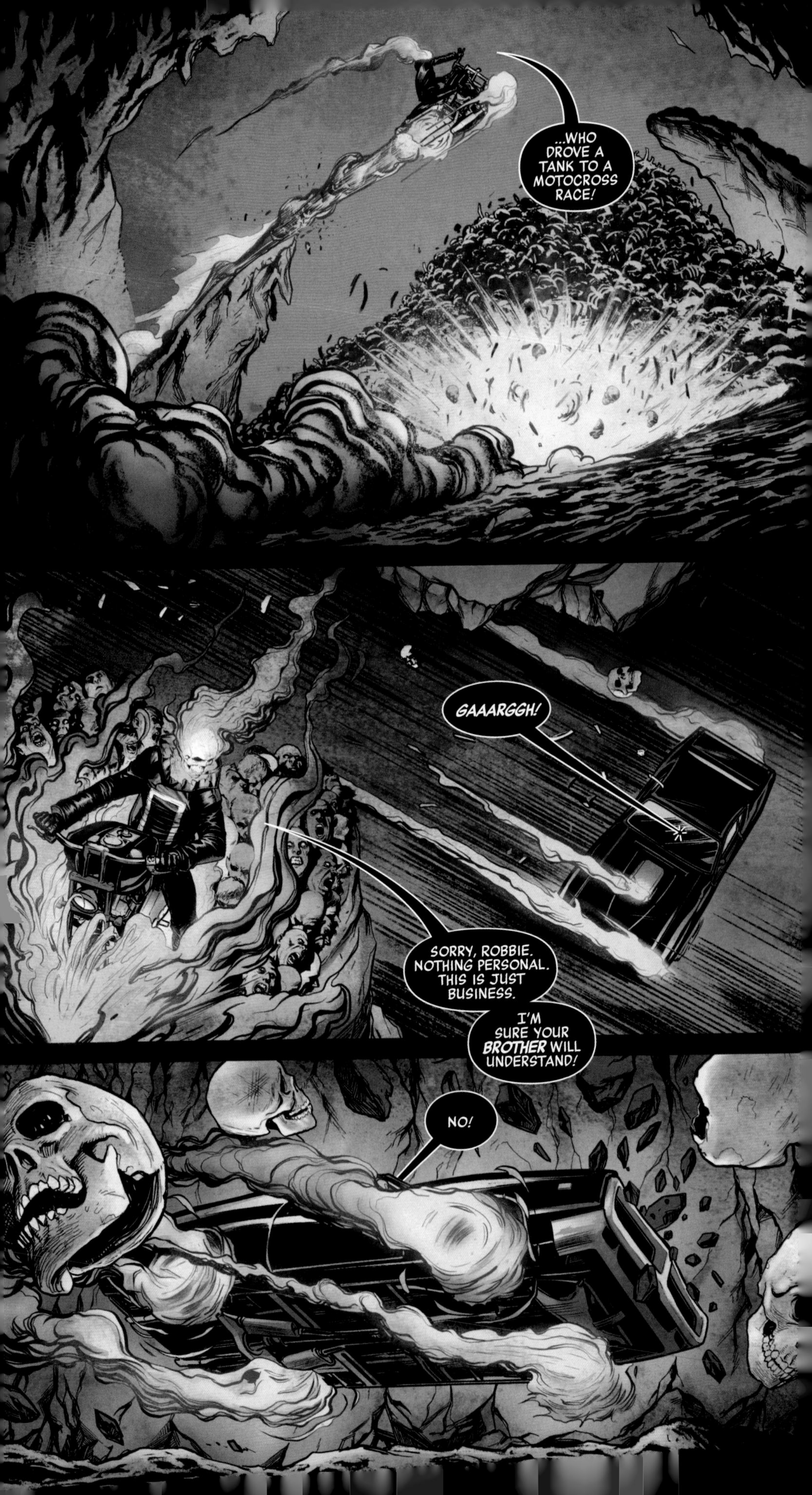
...WHO DROVE A TANK TO A MOTOCROSS RACE!
GAAARGGH!
SORRY, ROBBIE. NOTHING PERSONAL. THIS IS JUST BUSINESS.
I'M SURE YOUR BROTHER WILL UNDERSTAND!
NO!

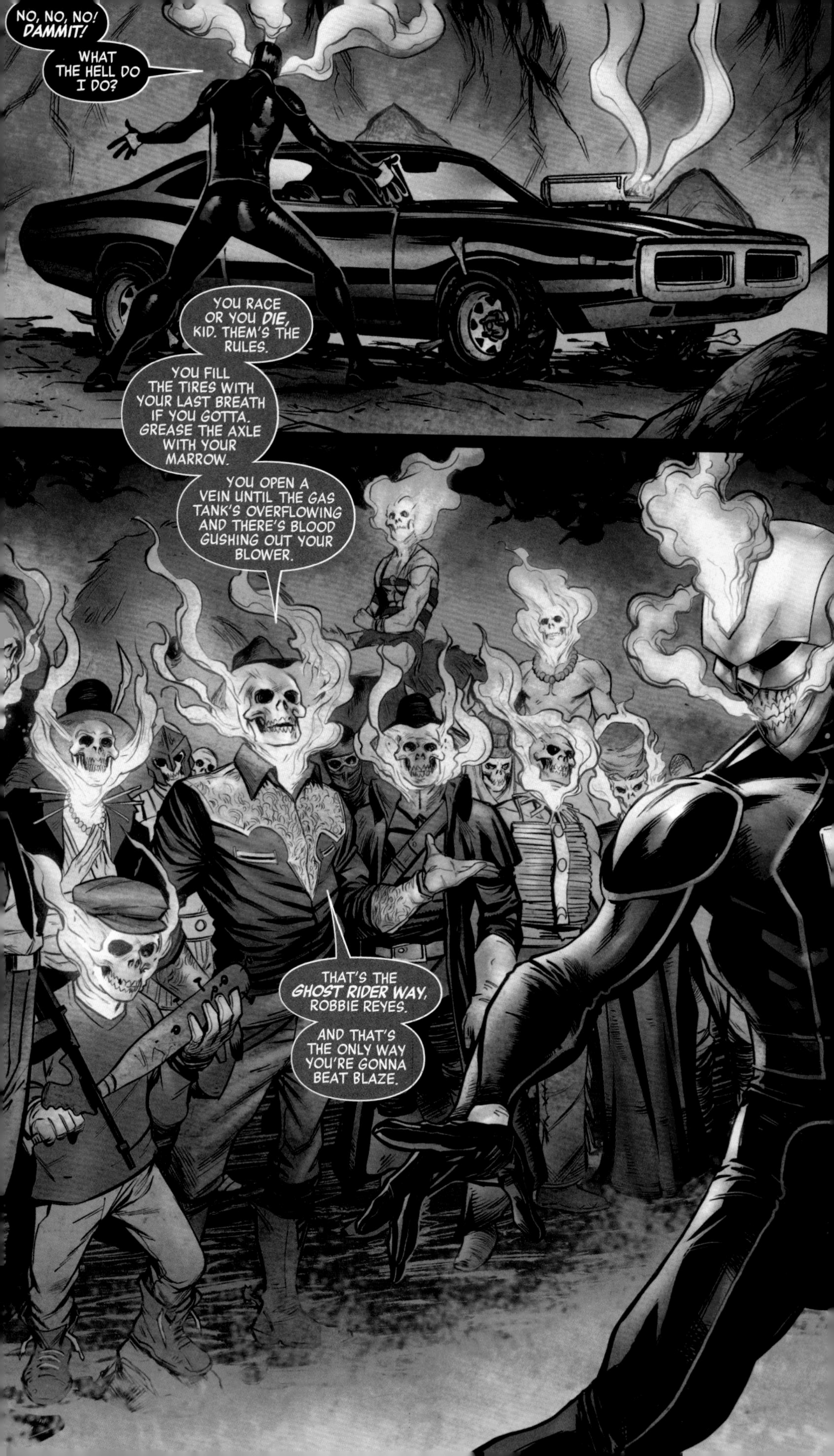
NO, NO, NO! DAMMIT!
WHAT THE HELL DO I DO?
YOU RACE OR YOU DIE, KID. THEM'S THE RULES.
YOU FILL THE TIRES WITH YOUR LAST BREATH IF YOU GOTTA. GREASE THE AXLE WITH YOUR MARROW.
YOU OPEN A VEIN UNTIL THE GAS TANK'S OVERFLOWING AND THERE'S BLOOD GUSHING OUT YOUR BLOWER.
THAT'S THE GHOST RIDER WAY, ROBBIE REYES.
AND THAT'S THE ONLY WAY YOU'RE GONNA BEAT BLAZE.

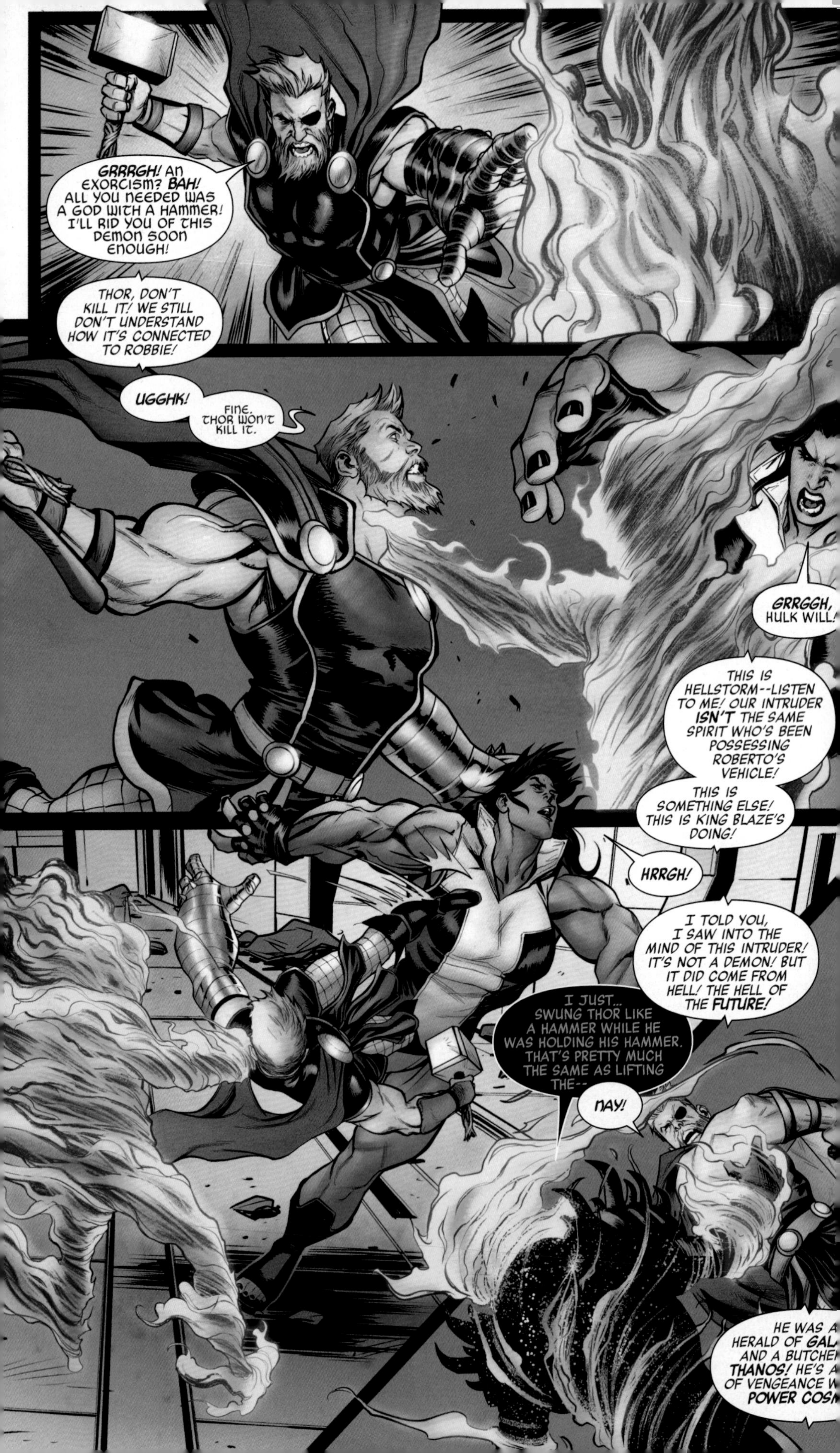
GRRRGH! AN EXORCISM? BAH! ALL YOU NEEDED WAS A GOD WITH A HAMMER! I'LL RID YOU OF THIS DEMON SOON ENOUGH!
THOR, DON'T KILL IT! WE STILL DON'T UNDERSTAND HOW IT'S CONNECTED TO ROBBIE!
UGGHK!
FINE. THOR WON'T KILL IT.
GRRGGH, HULK WILL!
THIS IS HELLSTORM--LISTEN TO ME! OUR INTRUDER ISN'T THE SAME SPIRIT WHO'S BEEN POSSESSING ROBERTO'S VEHICLE!
THIS IS SOMETHING ELSE! THIS IS KING BLAZE'S DOING!
HRRGH!
I TOLD YOU, I SAW INTO THE MIND OF THIS INTRUDER! IT'S NOT A DEMON! BUT IT DID COME FROM HELL! THE HELL OF THE FUTURE!
I JUST... SWUNG THOR LIKE A HAMMER WHILE HE WAS HOLDING HIS HAMMER. THAT'S PRETTY MUCH THE SAME AS LIFTING THE--
NAY!

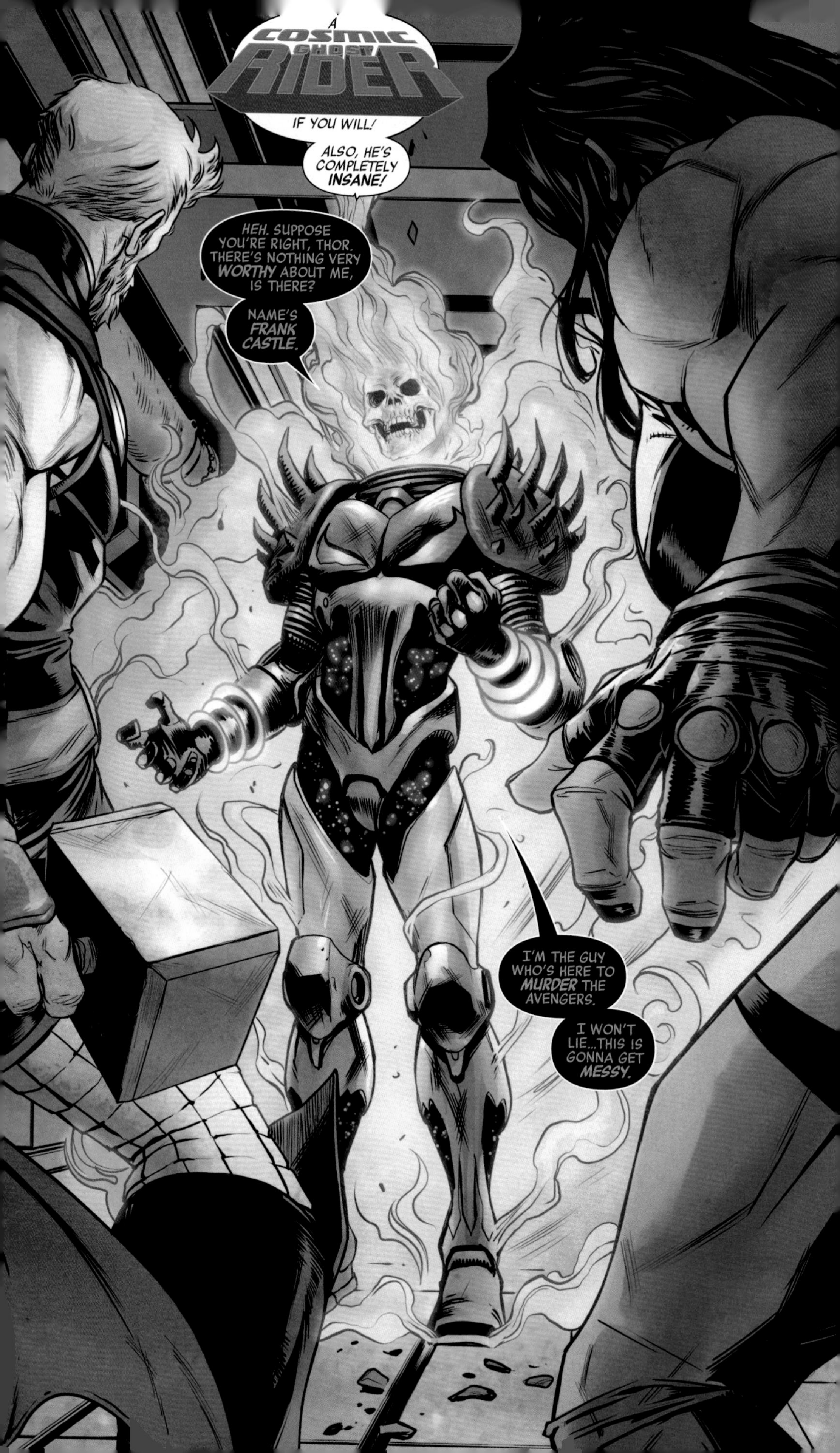
A COSMIC GHOST RIDER
IF YOU WILL!
ALSO, HE'S COMPLETELY INSANE!
HEH. SUPPOSE YOU'RE RIGHT, THOR. THERE'S NOTHING VERY WORTHY ABOUT ME, IS THERE?
NAME'S FRANK CASTLE.
I'M THE GUY WHO'S HERE TO MURDER THE AVENGERS.
I WON'T LIE...THIS IS GONNA GET MESSY.

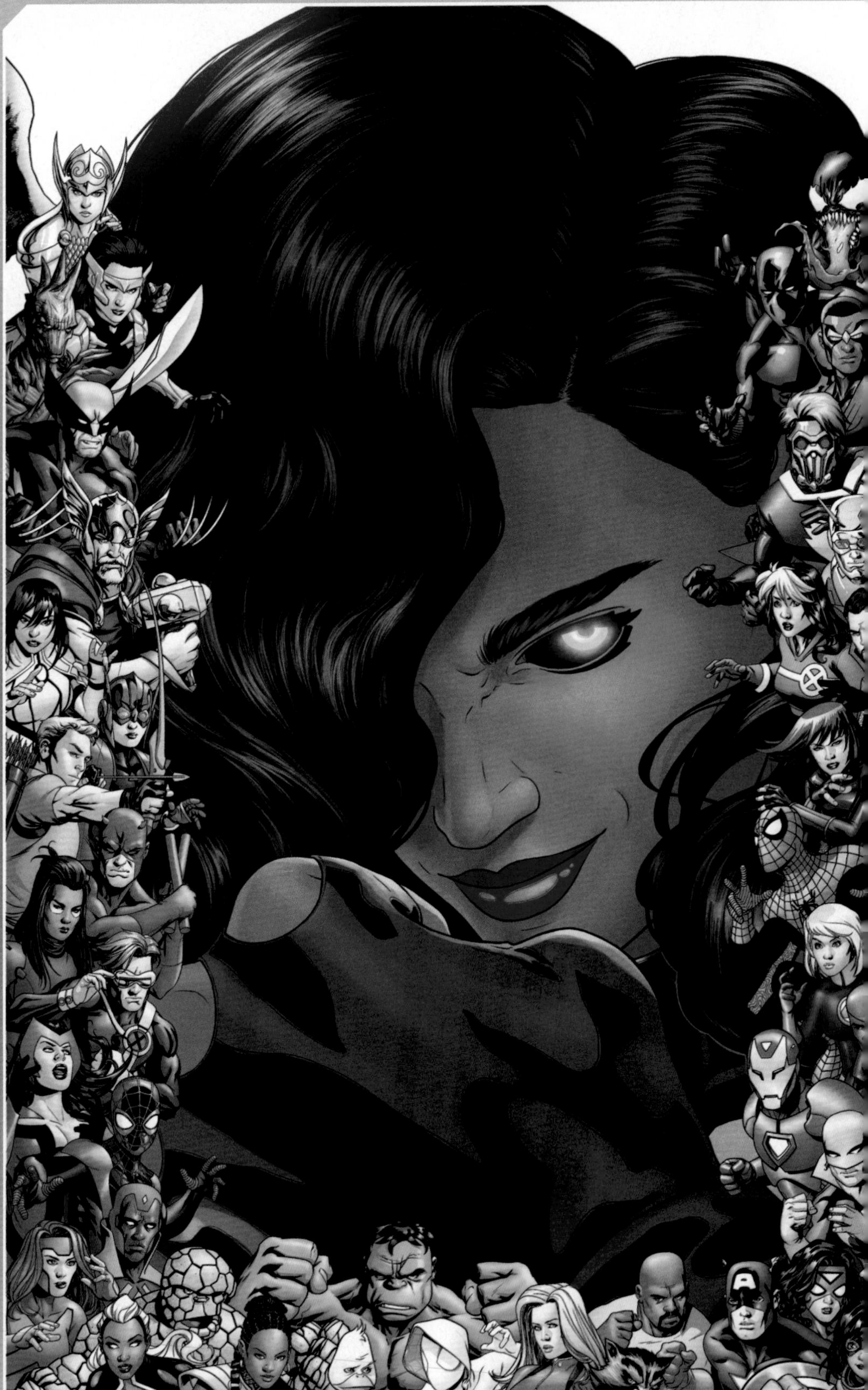

RUSSELL DAUTERMAN & MATTHEW WILSON
WITH MIKE McKONE & EDGAR DELGADO
23 FRAME VARIANT

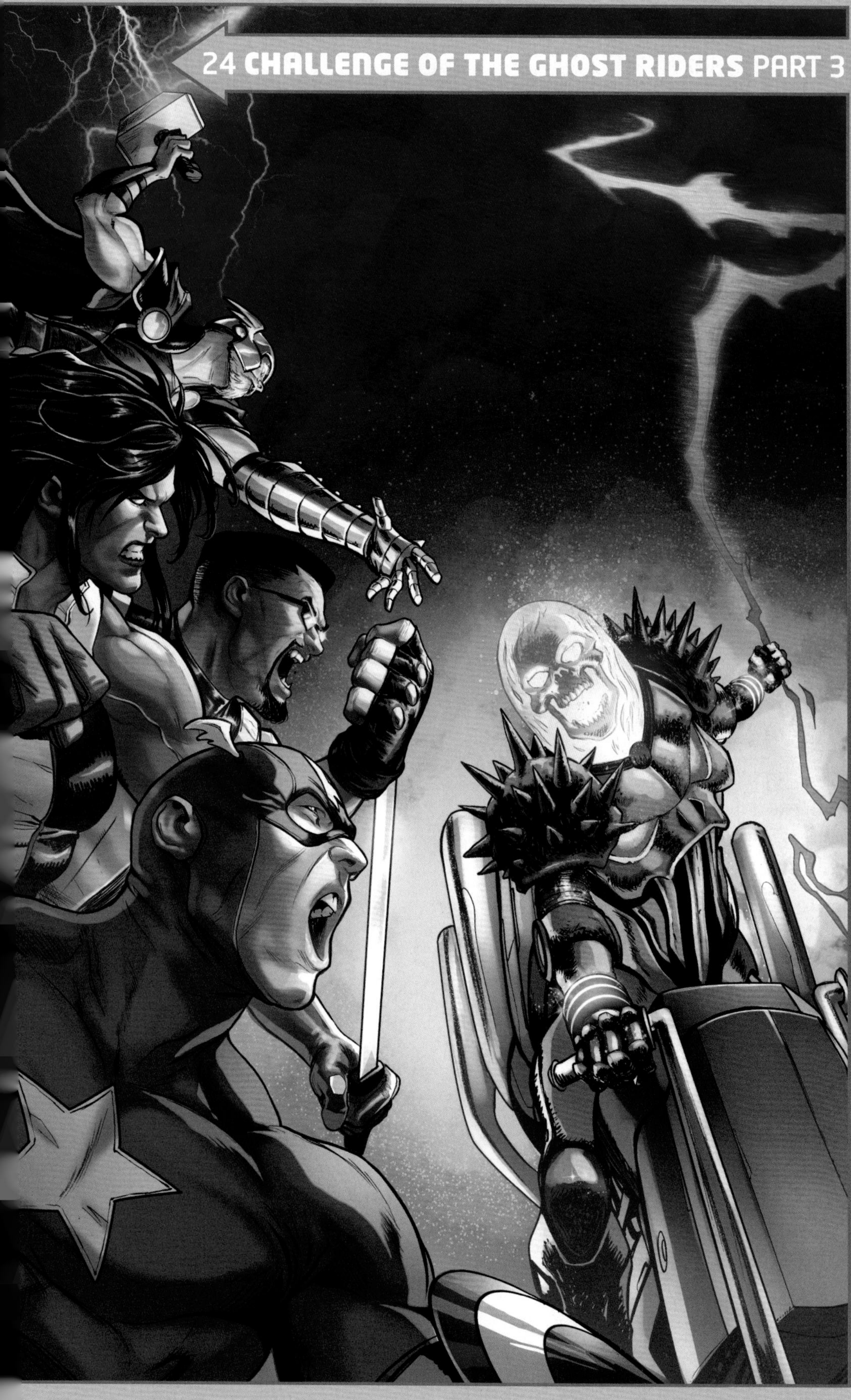
24 CHALLENGE OF THE GHOST RIDERS PART 3

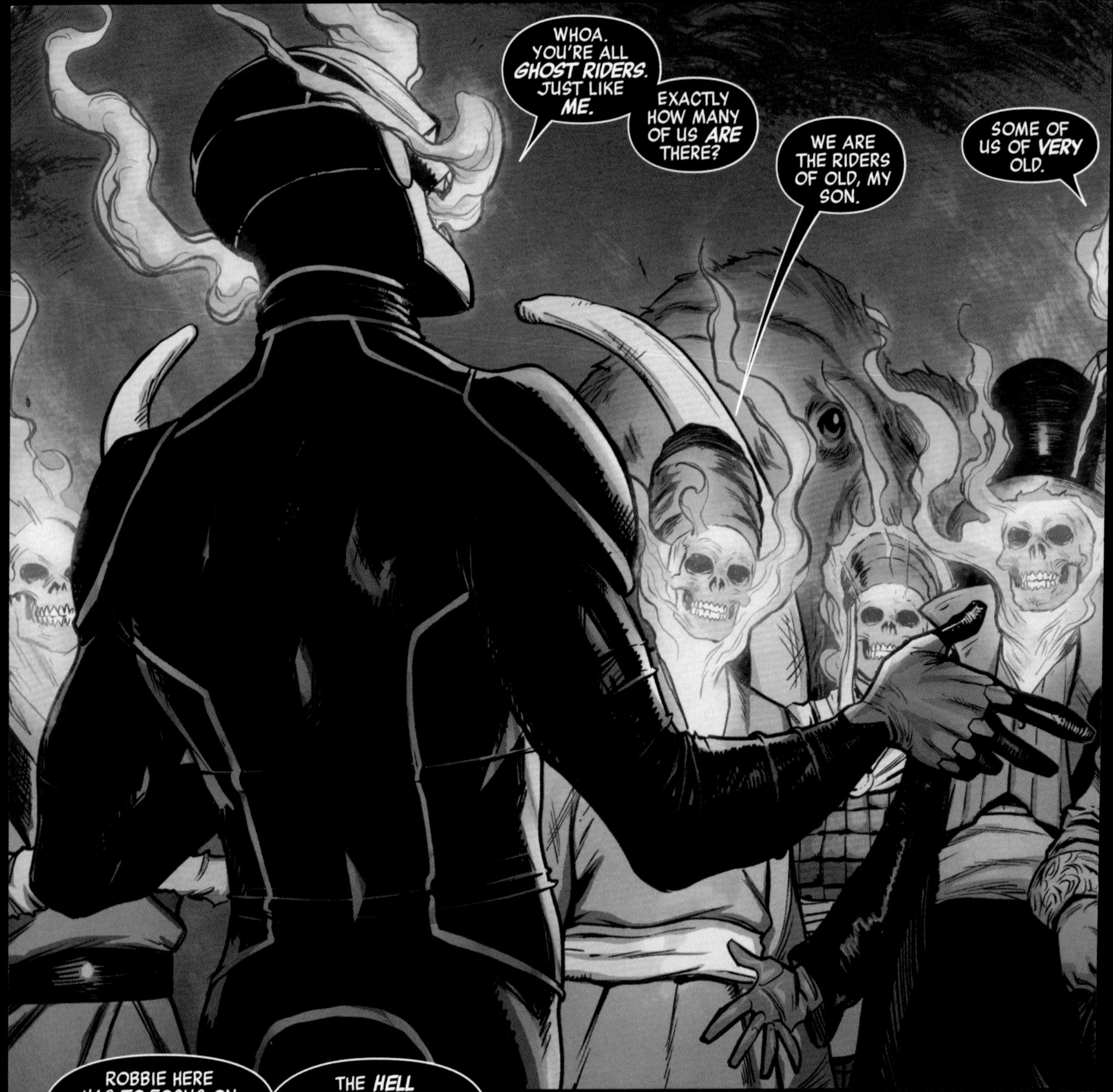
WHOA. YOU'RE ALL **GHOST RIDERS**. JUST LIKE **ME.**
EXACTLY HOW MANY OF US **ARE** THERE?
WE ARE THE RIDERS OF OLD, MY SON.
SOME OF US OF **VERY** OLD.

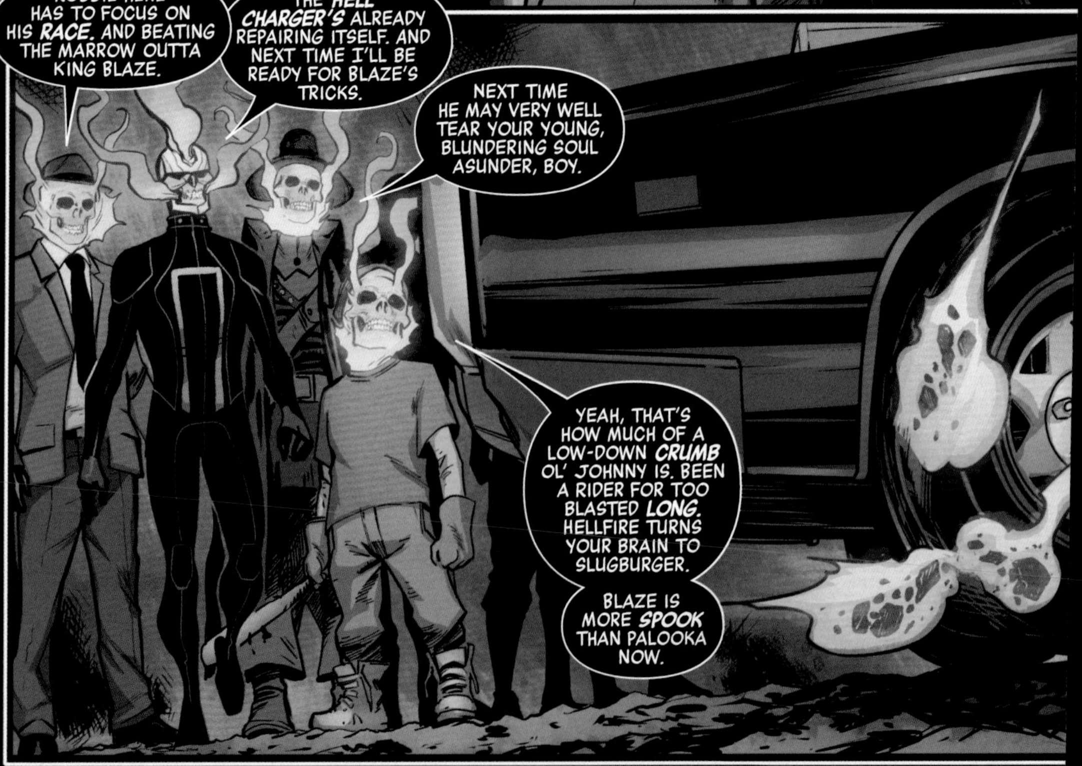
ROBBIE HERE HAS TO FOCUS ON HIS **RACE.** AND BEATING THE MARROW OUTTA KING BLAZE.
THE **HELL CHARGER'S** ALREADY REPAIRING ITSELF. AND NEXT TIME I'LL BE READY FOR BLAZE'S TRICKS.
NEXT TIME HE MAY VERY WELL TEAR YOUR YOUNG, BLUNDERING SOUL ASUNDER, BOY.
YEAH, THAT'S HOW MUCH OF A LOW-DOWN **CRUMB** OL' JOHNNY IS. BEEN A RIDER FOR TOO BLASTED **LONG.** HELLFIRE TURNS YOUR BRAIN TO SLUGBURGER.
BLAZE IS MORE **SPOOK** THAN PALOOKA NOW.

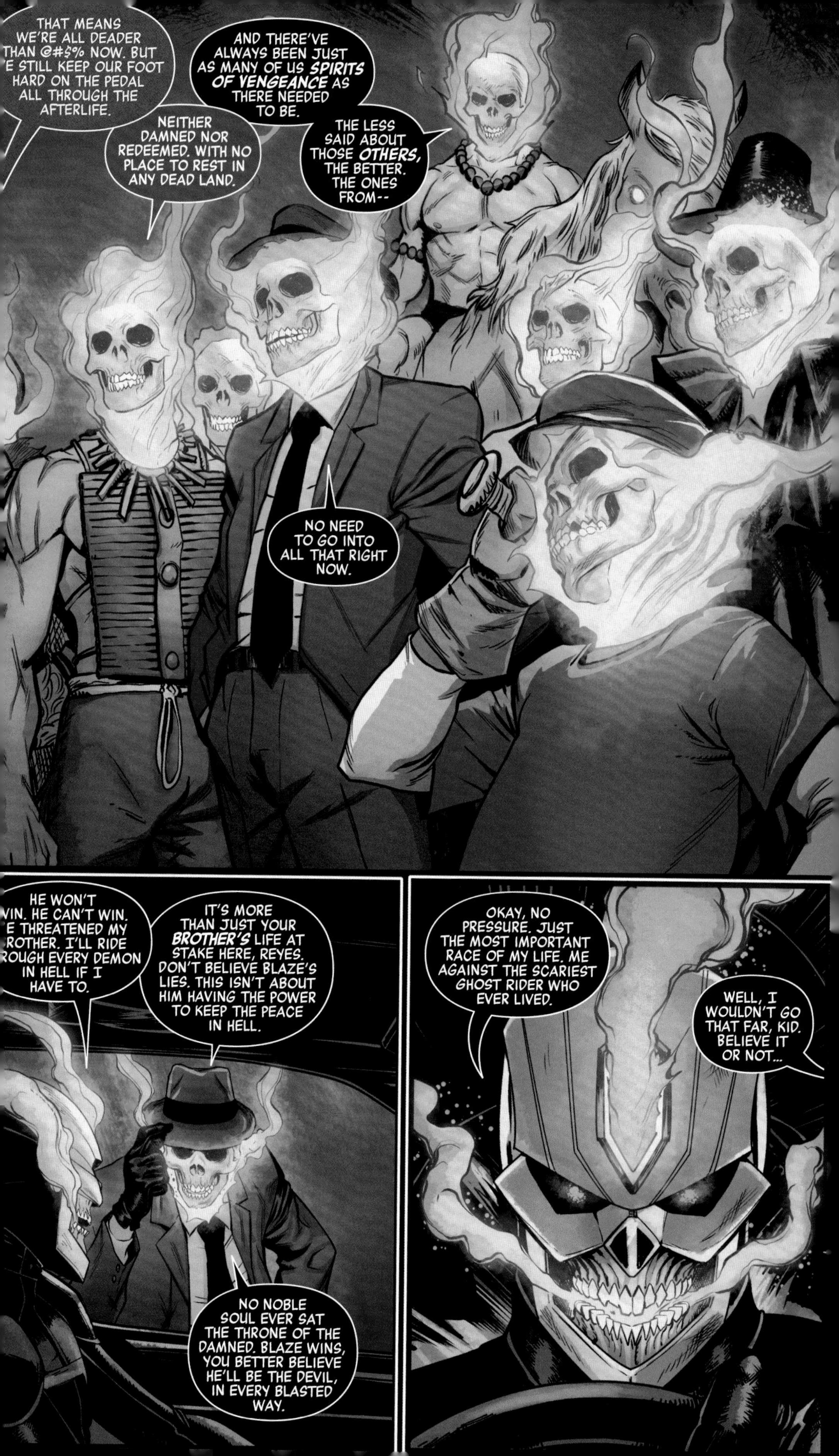

THAT MEANS WE'RE ALL DEADER THAN @#$% NOW. BUT 'E STILL KEEP OUR FOOT HARD ON THE PEDAL ALL THROUGH THE AFTERLIFE.
NEITHER DAMNED NOR REDEEMED. WITH NO PLACE TO REST IN ANY DEAD LAND.
AND THERE'VE ALWAYS BEEN JUST AS MANY OF US SPIRITS OF VENGEANCE AS THERE NEEDED TO BE.
THE LESS SAID ABOUT THOSE OTHERS, THE BETTER. THE ONES FROM--
NO NEED TO GO INTO ALL THAT RIGHT NOW.
HE WON'T VIN. HE CAN'T WIN. E THREATENED MY ROTHER. I'LL RIDE ROUGH EVERY DEMON IN HELL IF I HAVE TO.
IT'S MORE THAN JUST YOUR BROTHER'S LIFE AT STAKE HERE, REYES. DON'T BELIEVE BLAZE'S LIES. THIS ISN'T ABOUT HIM HAVING THE POWER TO KEEP THE PEACE IN HELL.
NO NOBLE SOUL EVER SAT THE THRONE OF THE DAMNED. BLAZE WINS, YOU BETTER BELIEVE HE'LL BE THE DEVIL, IN EVERY BLASTED WAY.
OKAY, NO PRESSURE. JUST THE MOST IMPORTANT RACE OF MY LIFE. ME AGAINST THE SCARIEST GHOST RIDER WHO EVER LIVED.
WELL, I WOULDN'T GO THAT FAR, KID. BELIEVE IT OR NOT...

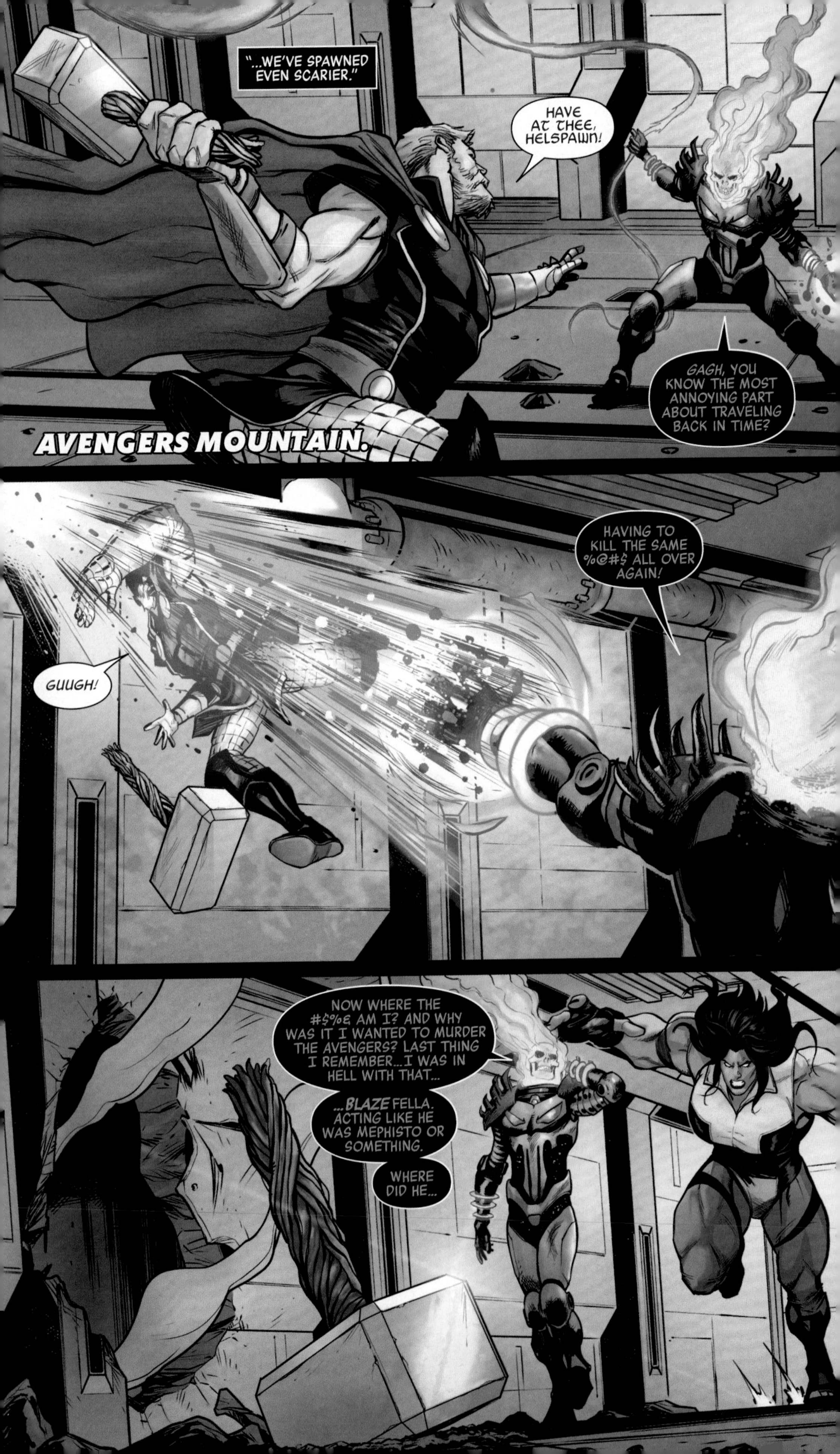
"...WE'VE SPAWNED EVEN SCARIER."
HAVE AT THEE, HELSPAWN!
GAGH, YOU KNOW THE MOST ANNOYING PART ABOUT TRAVELING BACK IN TIME?
AVENGERS MOUNTAIN.
HAVING TO KILL THE SAME %@#$ ALL OVER AGAIN!
GUUGH!
NOW WHERE THE #$%£ AM I? AND WHY WAS IT I WANTED TO MURDER THE AVENGERS? LAST THING I REMEMBER...I WAS IN HELL WITH THAT...
...BLAZE FELLA. ACTING LIKE HE WAS MEPHISTO OR SOMETHING.
WHERE DID HE...

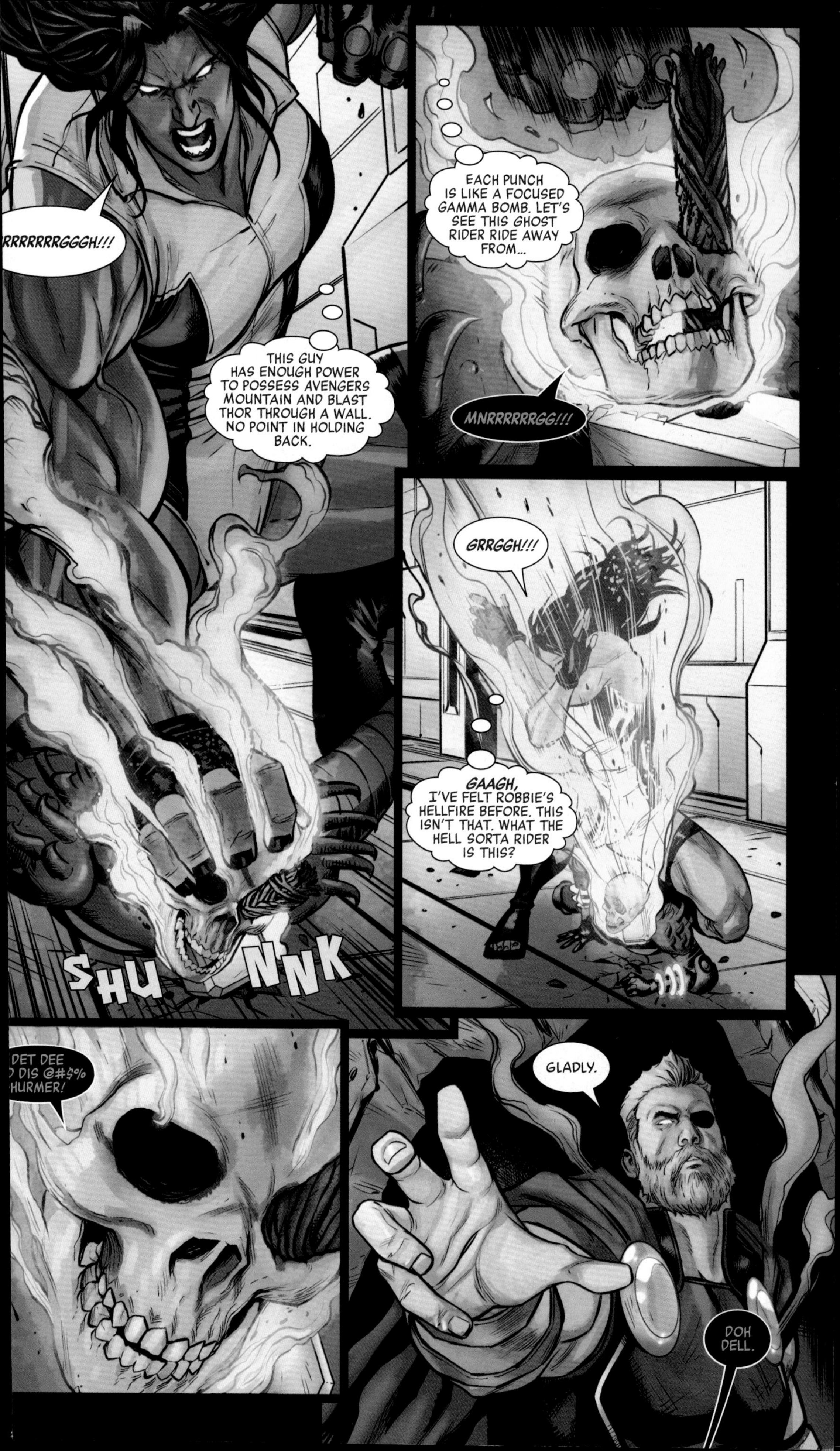
RRRRRRRRGGGH!!!
THIS GUY HAS ENOUGH POWER TO POSSESS AVENGERS MOUNTAIN AND BLAST THOR THROUGH A WALL. NO POINT IN HOLDING BACK.
SHU NNK
EACH PUNCH IS LIKE A FOCUSED GAMMA BOMB. LET'S SEE THIS GHOST RIDER RIDE AWAY FROM...
MNRRRRRRGG!!!
GRRGGH!!!
GAAGH, I'VE FELT ROBBIE'S HELLFIRE BEFORE. THIS ISN'T THAT. WHAT THE HELL SORTA RIDER IS THIS?
DET DEE D DIS @#$% HURMER!
GLADLY.
DOH DELL.

NNRRRRRRRRRGGGH!!!

PERHAPS *NOW* YOU MAY FEEL MORE APT TO EXPLAIN YOURSELF, TRESPASSER.

DUE DDRIPS RY *DEAD* OFD DAN WRANTS DEE DA DWALK.

DIE *DRESPAK* DAT. DUT *GHERE'S* RY WRANSWER.

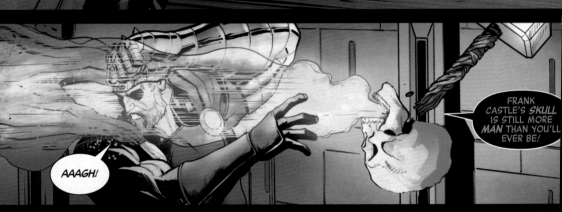

FRANK CASTLE'S *SKULL* IS STILL MORE *MAN* THAN YOU'LL EVER BE!

AAAGH!

AND HIS HEADLESS BODY AIN'T TOO SHABBY EITHER, *HUH,* HULK?

RRAAAGH!

YOU'VE GOTTA! BE! *KIDDING* ME!!!

VERY WELL! LET'S SEE HOW MUCH OF A MAN YOU FEEL LIKE ONCE I'VE HAMMERED YOUR INSOLENT SKULL INTO DUST!

YOU AND YOUR MAGIC FI HAMMER DON'T ME, PAL. BELIEV ANYTHING TH CAN DO...

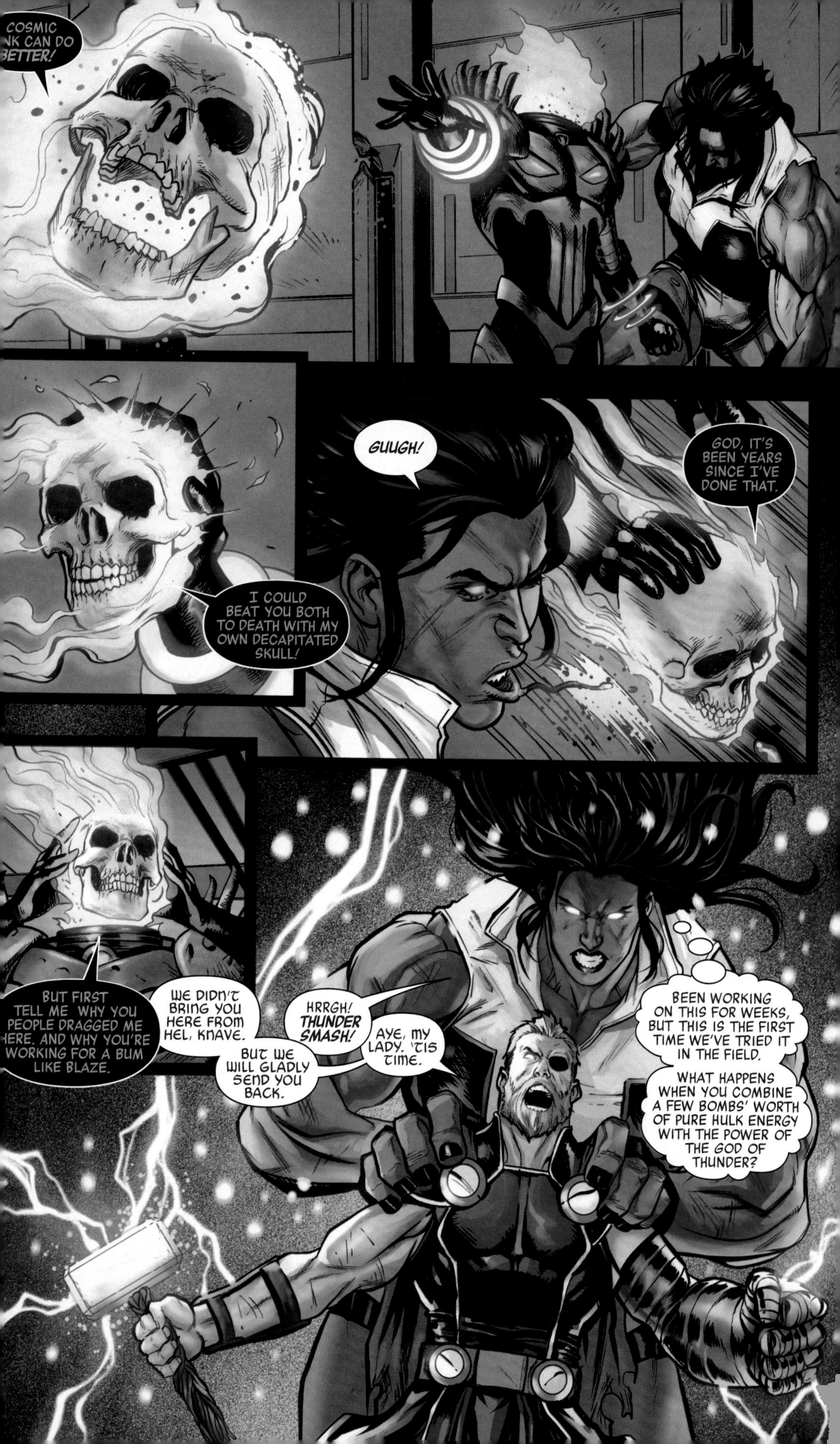
COSMIC
NK CAN DO
BETTER!
I COULD BEAT YOU BOTH TO DEATH WITH MY OWN DECAPITATED SKULL!
GUUGH!
GOD, IT'S BEEN YEARS SINCE I'VE DONE THAT.
BUT FIRST TELL ME WHY YOU PEOPLE DRAGGED ME HERE. AND WHY YOU'RE WORKING FOR A BUM LIKE BLAZE.
WE DIDN'T BRING YOU HERE FROM HEL, KNAVE.
BUT WE WILL GLADLY SEND YOU BACK.
HRRGH! THUNDER SMASH!
AYE, MY LADY. 'TIS TIME.
BEEN WORKING ON THIS FOR WEEKS, BUT THIS IS THE FIRST TIME WE'VE TRIED IT IN THE FIELD.
WHAT HAPPENS WHEN YOU COMBINE A FEW BOMBS' WORTH OF PURE HULK ENERGY WITH THE POWER OF THE GOD OF THUNDER?

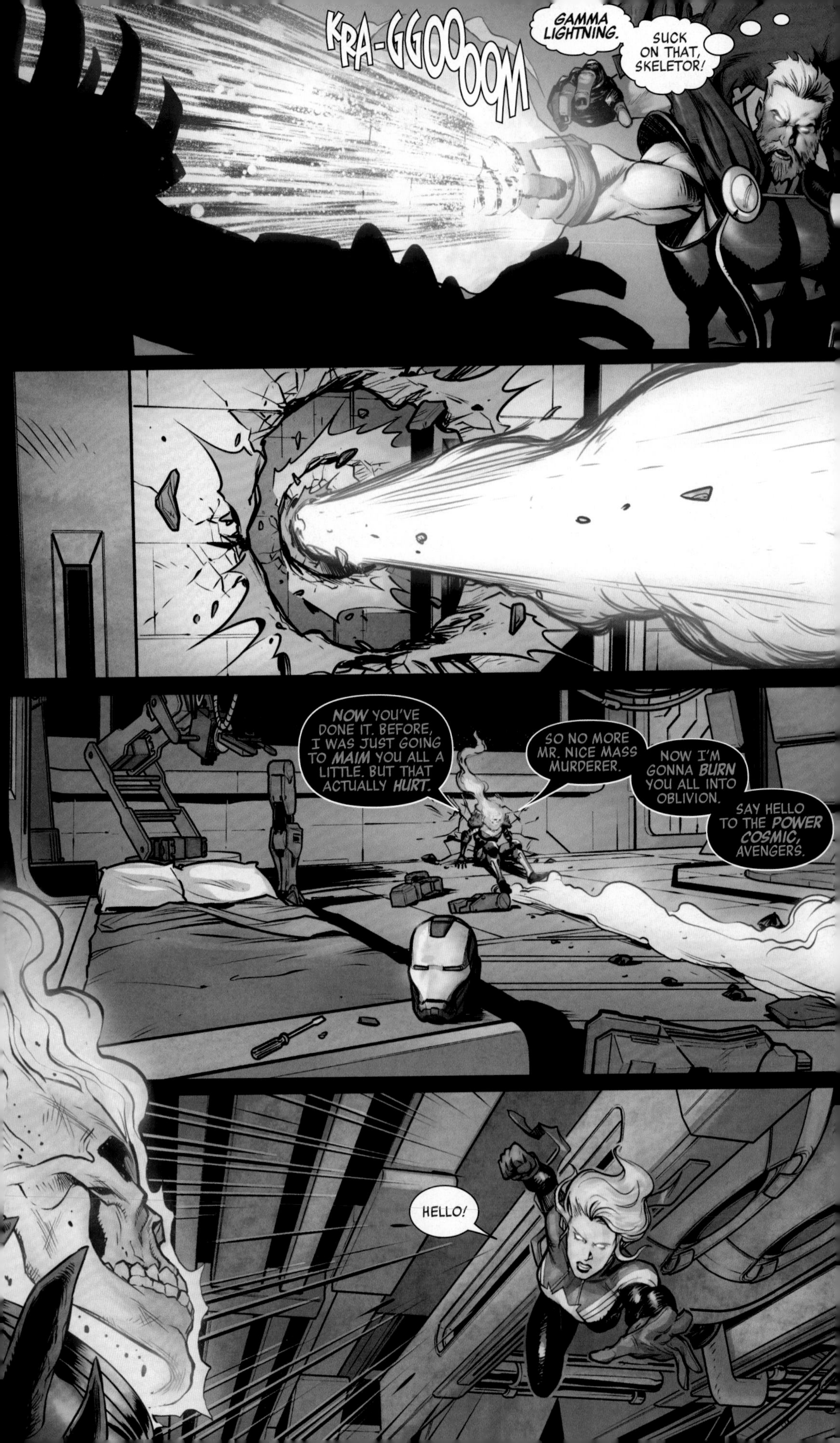
KRA-GGOOOOOM
GAMMA LIGHTNING.
SUCK ON THAT, SKELETOR!
NOW YOU'VE DONE IT. BEFORE, I WAS JUST GOING TO MAIM YOU ALL A LITTLE. BUT THAT ACTUALLY HURT.
SO NO MORE MR. NICE MASS MURDERER.
NOW I'M GONNA BURN YOU ALL INTO OBLIVION.
SAY HELLO TO THE POWER COSMIC, AVENGERS.
HELLO!

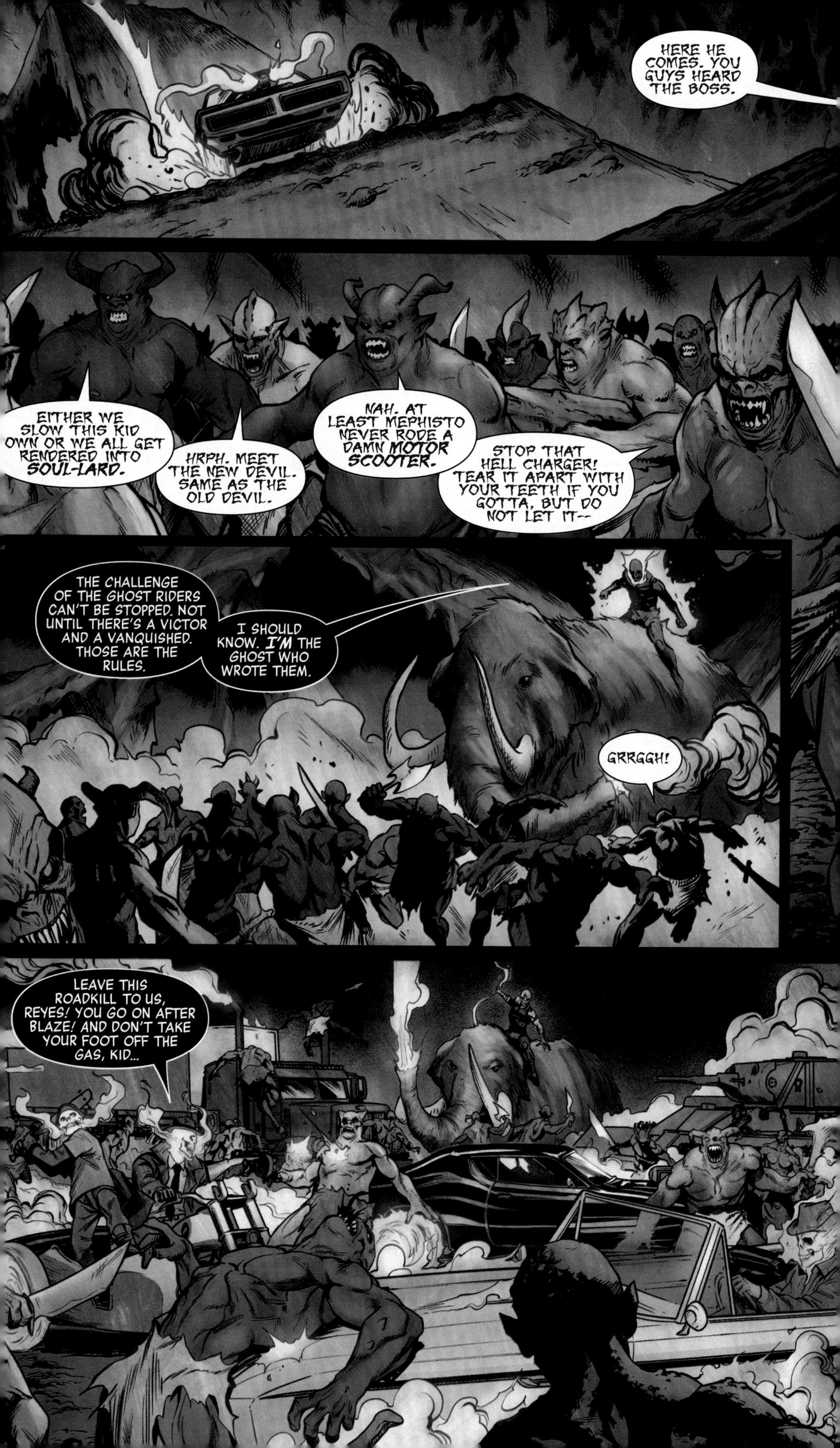
HERE HE COMES. YOU GUYS HEARD THE BOSS.
EITHER WE SLOW THIS KID OWN OR WE ALL GET RENDERED INTO SOUL-LARD.
HRPH. MEET THE NEW DEVIL. SAME AS THE OLD DEVIL.
NAH. AT LEAST MEPHISTO NEVER RODE A DAMN MOTOR SCOOTER.
STOP THAT HELL CHARGER! TEAR IT APART WITH YOUR TEETH IF YOU GOTTA, BUT DO NOT LET IT--
THE CHALLENGE OF THE GHOST RIDERS CAN'T BE STOPPED. NOT UNTIL THERE'S A VICTOR AND A VANQUISHED. THOSE ARE THE RULES.
I SHOULD KNOW. I'M THE GHOST WHO WROTE THEM.
GRRGGH!
LEAVE THIS ROADKILL TO US, REYES! YOU GO ON AFTER BLAZE! AND DON'T TAKE YOUR FOOT OFF THE GAS, KID...

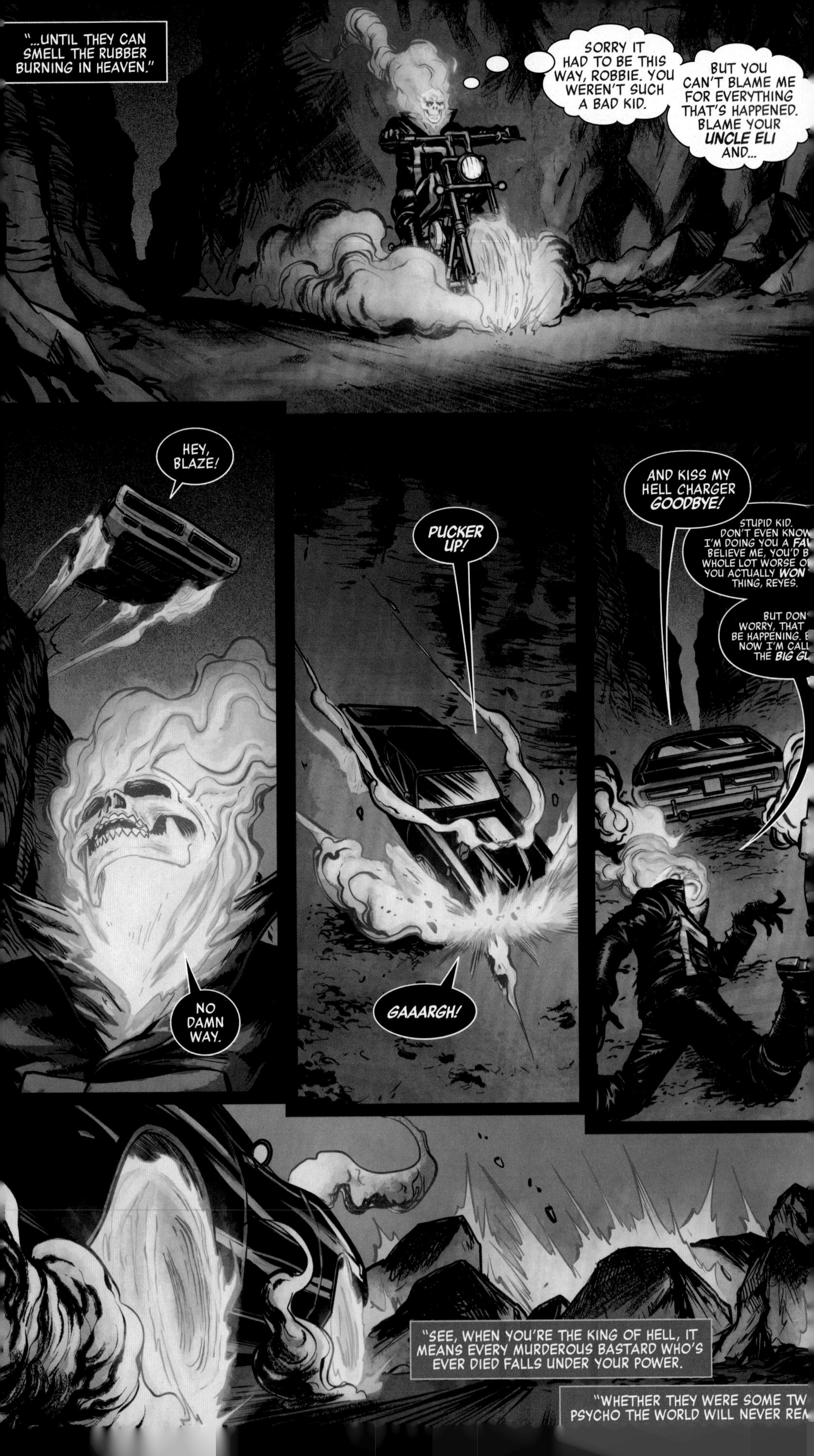
"...UNTIL THEY CAN SMELL THE RUBBER BURNING IN HEAVEN."
SORRY IT HAD TO BE THIS WAY, ROBBIE. YOU WEREN'T SUCH A BAD KID.
BUT YOU CAN'T BLAME ME FOR EVERYTHING THAT'S HAPPENED. BLAME YOUR UNCLE ELI AND...
HEY, BLAZE!
NO DAMN WAY.
PUCKER UP!
GAAARGH!
AND KISS MY HELL CHARGER GOODBYE!
STUPID KID. DON'T EVEN KNOW I'M DOING YOU A FA BELIEVE ME, YOU'D B WHOLE LOT WORSE OF YOU ACTUALLY WON THING, REYES.
BUT DON WORRY, THAT BE HAPPENING. NOW I'M CALL THE BIG GU
"SEE, WHEN YOU'RE THE KING OF HELL, IT MEANS EVERY MURDEROUS BASTARD WHO'S EVER DIED FALLS UNDER YOUR POWER.
"WHETHER THEY WERE SOME TW PSYCHO THE WORLD WILL NEVER REM

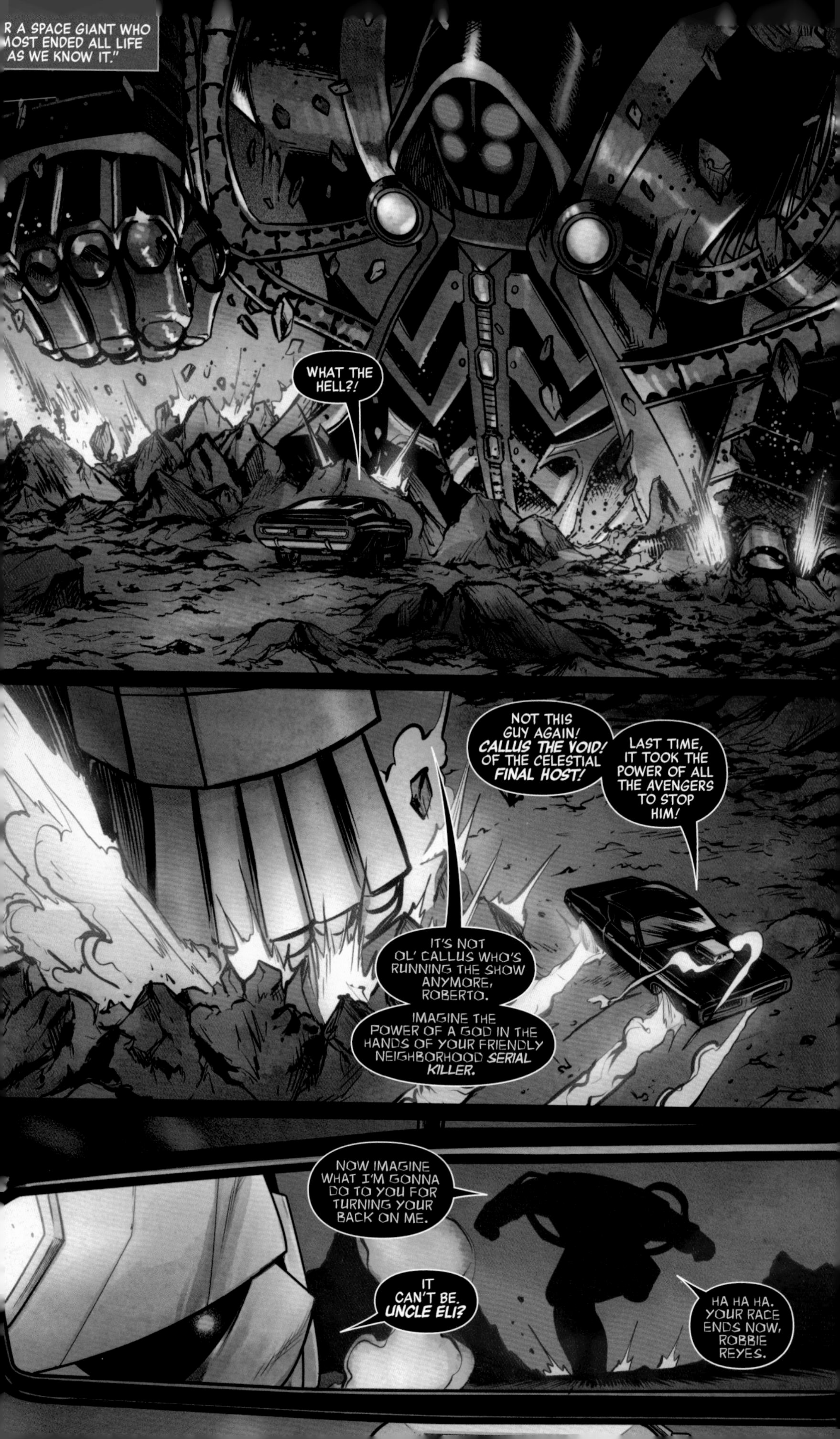
R A SPACE GIANT WHO
MOST ENDED ALL LIFE
AS WE KNOW IT."
WHAT THE HELL?!
NOT THIS GUY AGAIN! CALLUS THE VOID! OF THE CELESTIAL FINAL HOST!
LAST TIME, IT TOOK THE POWER OF ALL THE AVENGERS TO STOP HIM!
IT'S NOT OL' CALLUS WHO'S RUNNING THE SHOW ANYMORE, ROBERTO.
IMAGINE THE POWER OF A GOD IN THE HANDS OF YOUR FRIENDLY NEIGHBORHOOD SERIAL KILLER.
NOW IMAGINE WHAT I'M GONNA DO TO YOU FOR TURNING YOUR BACK ON ME.
IT CAN'T BE. UNCLE ELI?
HA HA HA. YOUR RACE ENDS NOW, ROBBIE REYES.

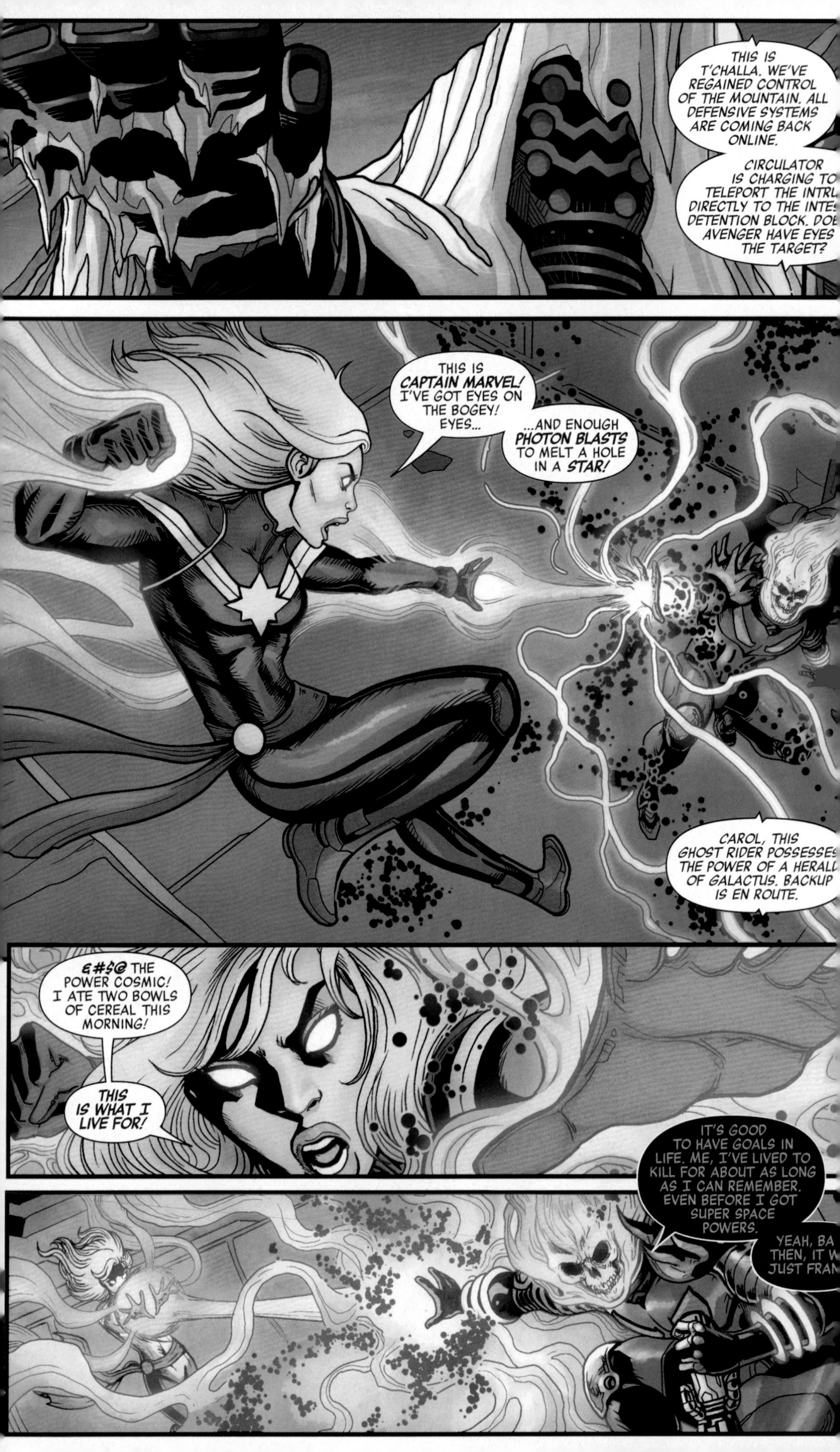
THIS IS T'CHALLA. WE'VE REGAINED CONTROL OF THE MOUNTAIN. ALL DEFENSIVE SYSTEMS ARE COMING BACK ONLINE.
CIRCULATOR IS CHARGING TO TELEPORT THE INTRU DIRECTLY TO THE INTE DETENTION BLOCK. DOE AVENGER HAVE EYES THE TARGET?
THIS IS CAPTAIN MARVEL! I'VE GOT EYES ON THE BOGEY! EYES...
...AND ENOUGH PHOTON BLASTS TO MELT A HOLE IN A STAR!
CAROL, THIS GHOST RIDER POSSESSES THE POWER OF A HERALD OF GALACTUS. BACKUP IS EN ROUTE.
&#$@ THE POWER COSMIC! I ATE TWO BOWLS OF CEREAL THIS MORNING!
THIS IS WHAT I LIVE FOR!
IT'S GOOD TO HAVE GOALS IN LIFE. ME, I'VE LIVED TO KILL FOR ABOUT AS LONG AS I CAN REMEMBER. EVEN BEFORE I GOT SUPER SPACE POWERS.
YEAH, BA THEN, IT W JUST FRAN

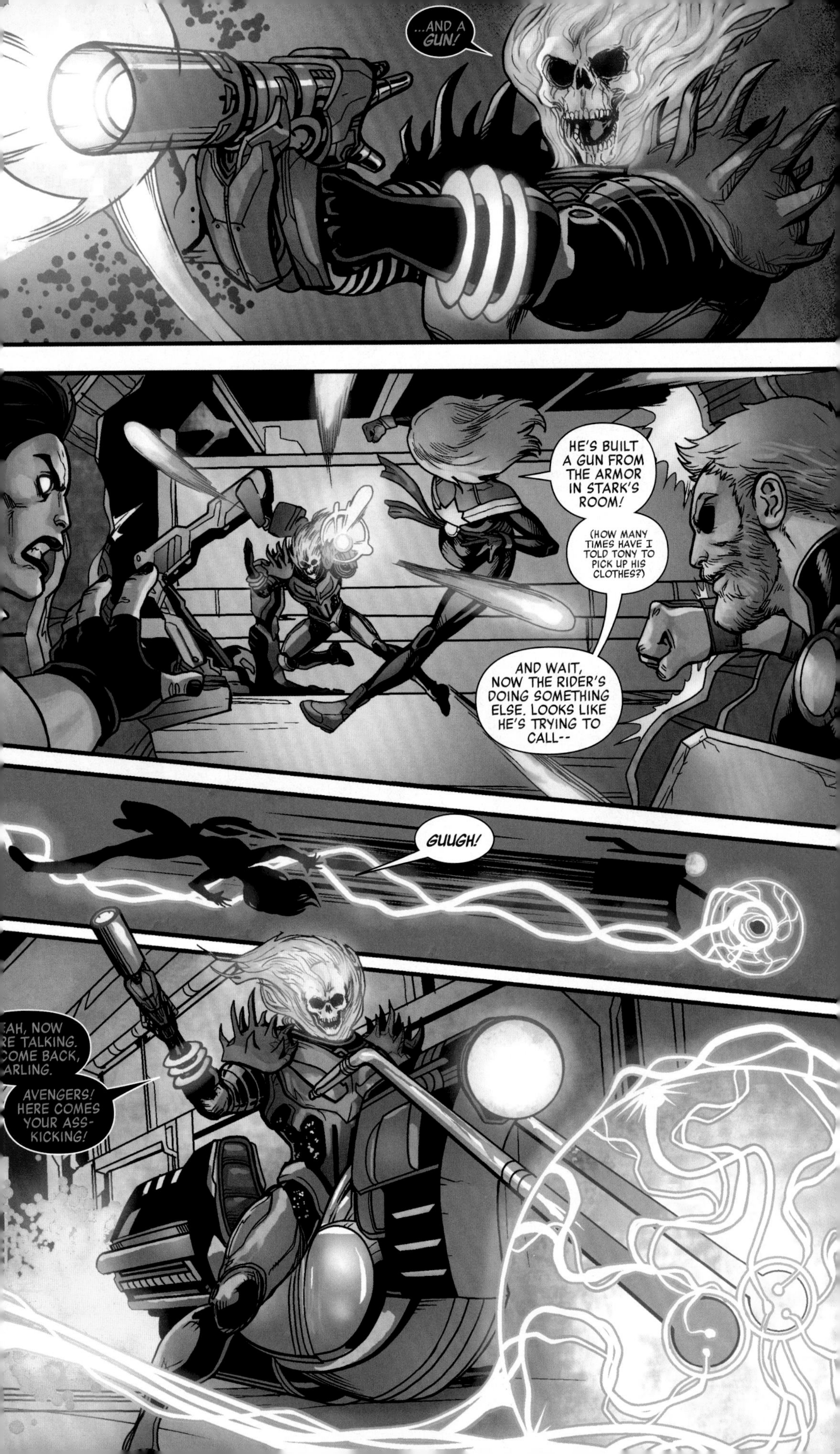

...AND A GUN!
HE'S BUILT A GUN FROM THE ARMOR IN STARK'S ROOM!
(HOW MANY TIMES HAVE I TOLD TONY TO PICK UP HIS CLOTHES?)
AND WAIT, NOW THE RIDER'S DOING SOMETHING ELSE. LOOKS LIKE HE'S TRYING TO CALL--
GUUGH!
EAH, NOW RE TALKING. COME BACK, ARLING.
AVENGERS! HERE COMES YOUR ASS-KICKING!

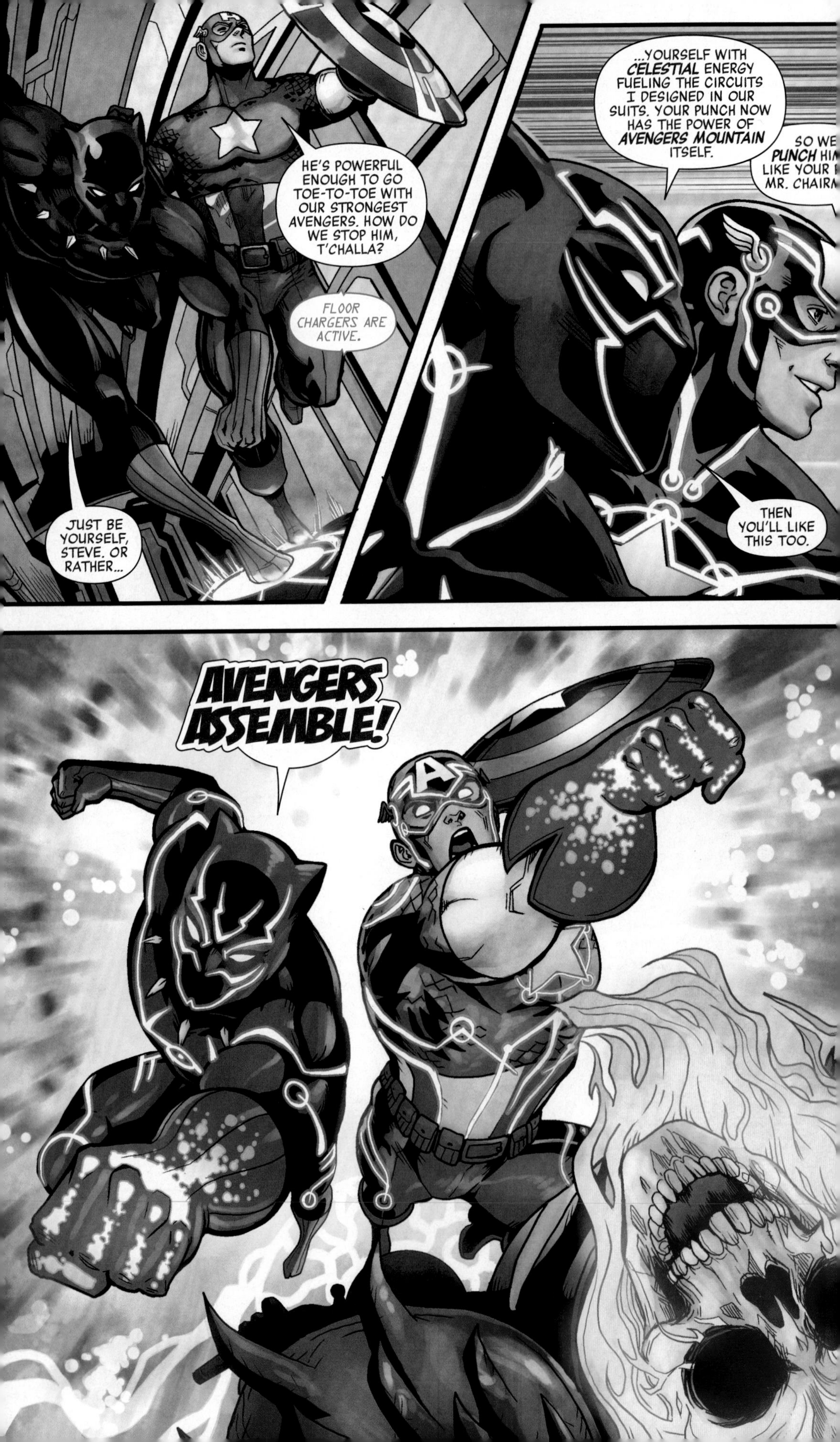
HE'S POWERFUL ENOUGH TO GO TOE-TO-TOE WITH OUR STRONGEST AVENGERS. HOW DO WE STOP HIM, T'CHALLA?
FLOOR CHARGERS ARE ACTIVE.
JUST BE YOURSELF, STEVE. OR RATHER...
...YOURSELF WITH CELESTIAL ENERGY FUELING THE CIRCUITS I DESIGNED IN OUR SUITS. YOUR PUNCH NOW HAS THE POWER OF AVENGERS MOUNTAIN ITSELF.
SO WE PUNCH HI LIKE YOUR MR. CHAIRM
THEN YOU'LL LIKE THIS TOO.
AVENGERS ASSEMBLE!

THESE WRETCHED GHOST RIDERS GET EVEN MORE ANNOYING WITH EACH NEW ITERATION. YET ANOTHER REASON TO DESPISE MEPHISTO.

BUT YOU DON'T SEEM VERY INTERESTED IN RIDERS RIGHT NOW, *BLADE.*

POWER COSMIC. SPACE GOD MUMBO JUMBO. THIS ISN'T MY KINDA FIGHT, HELLSTROM.

I'D RATHER WE GET BACK TO HELLFIRE AND POSSESSED HOT RODS AND...

BOY-THING'S GOT THE CREEP! NOW LET'S GET HIM INTO A CELL WHILE...

RP!

YOU'RE TRYING TO BEAT ME WITH YOUR *HOUSEPLANT?* YOU *SURE* YOU GUYS ARE THE AVENGERS?

NOT YOUR FIGHT, HUH?

NOW IT DAMN SURE IS.

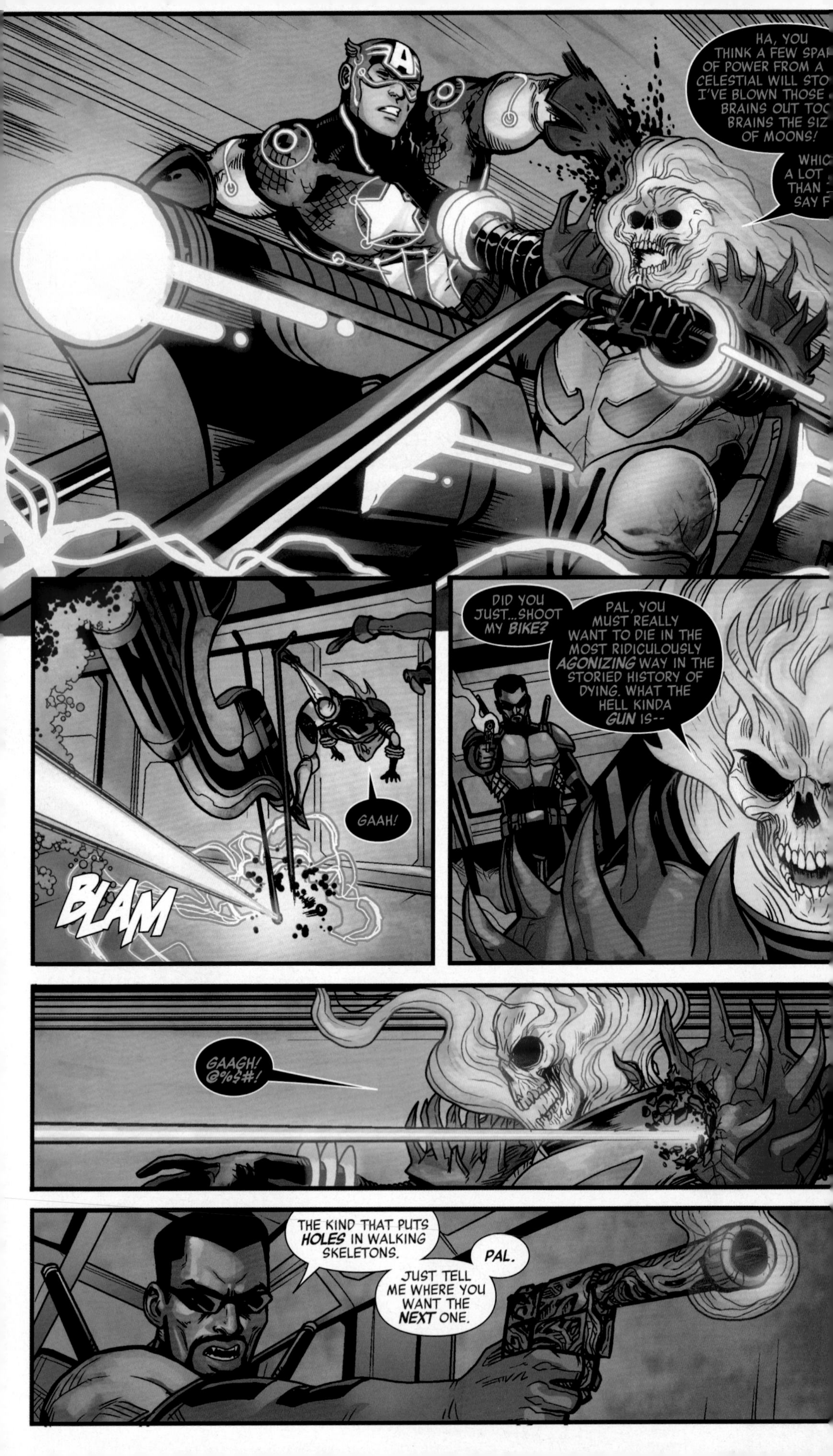
HA, YOU
THINK A FEW SPA
OF POWER FROM A
CELESTIAL WILL STO
I'VE BLOWN THOSE
BRAINS OUT TOO
BRAINS THE SIZ
OF MOONS!
WHIC
A LOT
THAN
SAY F
GAAH!
BLAM
DID YOU JUST...SHOOT MY BIKE?
PAL, YOU MUST REALLY WANT TO DIE IN THE MOST RIDICULOUSLY AGONIZING WAY IN THE STORIED HISTORY OF DYING. WHAT THE HELL KINDA GUN IS--
GAAGH! @%$#!
THE KIND THAT PUTS HOLES IN WALKING SKELETONS.
PAL.
JUST TELL ME WHERE YOU WANT THE NEXT ONE.

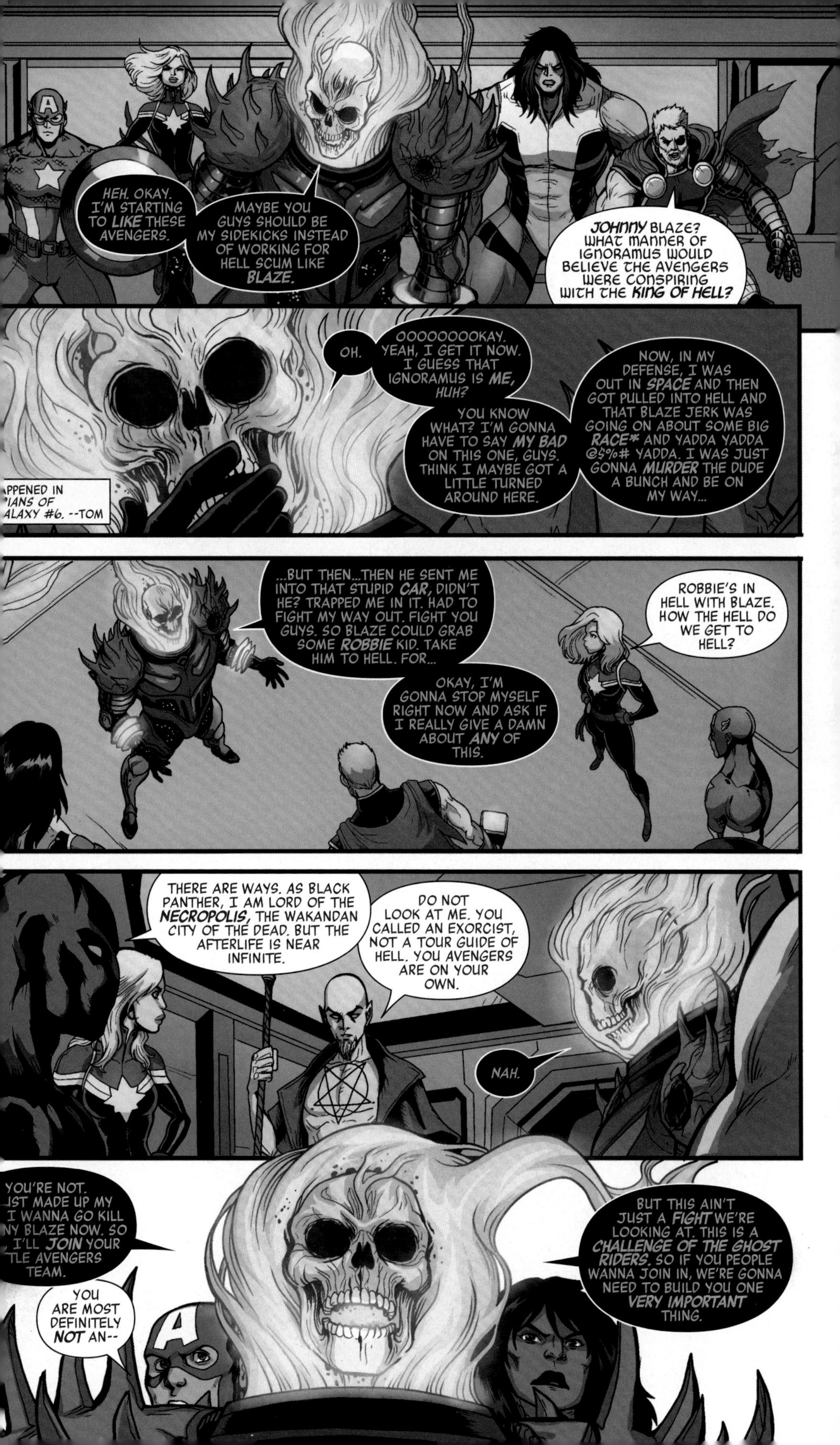
HEH. OKAY. I'M STARTING TO LIKE THESE AVENGERS.
MAYBE YOU GUYS SHOULD BE MY SIDEKICKS INSTEAD OF WORKING FOR HELL SCUM LIKE BLAZE.
JOHNNY BLAZE? WHAT MANNER OF IGNORAMUS WOULD BELIEVE THE AVENGERS WERE CONSPIRING WITH THE KING OF HELL?
OH.
OOOOOOOOKAY. YEAH, I GET IT NOW. I GUESS THAT IGNORAMUS IS ME, HUH?
YOU KNOW WHAT? I'M GONNA HAVE TO SAY MY BAD ON THIS ONE, GUYS. THINK I MAYBE GOT A LITTLE TURNED AROUND HERE.
NOW, IN MY DEFENSE, I WAS OUT IN SPACE AND THEN GOT PULLED INTO HELL AND THAT BLAZE JERK WAS GOING ON ABOUT SOME BIG RACE* AND YADDA YADDA @$%# YADDA. I WAS JUST GONNA MURDER THE DUDE A BUNCH AND BE ON MY WAY...
APPENED IN
IANS OF
ALAXY #6. --TOM
...BUT THEN...THEN HE SENT ME INTO THAT STUPID CAR, DIDN'T HE? TRAPPED ME IN IT. HAD TO FIGHT MY WAY OUT. FIGHT YOU GUYS. SO BLAZE COULD GRAB SOME ROBBIE KID. TAKE HIM TO HELL. FOR...
OKAY, I'M GONNA STOP MYSELF RIGHT NOW AND ASK IF I REALLY GIVE A DAMN ABOUT ANY OF THIS.
ROBBIE'S IN HELL WITH BLAZE. HOW THE HELL DO WE GET TO HELL?
THERE ARE WAYS. AS BLACK PANTHER, I AM LORD OF THE NECROPOLIS, THE WAKANDAN CITY OF THE DEAD. BUT THE AFTERLIFE IS NEAR INFINITE.
DO NOT LOOK AT ME. YOU CALLED AN EXORCIST, NOT A TOUR GUIDE OF HELL. YOU AVENGERS ARE ON YOUR OWN.
NAH.
YOU'RE NOT.
JST MADE UP MY
I WANNA GO KILL
NY BLAZE NOW. SO
I'LL JOIN YOUR
TLE AVENGERS
TEAM.
YOU ARE MOST DEFINITELY NOT AN--
BUT THIS AIN'T JUST A FIGHT WE'RE LOOKING AT. THIS IS A CHALLENGE OF THE GHOST RIDERS. SO IF YOU PEOPLE WANNA JOIN IN, WE'RE GONNA NEED TO BUILD YOU ONE VERY IMPORTANT THING.

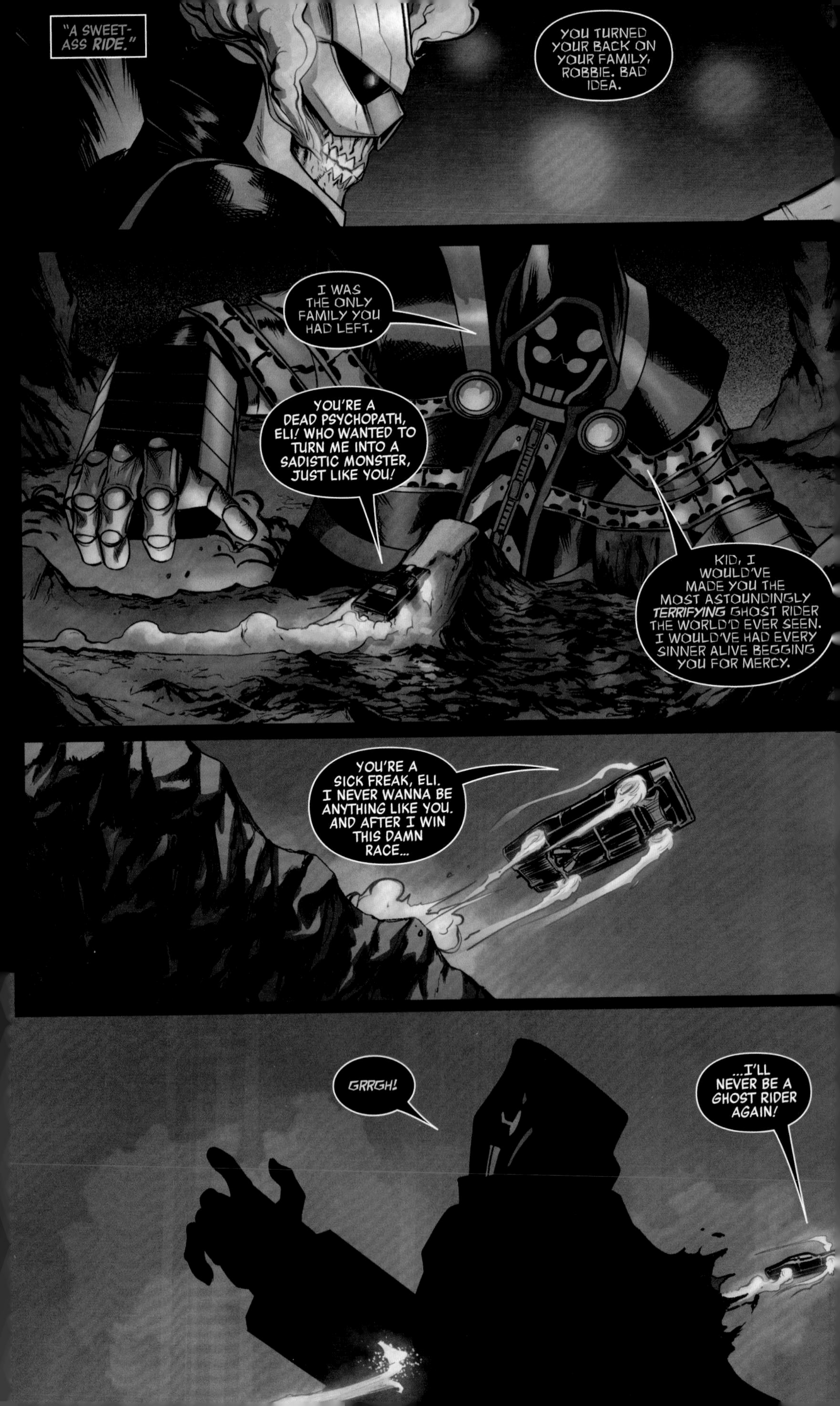
"A SWEET-ASS RIDE."
YOU TURNED YOUR BACK ON YOUR FAMILY, ROBBIE. BAD IDEA.
I WAS THE ONLY FAMILY YOU HAD LEFT.
YOU'RE A DEAD PSYCHOPATH, ELI! WHO WANTED TO TURN ME INTO A SADISTIC MONSTER, JUST LIKE YOU!
KID, I WOULD'VE MADE YOU THE MOST ASTOUNDINGLY TERRIFYING GHOST RIDER THE WORLD'D EVER SEEN. I WOULD'VE HAD EVERY SINNER ALIVE BEGGING YOU FOR MERCY.
YOU'RE A SICK FREAK, ELI. I NEVER WANNA BE ANYTHING LIKE YOU. AND AFTER I WIN THIS DAMN RACE...
GRRGH!
...I'LL NEVER BE A GHOST RIDER AGAIN!

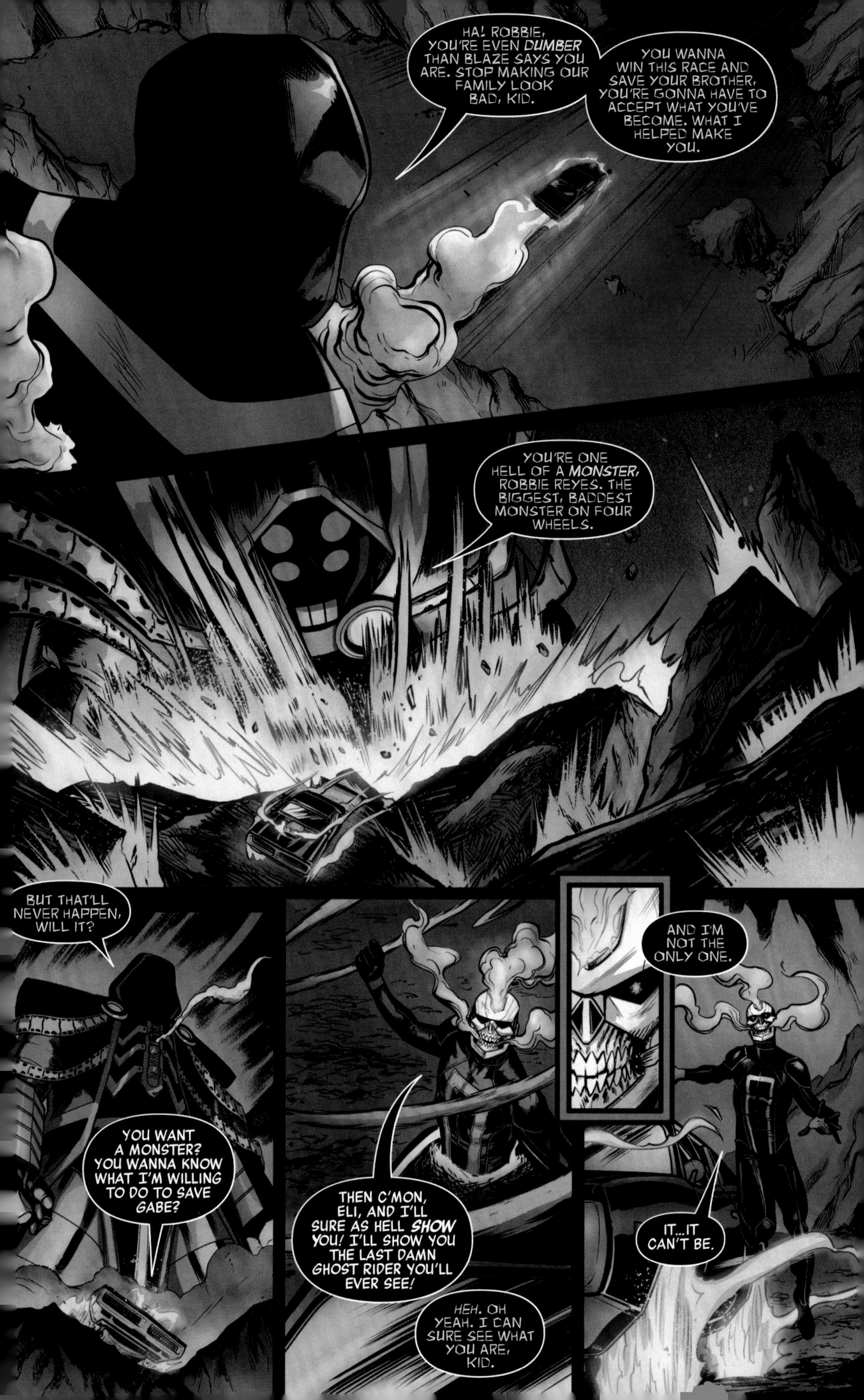
HA! ROBBIE, YOU'RE EVEN DUMBER THAN BLAZE SAYS YOU ARE. STOP MAKING OUR FAMILY LOOK BAD, KID.
YOU WANNA WIN THIS RACE AND SAVE YOUR BROTHER, YOU'RE GONNA HAVE TO ACCEPT WHAT YOU'VE BECOME. WHAT I HELPED MAKE YOU.
YOU'RE ONE HELL OF A MONSTER, ROBBIE REYES. THE BIGGEST, BADDEST MONSTER ON FOUR WHEELS.
BUT THAT'LL NEVER HAPPEN, WILL IT?
YOU WANT A MONSTER? YOU WANNA KNOW WHAT I'M WILLING TO DO TO SAVE GABE?
THEN C'MON, ELI, AND I'LL SURE AS HELL SHOW YOU! I'LL SHOW YOU THE LAST DAMN GHOST RIDER YOU'LL EVER SEE!
HEH. OH YEAH. I CAN SURE SEE WHAT YOU ARE, KID.
AND I'M NOT THE ONLY ONE.
IT...IT CAN'T BE.

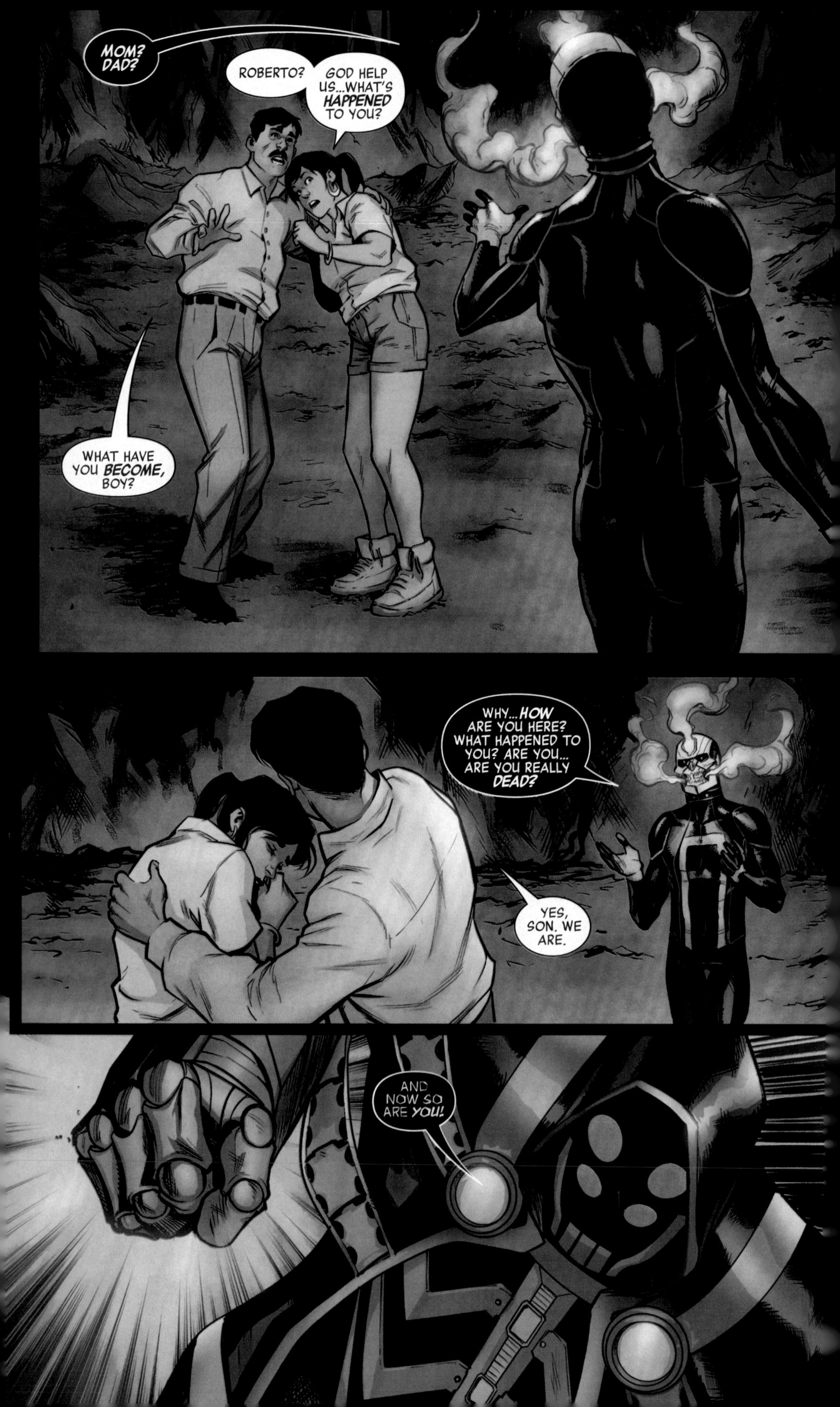
MOM? DAD?
ROBERTO?
GOD HELP US...WHAT'S HAPPENED TO YOU?
WHAT HAVE YOU BECOME, BOY?
WHY...HOW ARE YOU HERE? WHAT HAPPENED TO YOU? ARE YOU... ARE YOU REALLY DEAD?
YES, SON. WE ARE.
AND NOW SO ARE YOU!

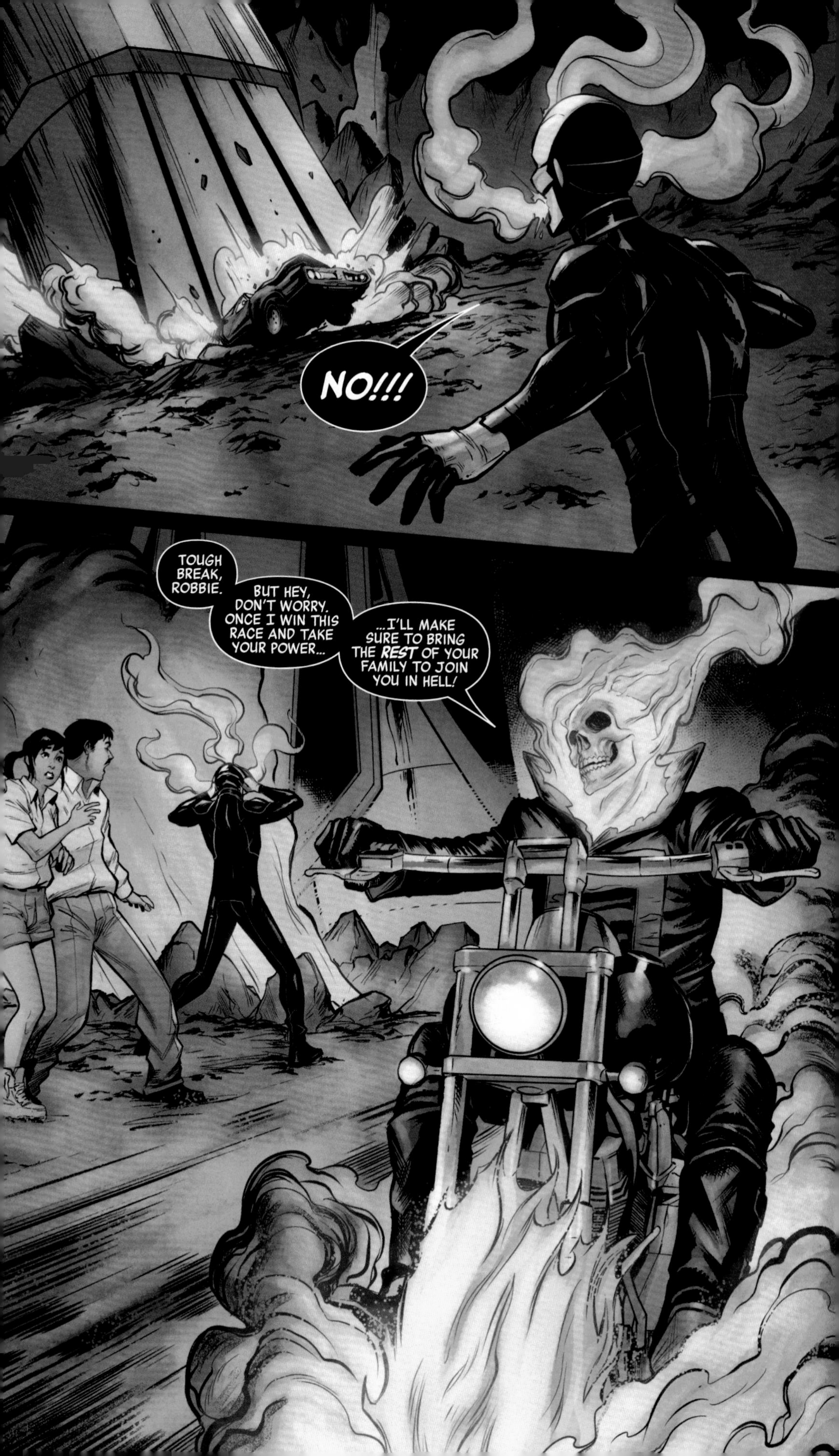
NO!!!
TOUGH BREAK, ROBBIE.
BUT HEY, DON'T WORRY. ONCE I WIN THIS RACE AND TAKE YOUR POWER...
...I'LL MAKE SURE TO BRING THE REST OF YOUR FAMILY TO JOIN YOU IN HELL!

25 CHALLENGE OF THE GHOST RIDERS PART 4

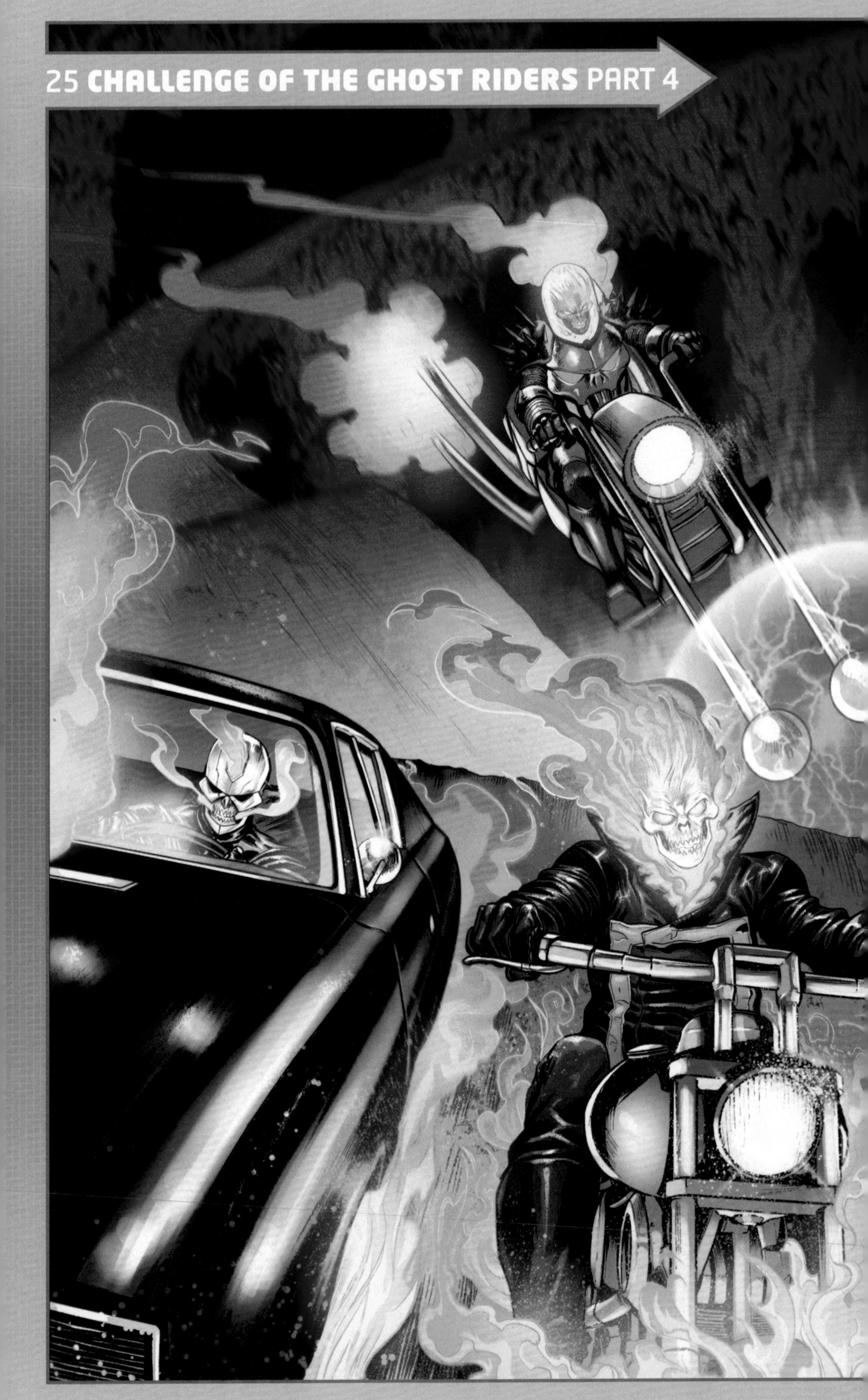

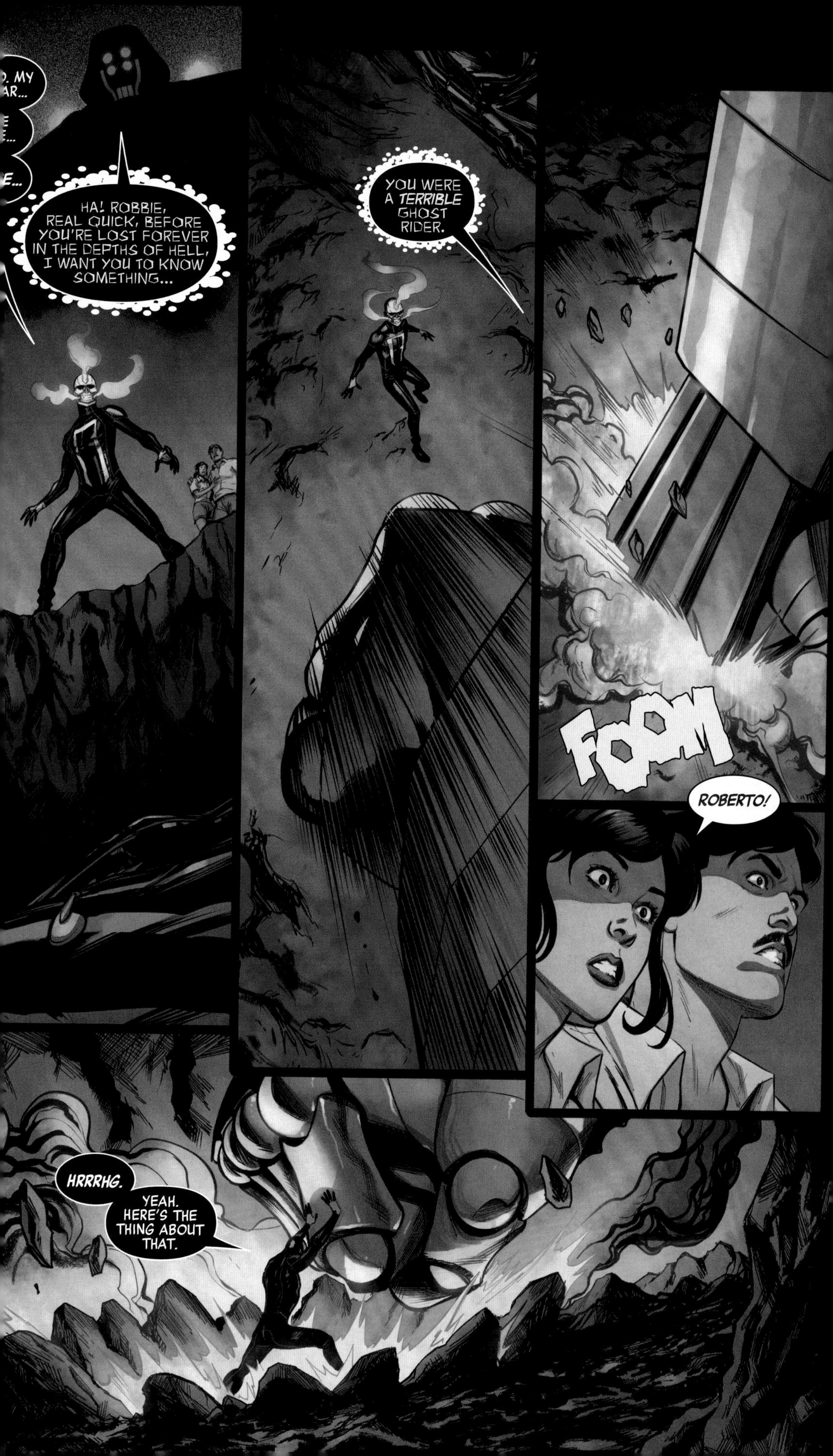
HA! ROBBIE, REAL QUICK, BEFORE YOU'RE LOST FOREVER IN THE DEPTHS OF HELL, I WANT YOU TO KNOW SOMETHING...
YOU WERE A *TERRIBLE* GHOST RIDER.
FOOM
ROBERTO!
HRRRHG.
YEAH. HERE'S THE THING ABOUT THAT.

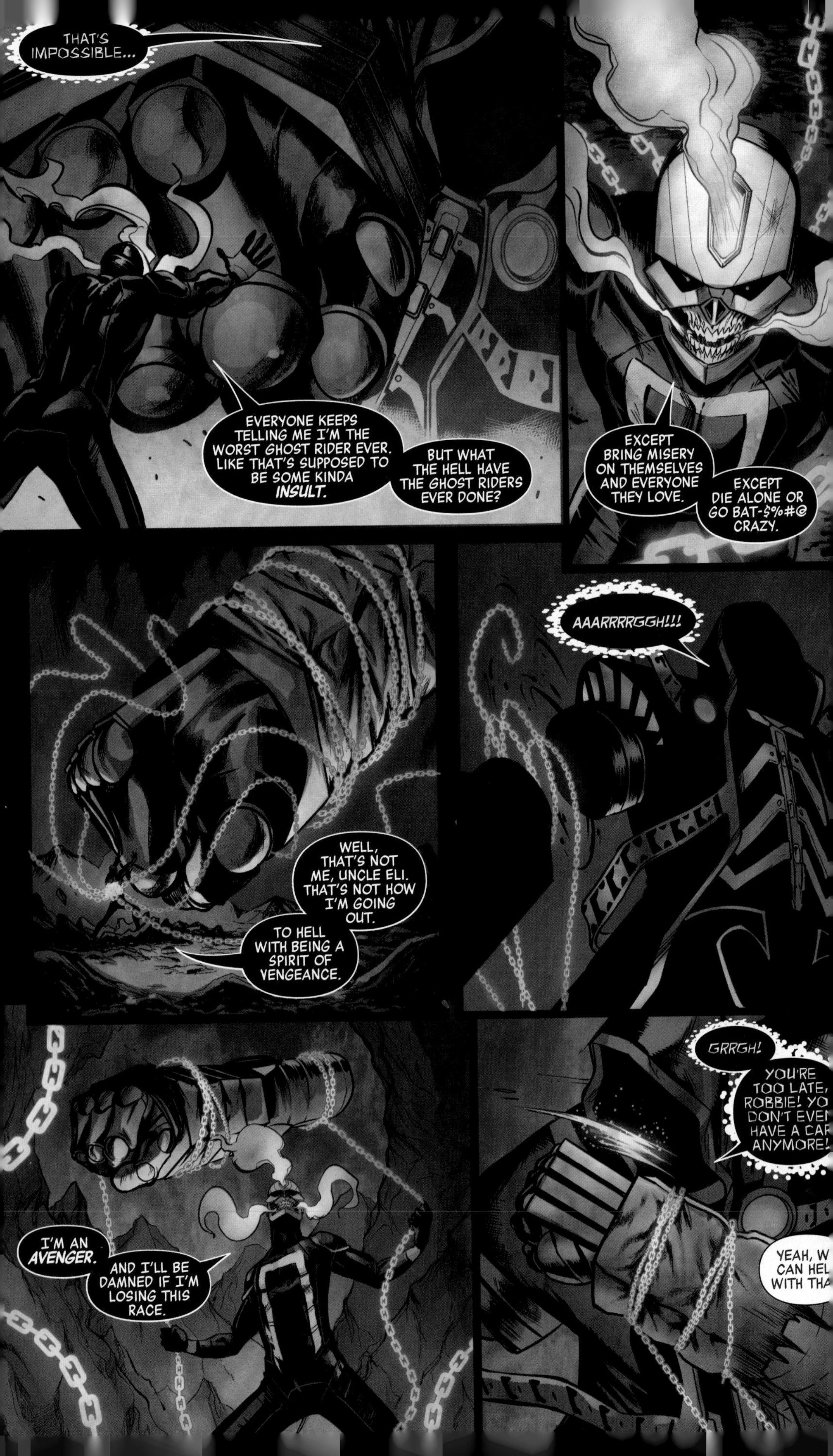
THAT'S IMPOSSIBLE...
EVERYONE KEEPS TELLING ME I'M THE WORST GHOST RIDER EVER. LIKE THAT'S SUPPOSED TO BE SOME KINDA INSULT.
BUT WHAT THE HELL HAVE THE GHOST RIDERS EVER DONE?
EXCEPT BRING MISERY ON THEMSELVES AND EVERYONE THEY LOVE.
EXCEPT DIE ALONE OR GO BAT-$%#@ CRAZY.
WELL, THAT'S NOT ME, UNCLE ELI. THAT'S NOT HOW I'M GOING OUT.
TO HELL WITH BEING A SPIRIT OF VENGEANCE.
AAARRRRGGH!!!
I'M AN AVENGER.
AND I'LL BE DAMNED IF I'M LOSING THIS RACE.
GRRGH!
YOU'RE TOO LATE, ROBBIE! YO DON'T EVEN HAVE A CAR ANYMORE!
YEAH, W CAN HEL WITH THA

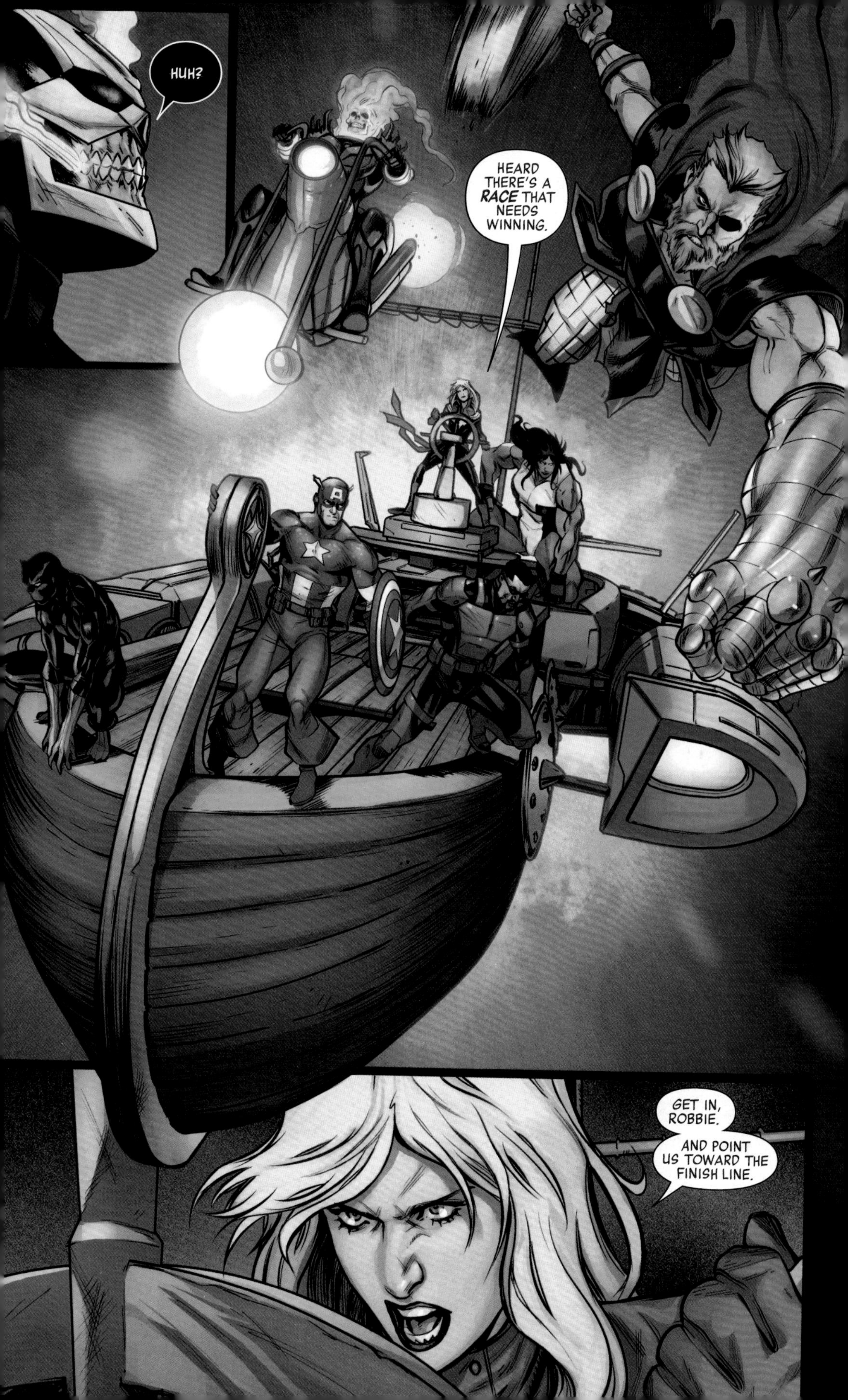
HUH?
HEARD THERE'S A *RACE* THAT NEEDS WINNING.
GET IN, ROBBIE.
AND POINT US TOWARD THE FINISH LINE.

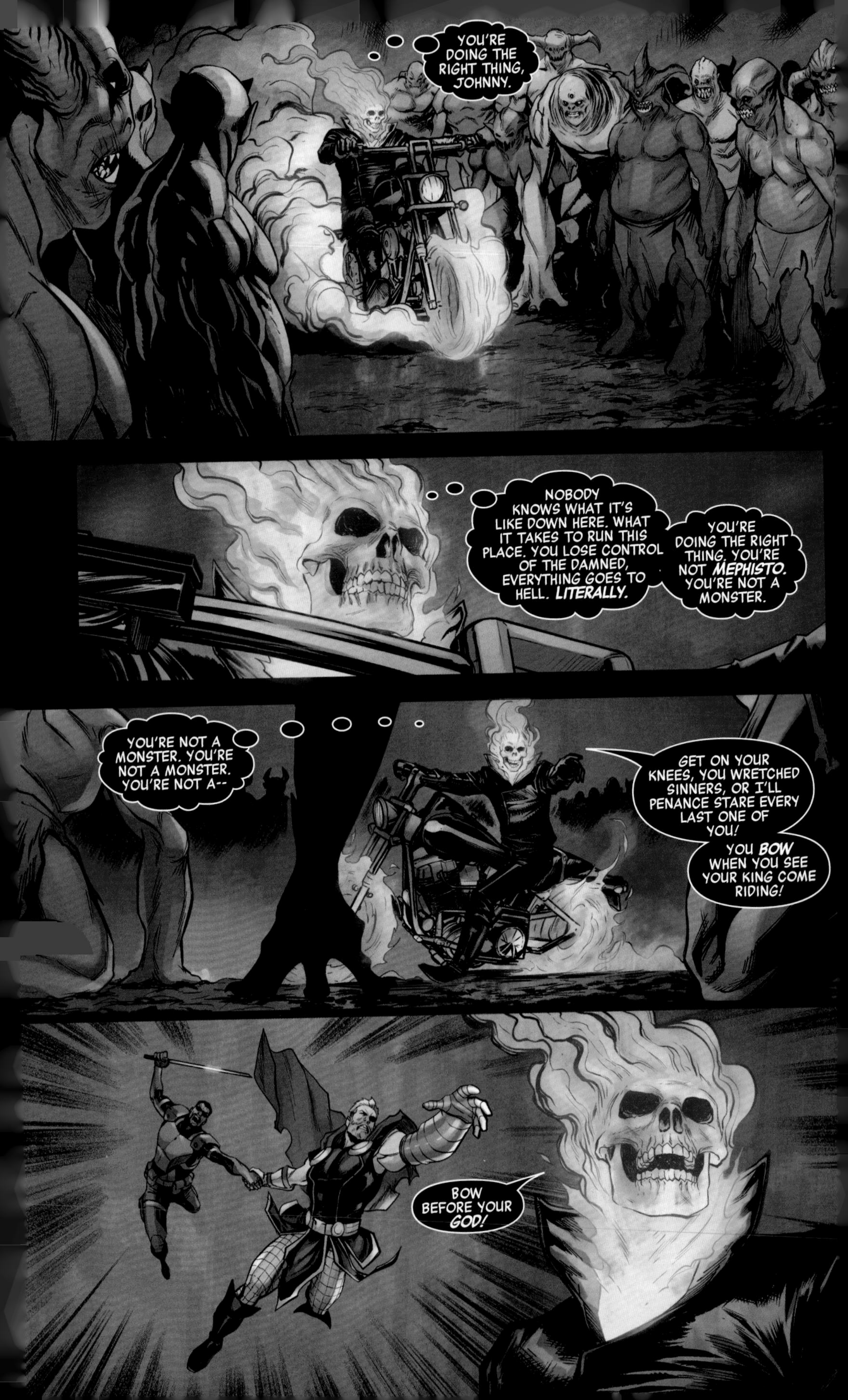
YOU'RE DOING THE RIGHT THING, JOHNNY.
NOBODY KNOWS WHAT IT'S LIKE DOWN HERE. WHAT IT TAKES TO RUN THIS PLACE. YOU LOSE CONTROL OF THE DAMNED, EVERYTHING GOES TO HELL. LITERALLY.
YOU'RE DOING THE RIGHT THING. YOU'RE NOT MEPHISTO. YOU'RE NOT A MONSTER.
YOU'RE NOT A MONSTER. YOU'RE NOT A MONSTER. YOU'RE NOT A--
GET ON YOUR KNEES, YOU WRETCHED SINNERS, OR I'LL PENANCE STARE EVERY LAST ONE OF YOU!
YOU BOW WHEN YOU SEE YOUR KING COME RIDING!
BOW BEFORE YOUR GOD!

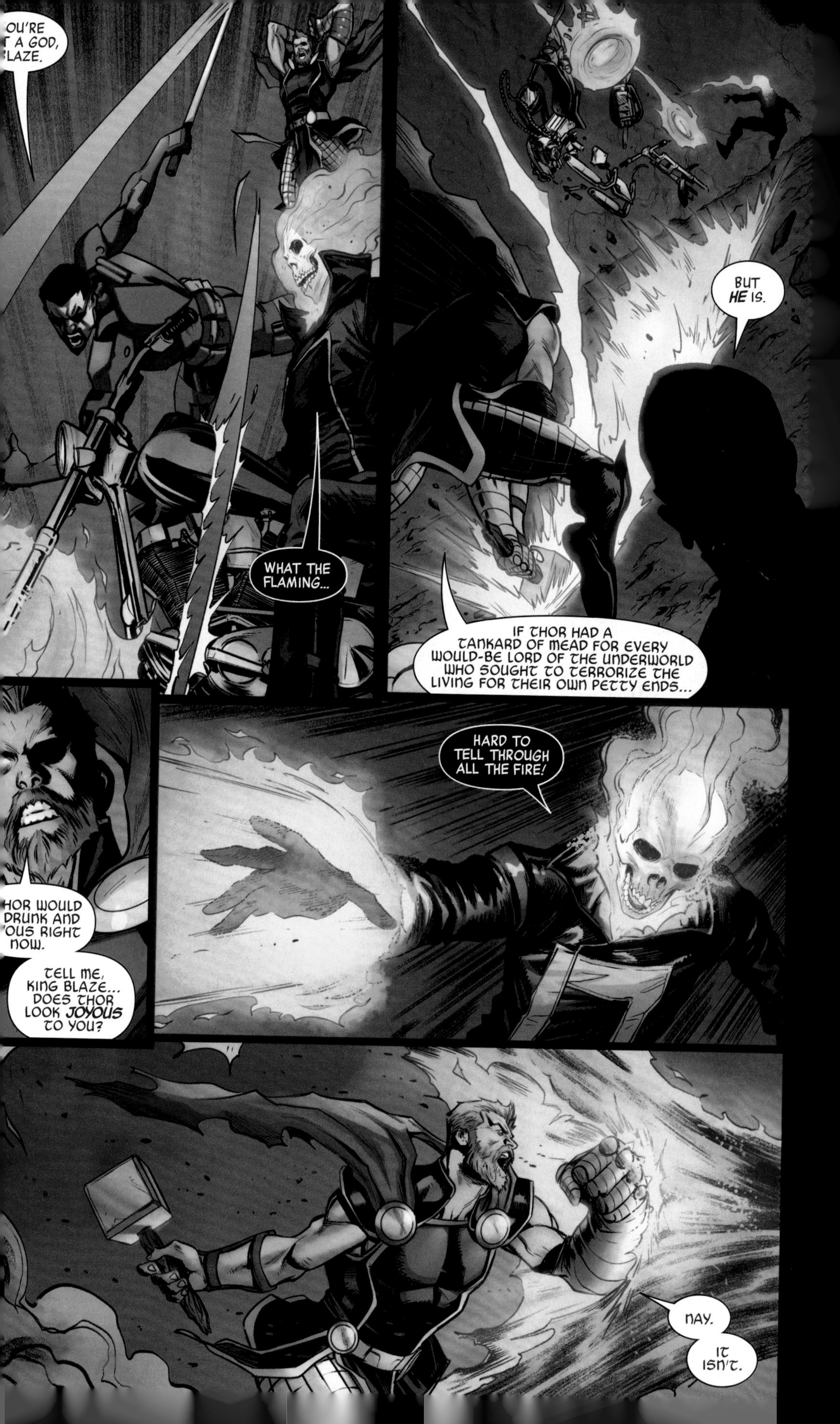
OU'RE
T A GOD,
LAZE.
WHAT THE
FLAMING...
BUT
HE IS.
IF THOR HAD A
TANKARD OF MEAD FOR EVERY
WOULD-BE LORD OF THE UNDERWORLD
WHO SOUGHT TO TERRORIZE THE
LIVING FOR THEIR OWN PETTY ENDS...
HOR WOULD
DRUNK AND
OUS RIGHT
NOW.
TELL ME,
KING BLAZE...
DOES THOR
LOOK JOYOUS
TO YOU?
HARD TO
TELL THROUGH
ALL THE FIRE!
NAY.
IT
ISN'T.

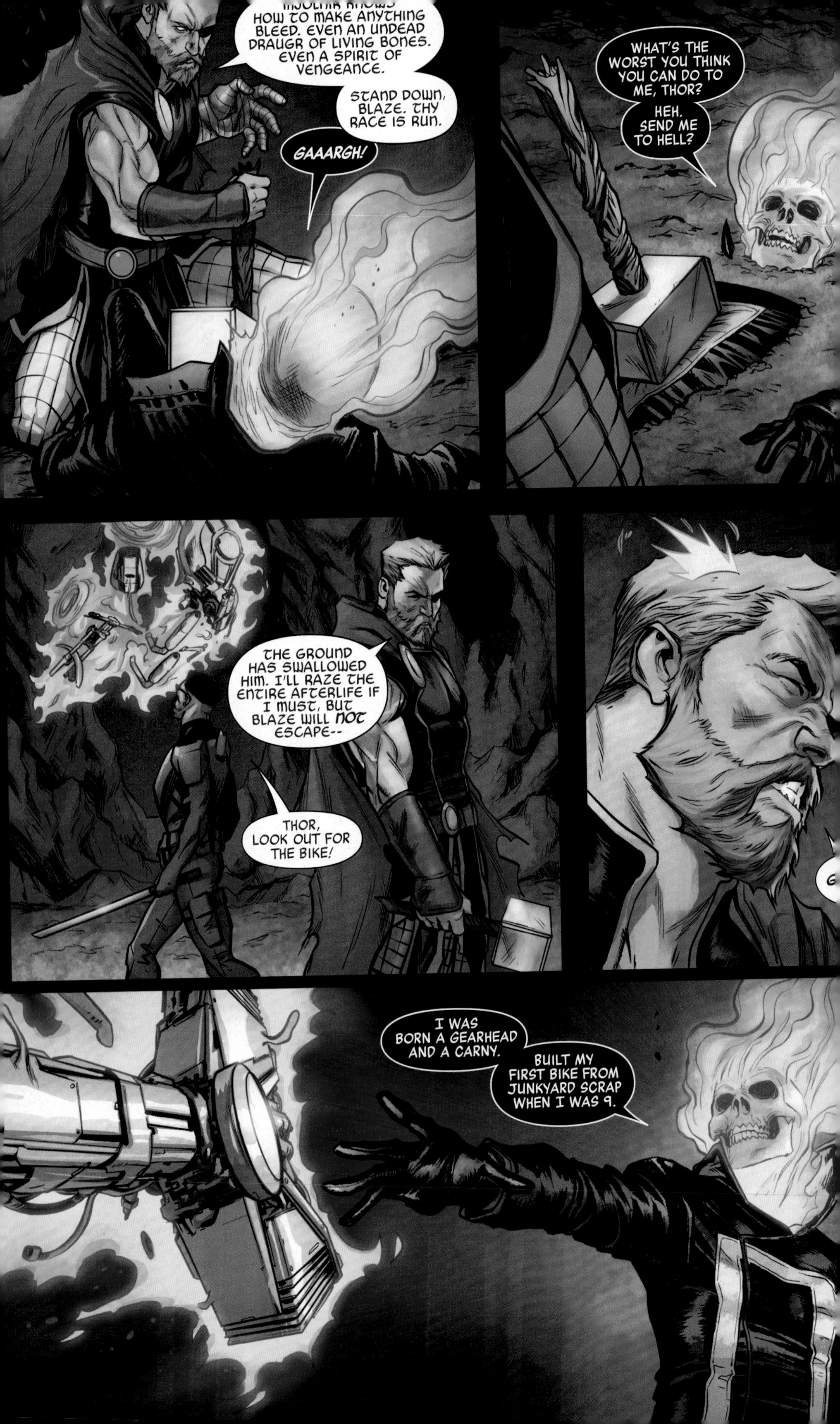
HOW TO MAKE ANYTHING BLEED. EVEN AN UNDEAD DRAUGR OF LIVING BONES. EVEN A SPIRIT OF VENGEANCE.
STAND DOWN, BLAZE. THY RACE IS RUN.
GAAARGH!
WHAT'S THE WORST YOU THINK YOU CAN DO TO ME, THOR?
HEH. SEND ME TO HELL?
THE GROUND HAS SWALLOWED HIM. I'LL RAZE THE ENTIRE AFTERLIFE IF I MUST, BUT BLAZE WILL NOT ESCAPE--
THOR, LOOK OUT FOR THE BIKE!
I WAS BORN A GEARHEAD AND A CARNY.
BUILT MY FIRST BIKE FROM JUNKYARD SCRAP WHEN I WAS 9.

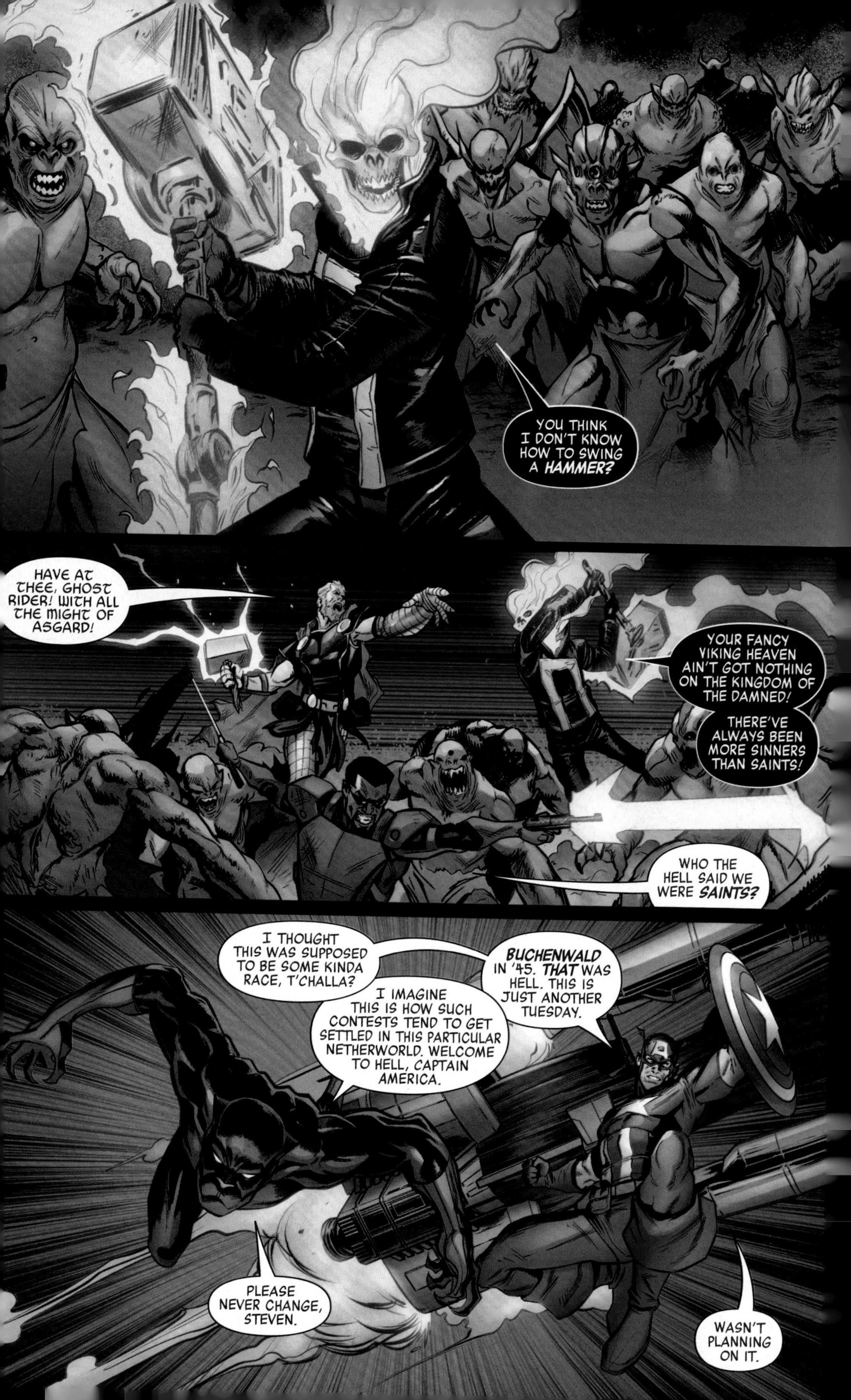
YOU THINK I DON'T KNOW HOW TO SWING A HAMMER?
HAVE AT THEE, GHOST RIDER! WITH ALL THE MIGHT OF ASGARD!
YOUR FANCY VIKING HEAVEN AIN'T GOT NOTHING ON THE KINGDOM OF THE DAMNED!
THERE'VE ALWAYS BEEN MORE SINNERS THAN SAINTS!
WHO THE HELL SAID WE WERE SAINTS?
I THOUGHT THIS WAS SUPPOSED TO BE SOME KINDA RACE, T'CHALLA?
I IMAGINE THIS IS HOW SUCH CONTESTS TEND TO GET SETTLED IN THIS PARTICULAR NETHERWORLD. WELCOME TO HELL, CAPTAIN AMERICA.
BUCHENWALD IN '45. THAT WAS HELL. THIS IS JUST ANOTHER TUESDAY.
PLEASE NEVER CHANGE, STEVEN.
WASN'T PLANNING ON IT.

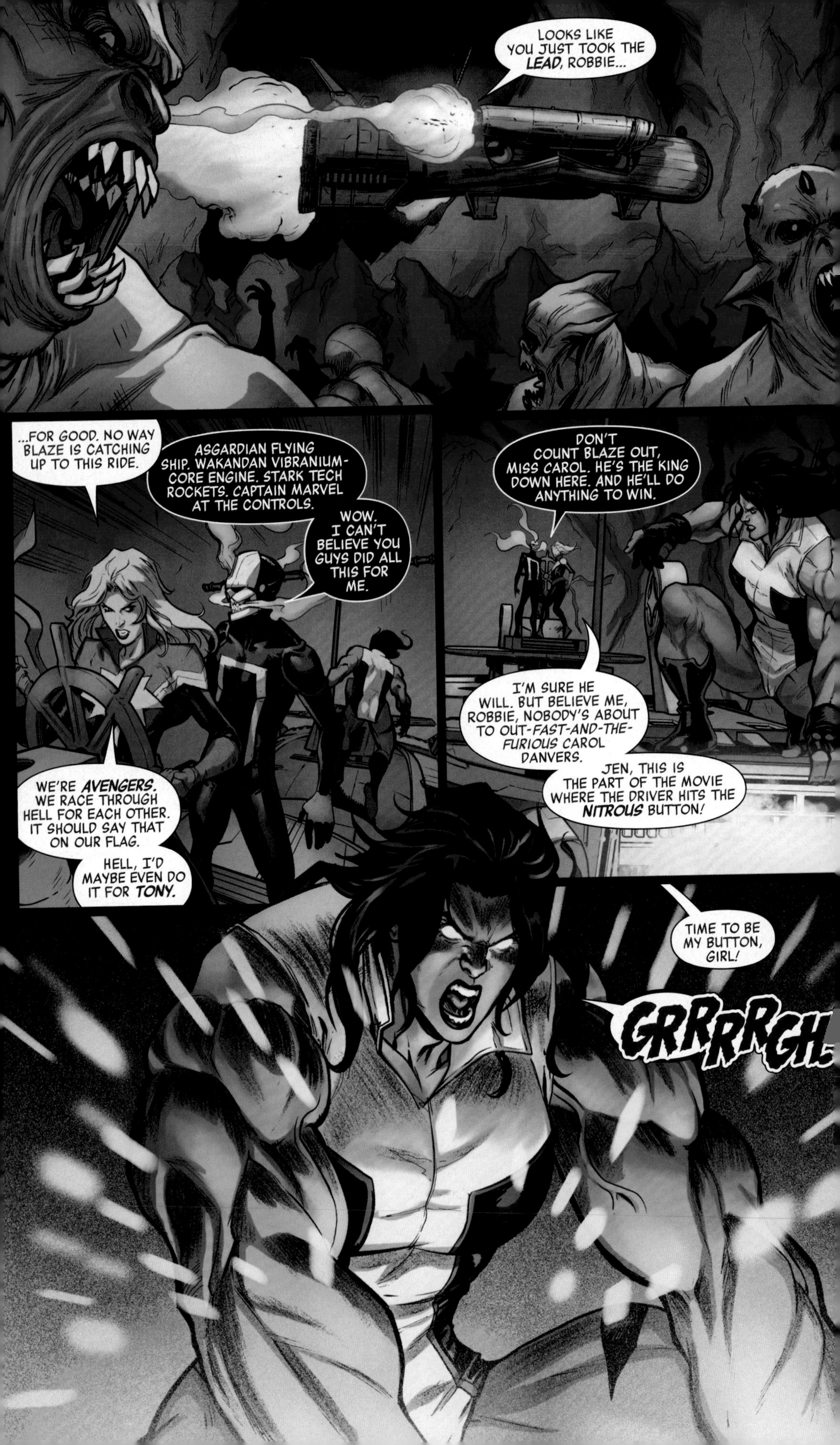
LOOKS LIKE YOU JUST TOOK THE *LEAD*, ROBBIE...
...FOR GOOD. NO WAY BLAZE IS CATCHING UP TO THIS RIDE.
ASGARDIAN FLYING SHIP. WAKANDAN VIBRANIUM-CORE ENGINE. STARK TECH ROCKETS. CAPTAIN MARVEL AT THE CONTROLS.
WOW. I CAN'T BELIEVE YOU GUYS DID ALL THIS FOR ME.
WE'RE *AVENGERS.* WE RACE THROUGH HELL FOR EACH OTHER. IT SHOULD SAY THAT ON OUR FLAG.
HELL, I'D MAYBE EVEN DO IT FOR *TONY.*
DON'T COUNT BLAZE OUT, MISS CAROL. HE'S THE KING DOWN HERE. AND HE'LL DO ANYTHING TO WIN.
I'M SURE HE WILL. BUT BELIEVE ME, ROBBIE, NOBODY'S ABOUT TO OUT-*FAST-AND-THE-FURIOUS* CAROL DANVERS.
JEN, THIS IS THE PART OF THE MOVIE WHERE THE DRIVER HITS THE *NITROUS* BUTTON!
TIME TO BE MY BUTTON, GIRL!
GRRRRGH

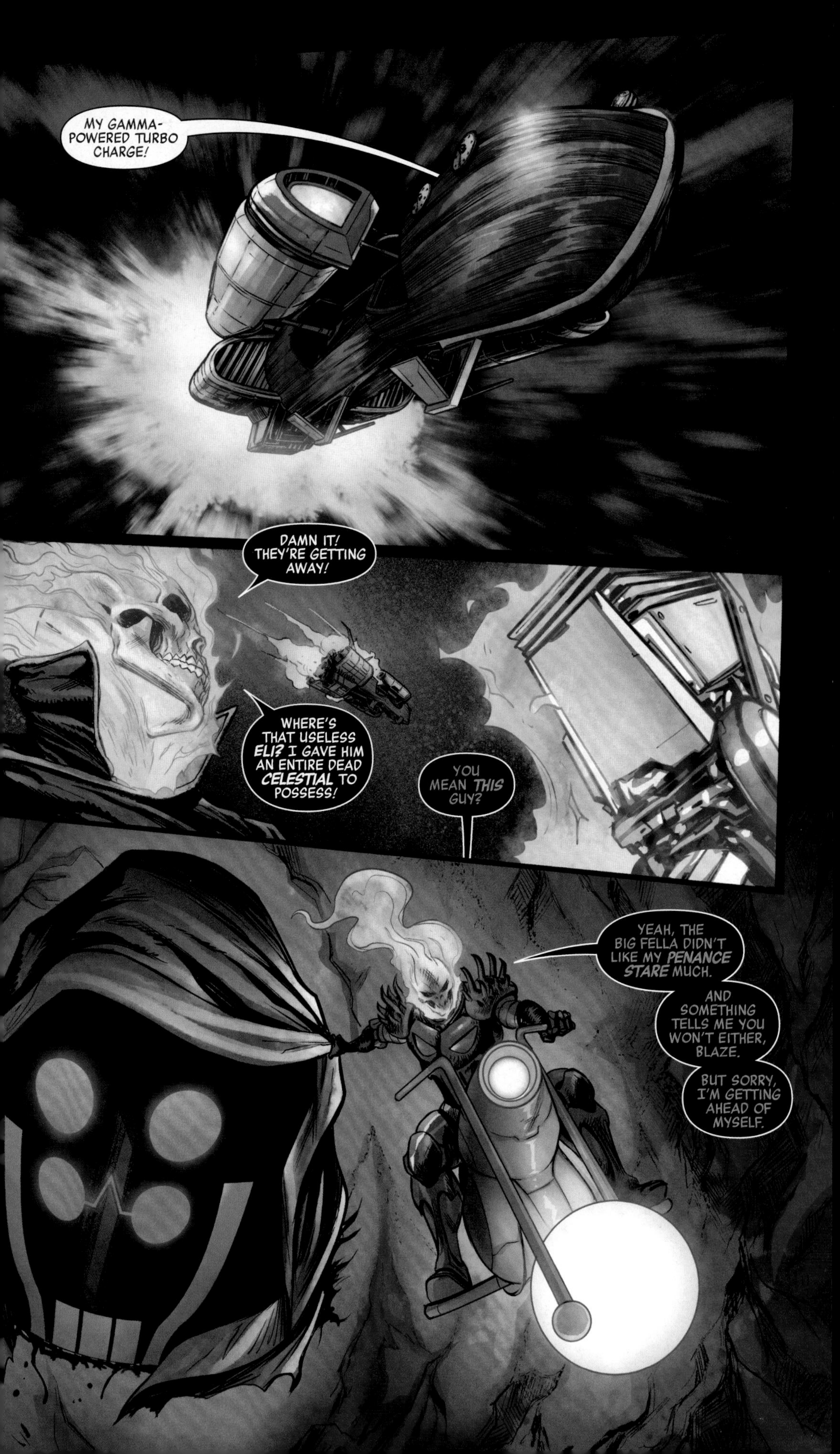
MY GAMMA-POWERED TURBO CHARGE!
DAMN IT! THEY'RE GETTING AWAY!
WHERE'S THAT USELESS ELI? I GAVE HIM AN ENTIRE DEAD CELESTIAL TO POSSESS!
YOU MEAN THIS GUY?
YEAH, THE BIG FELLA DIDN'T LIKE MY PENANCE STARE MUCH.
AND SOMETHING TELLS ME YOU WON'T EITHER, BLAZE.
BUT SORRY, I'M GETTING AHEAD OF MYSELF.

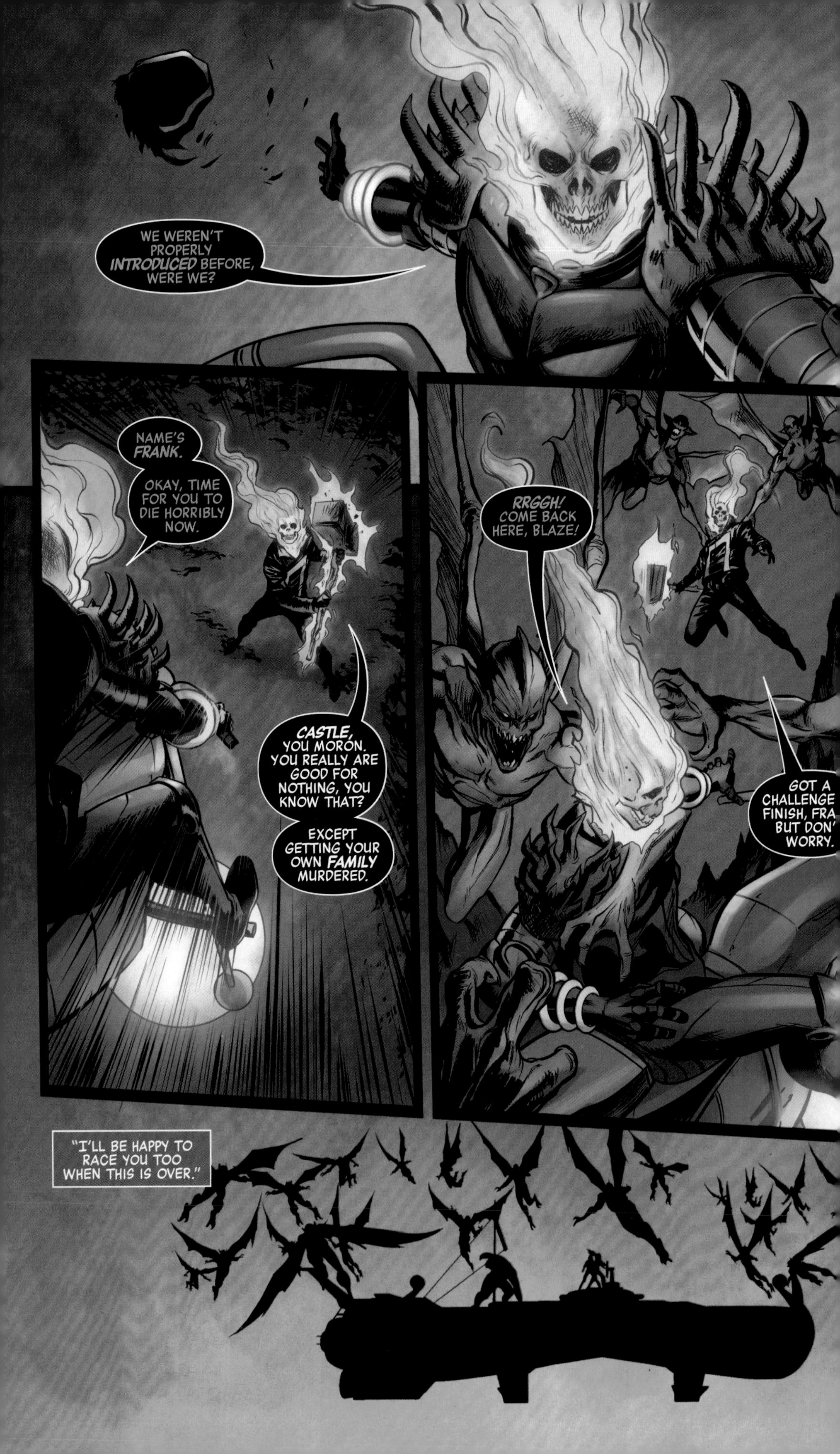
WE WEREN'T PROPERLY INTRODUCED BEFORE, WERE WE?
NAME'S FRANK.
OKAY, TIME FOR YOU TO DIE HORRIBLY NOW.
CASTLE, YOU MORON. YOU REALLY ARE GOOD FOR NOTHING, YOU KNOW THAT?
EXCEPT GETTING YOUR OWN FAMILY MURDERED.
RRGGH! COME BACK HERE, BLAZE!
GOT A CHALLENGE FINISH, FRA BUT DON' WORRY.
"I'LL BE HAPPY TO RACE YOU TOO WHEN THIS IS OVER."

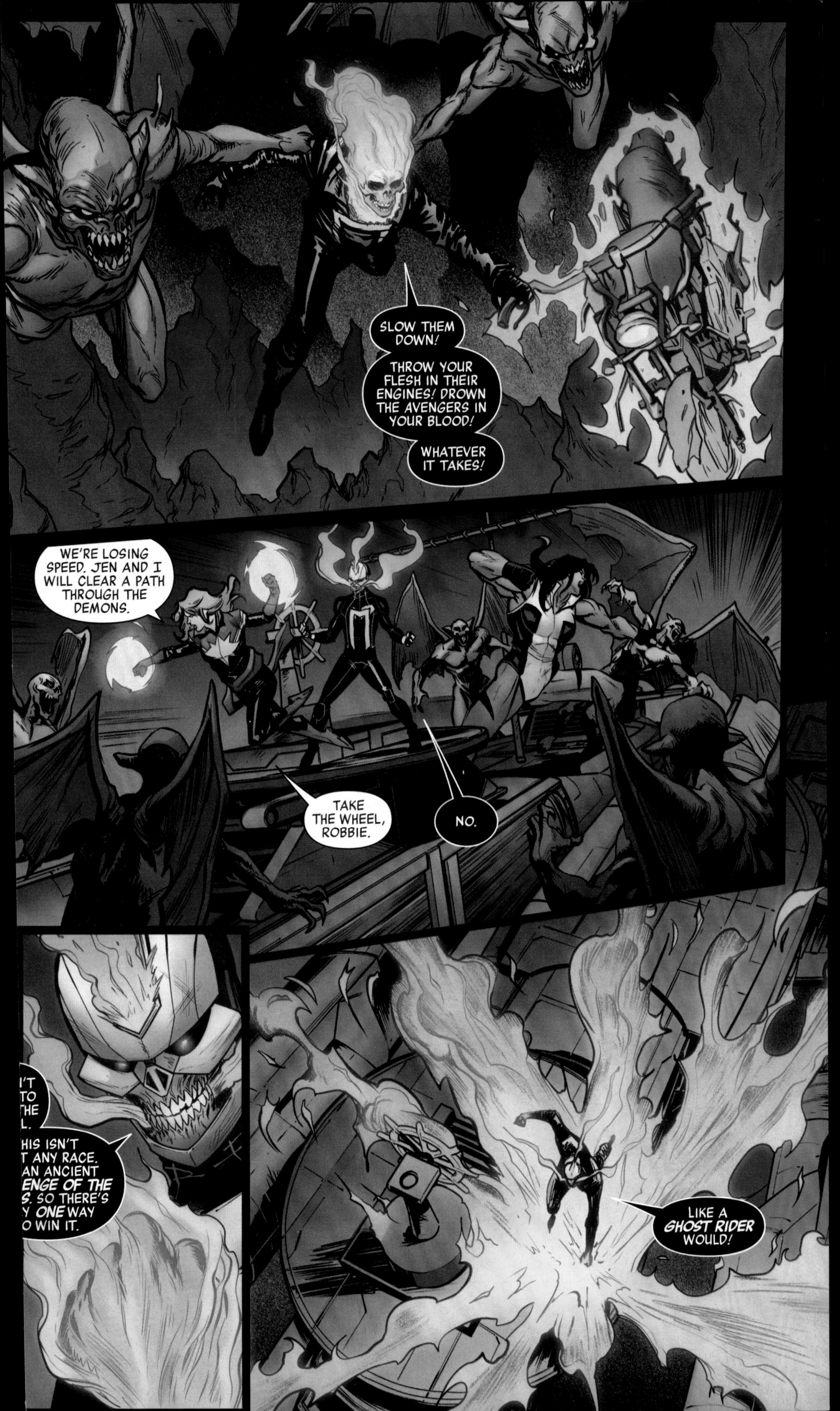
SLOW THEM DOWN!
THROW YOUR FLESH IN THEIR ENGINES! DROWN THE AVENGERS IN YOUR BLOOD!
WHATEVER IT TAKES!
WE'RE LOSING SPEED. JEN AND I WILL CLEAR A PATH THROUGH THE DEMONS.
TAKE THE WHEEL, ROBBIE.
NO.
LIKE A *GHOST RIDER* WOULD!

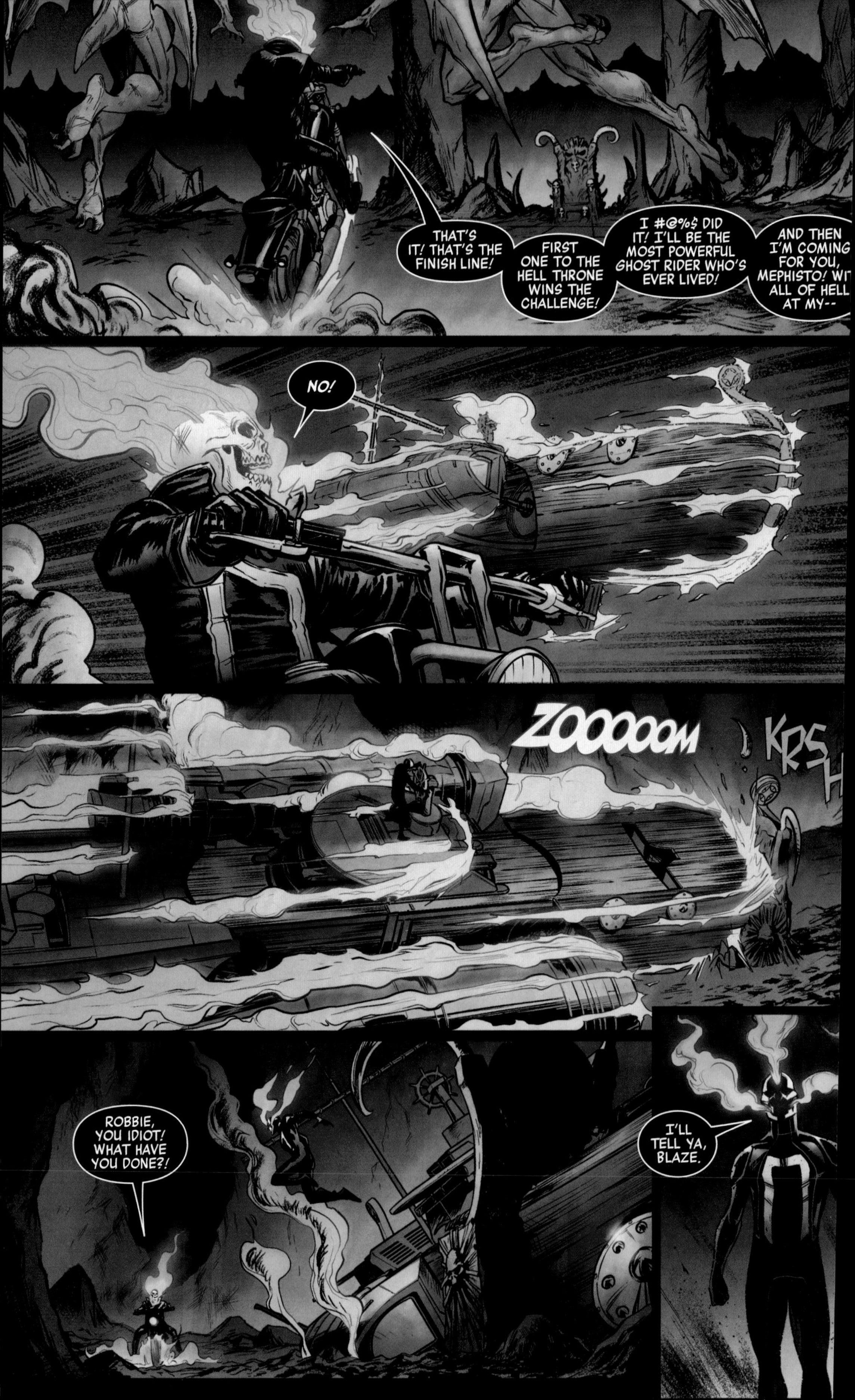
THAT'S IT! THAT'S THE FINISH LINE!
FIRST ONE TO THE HELL THRONE WINS THE CHALLENGE!
I #@%$ DID IT! I'LL BE THE MOST POWERFUL GHOST RIDER WHO'S EVER LIVED!
AND THEN I'M COMING FOR YOU, MEPHISTO! WIT ALL OF HELL AT MY--
NO!
ZOOOOOM
KRSH
ROBBIE, YOU IDIOT! WHAT HAVE YOU DONE?!
I'LL TELL YA, BLAZE.

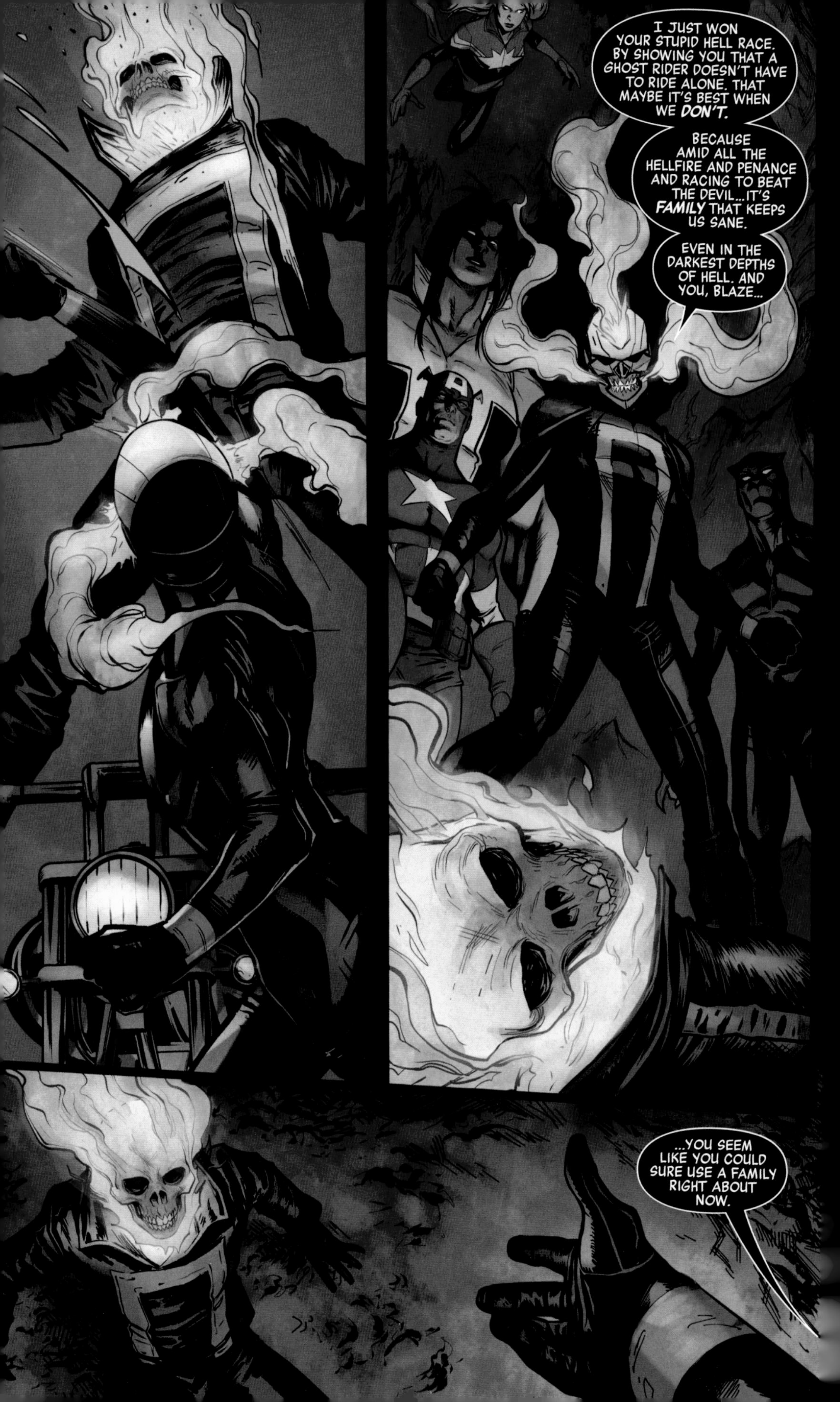
I JUST WON YOUR STUPID HELL RACE. BY SHOWING YOU THAT A GHOST RIDER DOESN'T HAVE TO RIDE ALONE. THAT MAYBE IT'S BEST WHEN WE DON'T.
BECAUSE AMID ALL THE HELLFIRE AND PENANCE AND RACING TO BEAT THE DEVIL...IT'S FAMILY THAT KEEPS US SANE.
EVEN IN THE DARKEST DEPTHS OF HELL. AND YOU, BLAZE...
...YOU SEEM LIKE YOU COULD SURE USE A FAMILY RIGHT ABOUT NOW.

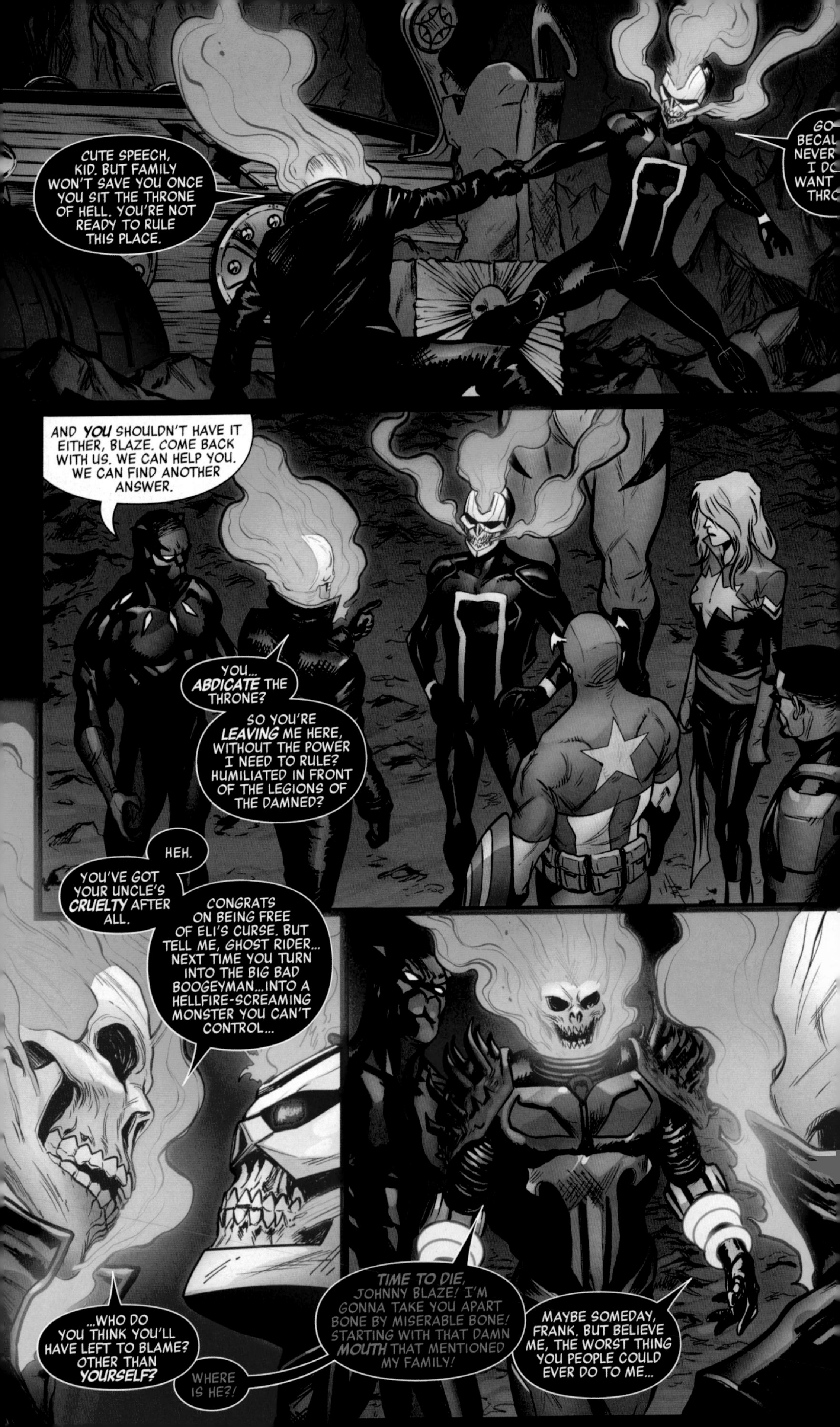
CUTE SPEECH, KID. BUT FAMILY WON'T SAVE YOU ONCE YOU SIT THE THRONE OF HELL. YOU'RE NOT READY TO RULE THIS PLACE.
AND *YOU* SHOULDN'T HAVE IT EITHER, BLAZE. COME BACK WITH US. WE CAN HELP YOU. WE CAN FIND ANOTHER ANSWER.
YOU... *ABDICATE* THE THRONE?
SO YOU'RE *LEAVING* ME HERE, WITHOUT THE POWER I NEED TO RULE? HUMILIATED IN FRONT OF THE LEGIONS OF THE DAMNED?
HEH.
YOU'VE GOT YOUR UNCLE'S *CRUELTY* AFTER ALL.
CONGRATS ON BEING FREE OF ELI'S CURSE. BUT TELL ME, GHOST RIDER... NEXT TIME YOU TURN INTO THE BIG BAD BOOGEYMAN...INTO A HELLFIRE-SCREAMING MONSTER YOU CAN'T CONTROL...
...WHO DO YOU THINK YOU'LL HAVE LEFT TO BLAME? OTHER THAN *YOURSELF?*
WHERE IS HE?!
TIME TO DIE, JOHNNY BLAZE! I'M GONNA TAKE YOU APART BONE BY MISERABLE BONE! STARTING WITH THAT DAMN *MOUTH* THAT MENTIONED MY FAMILY!
MAYBE SOMEDAY, FRANK. BUT BELIEVE ME, THE WORST THING YOU PEOPLE COULD EVER DO TO ME...

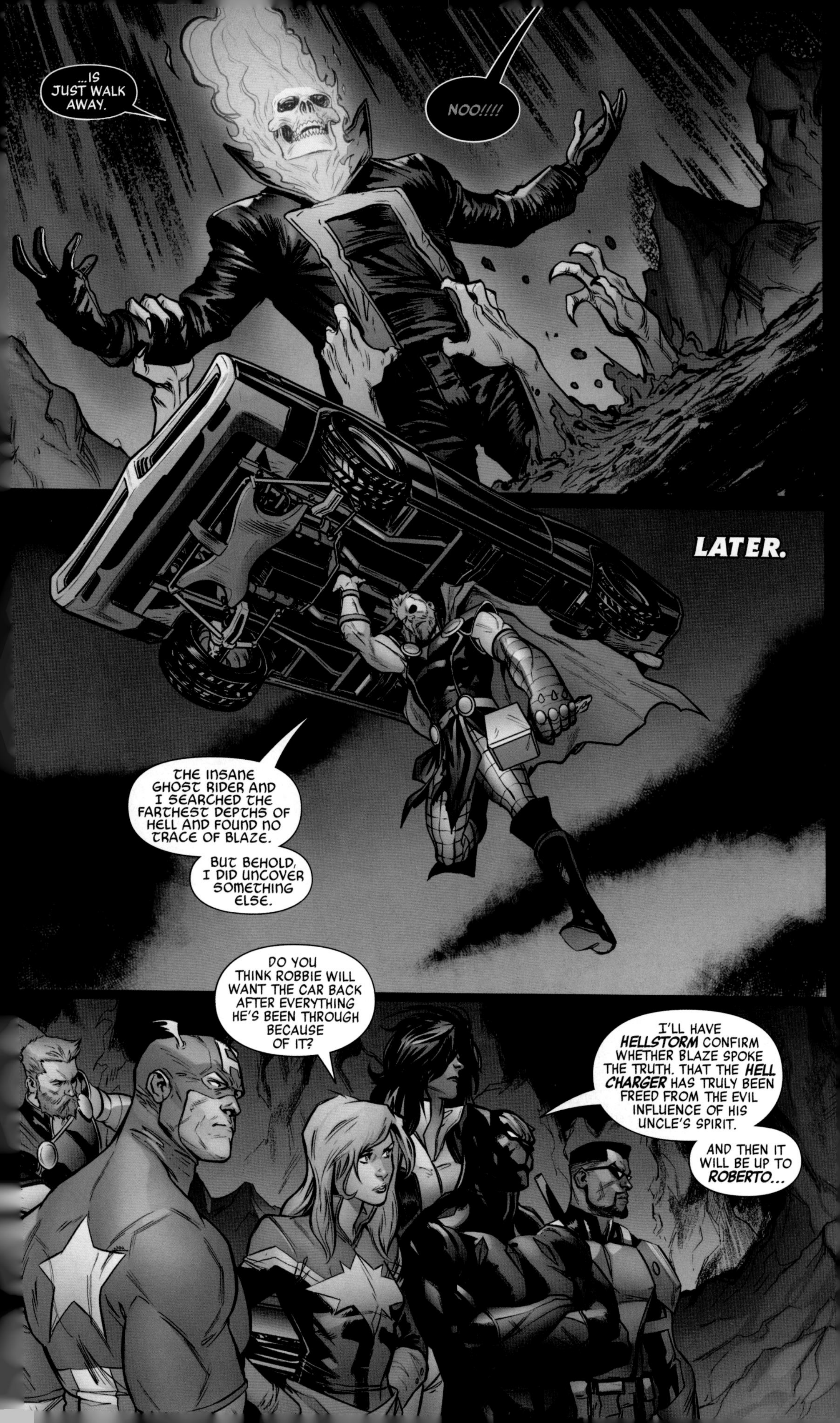
...IS JUST WALK AWAY.
NOO!!!!
LATER.
THE INSANE GHOST RIDER AND I SEARCHED THE FARTHEST DEPTHS OF HELL AND FOUND NO TRACE OF BLAZE.
BUT BEHOLD, I DID UNCOVER SOMETHING ELSE.
DO YOU THINK ROBBIE WILL WANT THE CAR BACK AFTER EVERYTHING HE'S BEEN THROUGH BECAUSE OF IT?
I'LL HAVE HELLSTORM CONFIRM WHETHER BLAZE SPOKE THE TRUTH. THAT THE HELL CHARGER HAS TRULY BEEN FREED FROM THE EVIL INFLUENCE OF HIS UNCLE'S SPIRIT.
AND THEN IT WILL BE UP TO ROBERTO...

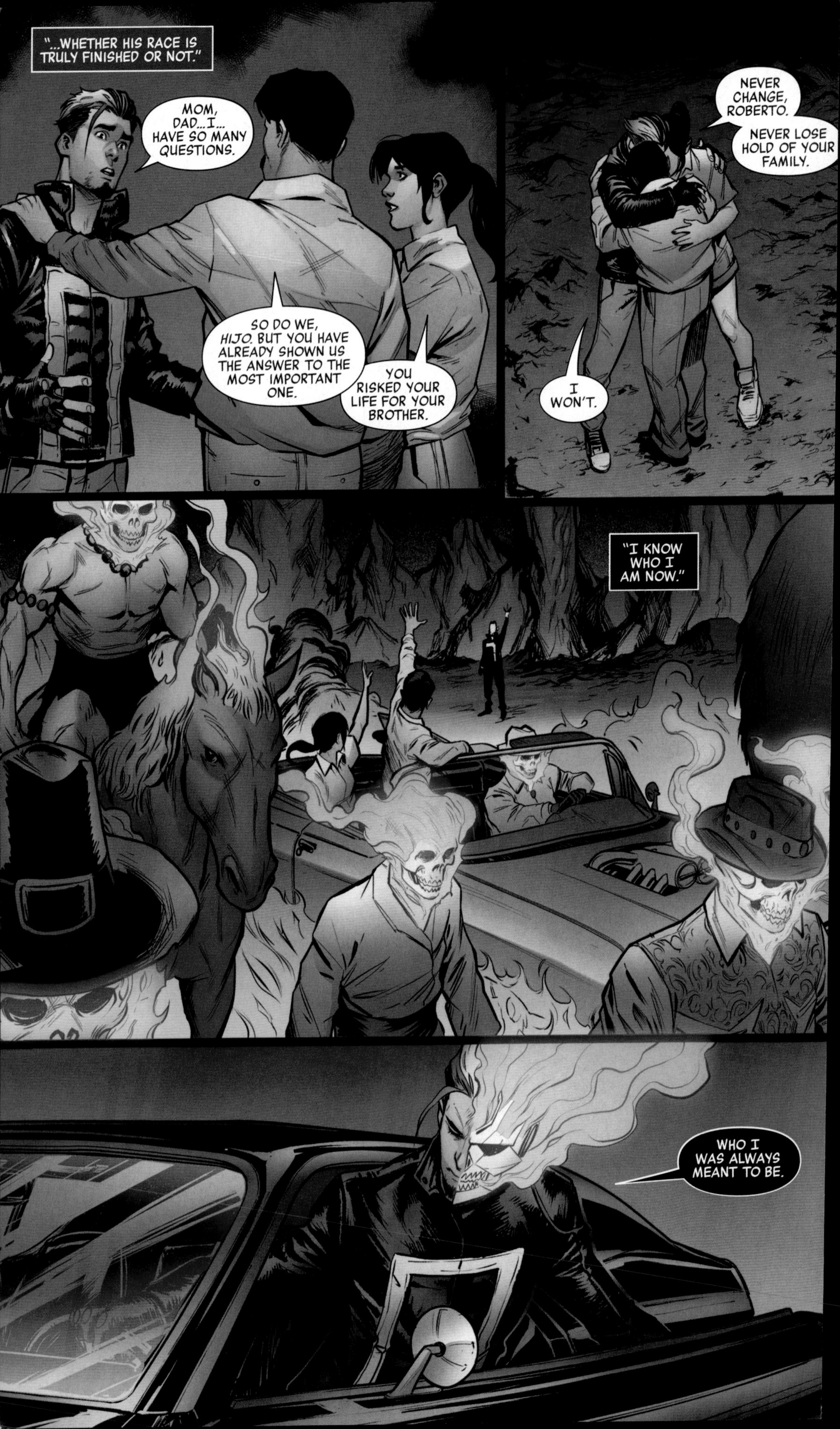
"...WHETHER HIS RACE IS TRULY FINISHED OR NOT."
MOM, DAD... I... HAVE SO MANY QUESTIONS.
SO DO WE, HIJO. BUT YOU HAVE ALREADY SHOWN US THE ANSWER TO THE MOST IMPORTANT ONE.
YOU RISKED YOUR LIFE FOR YOUR BROTHER.
NEVER CHANGE, ROBERTO.
NEVER LOSE HOLD OF YOUR FAMILY.
I WON'T.
"I KNOW WHO I AM NOW."
WHO I WAS ALWAYS MEANT TO BE.

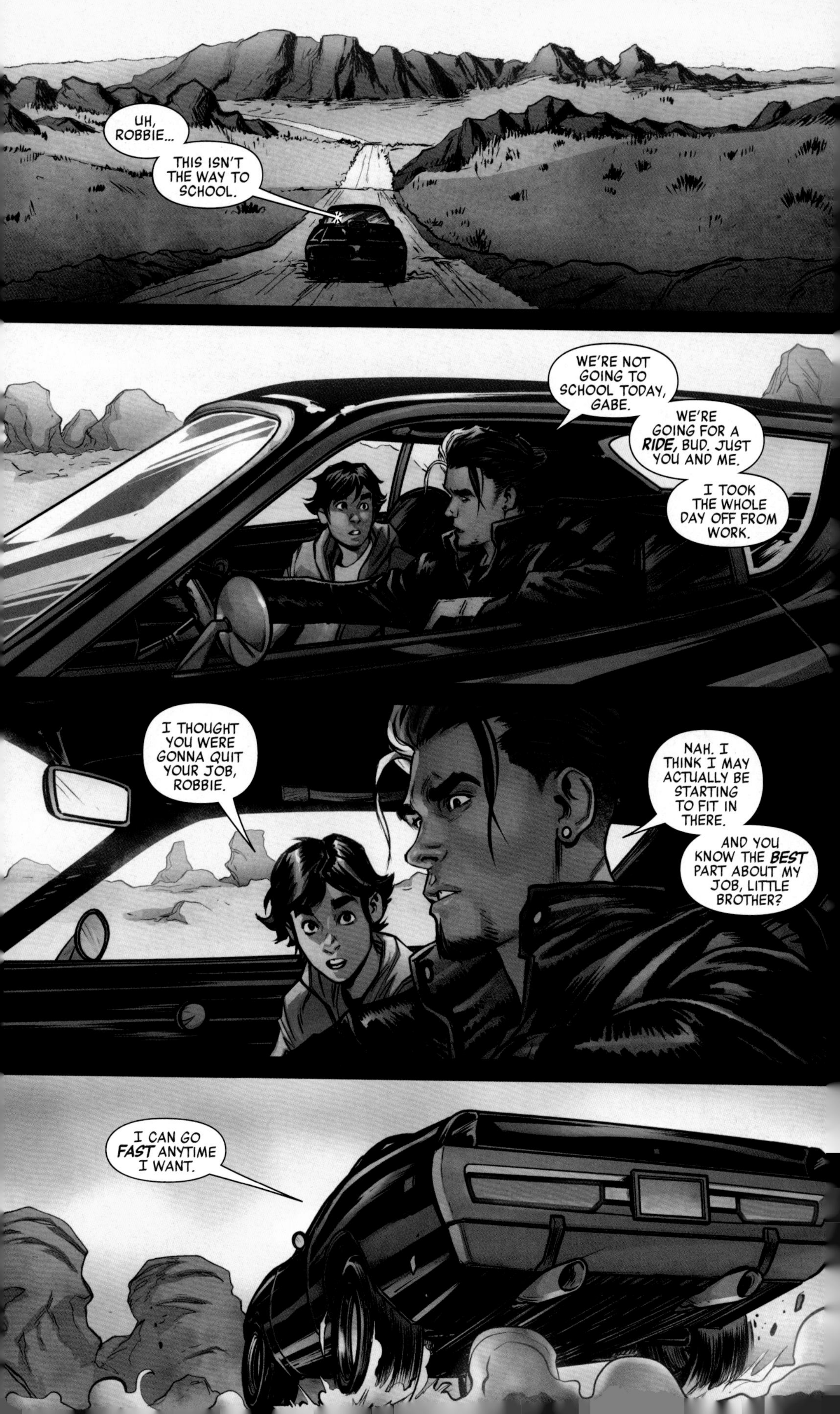
UH, ROBBIE...
THIS ISN'T THE WAY TO SCHOOL.
WE'RE NOT GOING TO SCHOOL TODAY, GABE.
WE'RE GOING FOR A **RIDE,** BUD. JUST YOU AND ME.
I TOOK THE WHOLE DAY OFF FROM WORK.
I THOUGHT YOU WERE GONNA QUIT YOUR JOB, ROBBIE.
NAH. I THINK I MAY ACTUALLY BE STARTING TO FIT IN THERE.
AND YOU KNOW THE **BEST** PART ABOUT MY JOB, LITTLE BROTHER?
I CAN GO **FAST** ANYTIME I WANT.

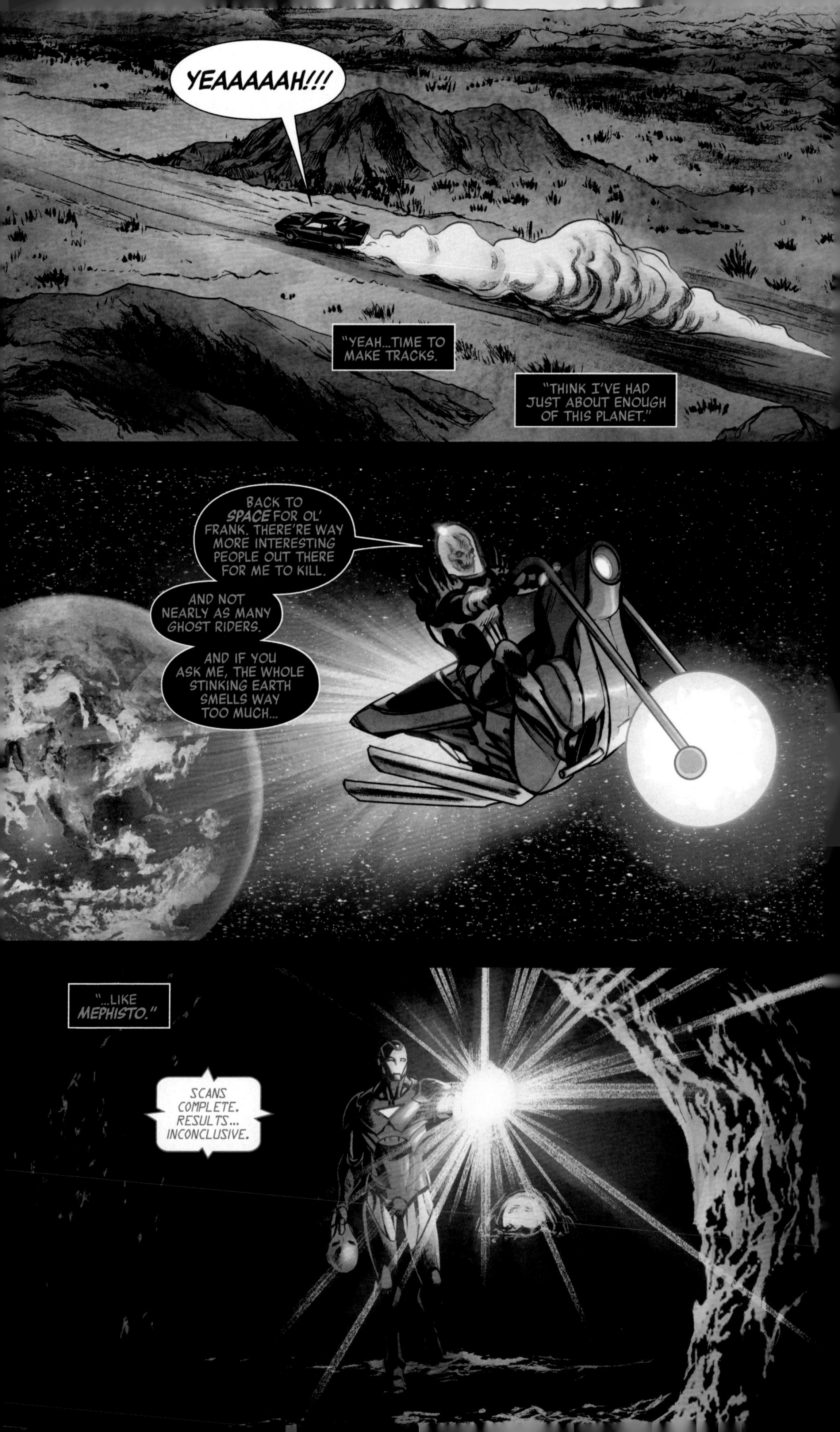
YEAAAAAH!!!
"YEAH...TIME TO MAKE TRACKS.
"THINK I'VE HAD JUST ABOUT ENOUGH OF THIS PLANET."
BACK TO *SPACE* FOR OL' FRANK. THERE'RE WAY MORE INTERESTING PEOPLE OUT THERE FOR ME TO KILL.
AND NOT NEARLY AS MANY GHOST RIDERS.
AND IF YOU ASK ME, THE WHOLE STINKING EARTH SMELLS WAY TOO MUCH...
"...LIKE *MEPHISTO.*"
SCANS COMPLETE. RESULTS... INCONCLUSIVE.

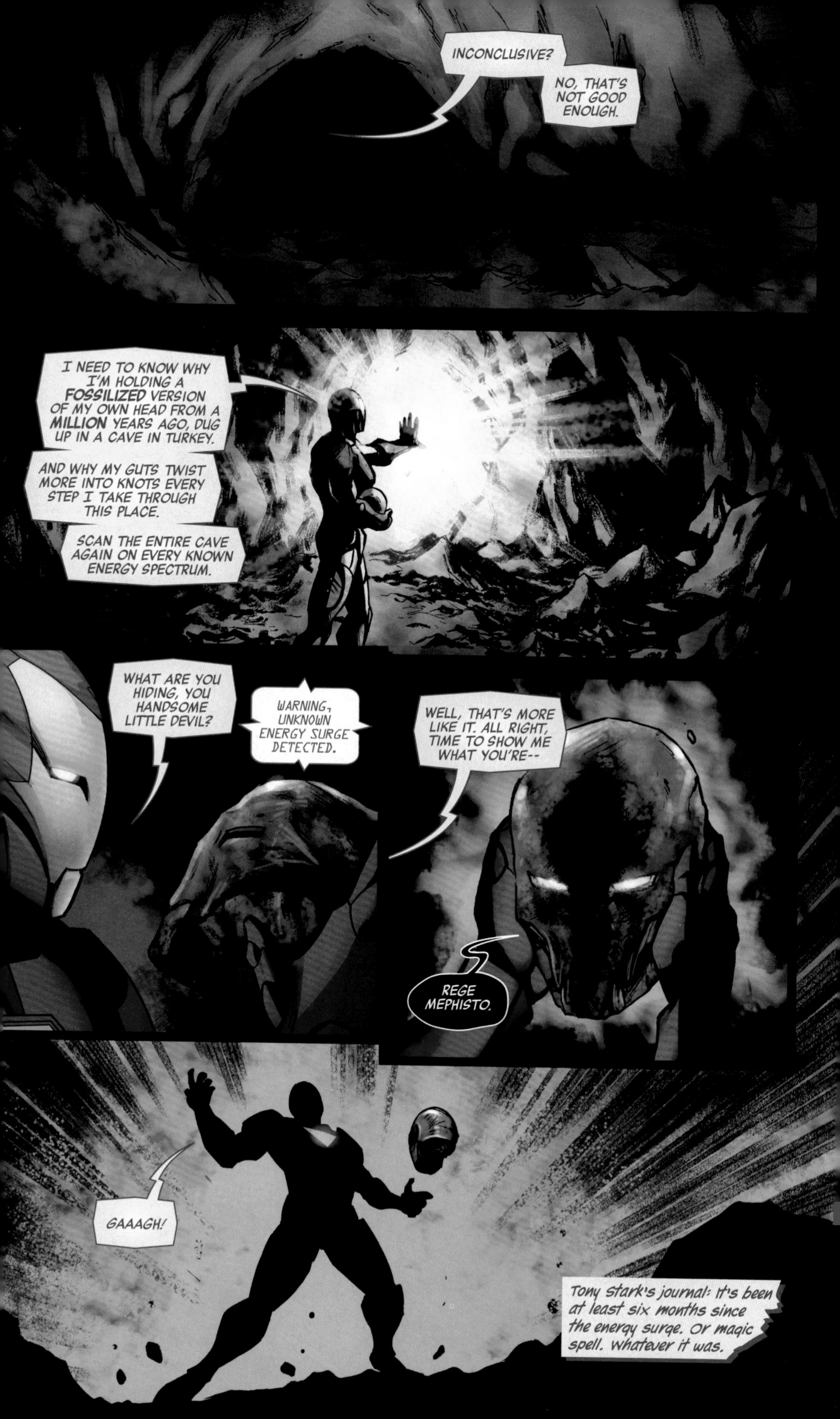
INCONCLUSIVE?
NO, THAT'S NOT GOOD ENOUGH.
I NEED TO KNOW WHY I'M HOLDING A FOSSILIZED VERSION OF MY OWN HEAD FROM A MILLION YEARS AGO, DUG UP IN A CAVE IN TURKEY.
AND WHY MY GUTS TWIST MORE INTO KNOTS EVERY STEP I TAKE THROUGH THIS PLACE.
SCAN THE ENTIRE CAVE AGAIN ON EVERY KNOWN ENERGY SPECTRUM.
WHAT ARE YOU HIDING, YOU HANDSOME LITTLE DEVIL?
WARNING, UNKNOWN ENERGY SURGE DETECTED.
WELL, THAT'S MORE LIKE IT. ALL RIGHT, TIME TO SHOW ME WHAT YOU'RE--
REGE MEPHISTO.
GAAAGH!
Tony Stark's journal: It's been at least six months since the energy surge. Or magic spell. Whatever it was.

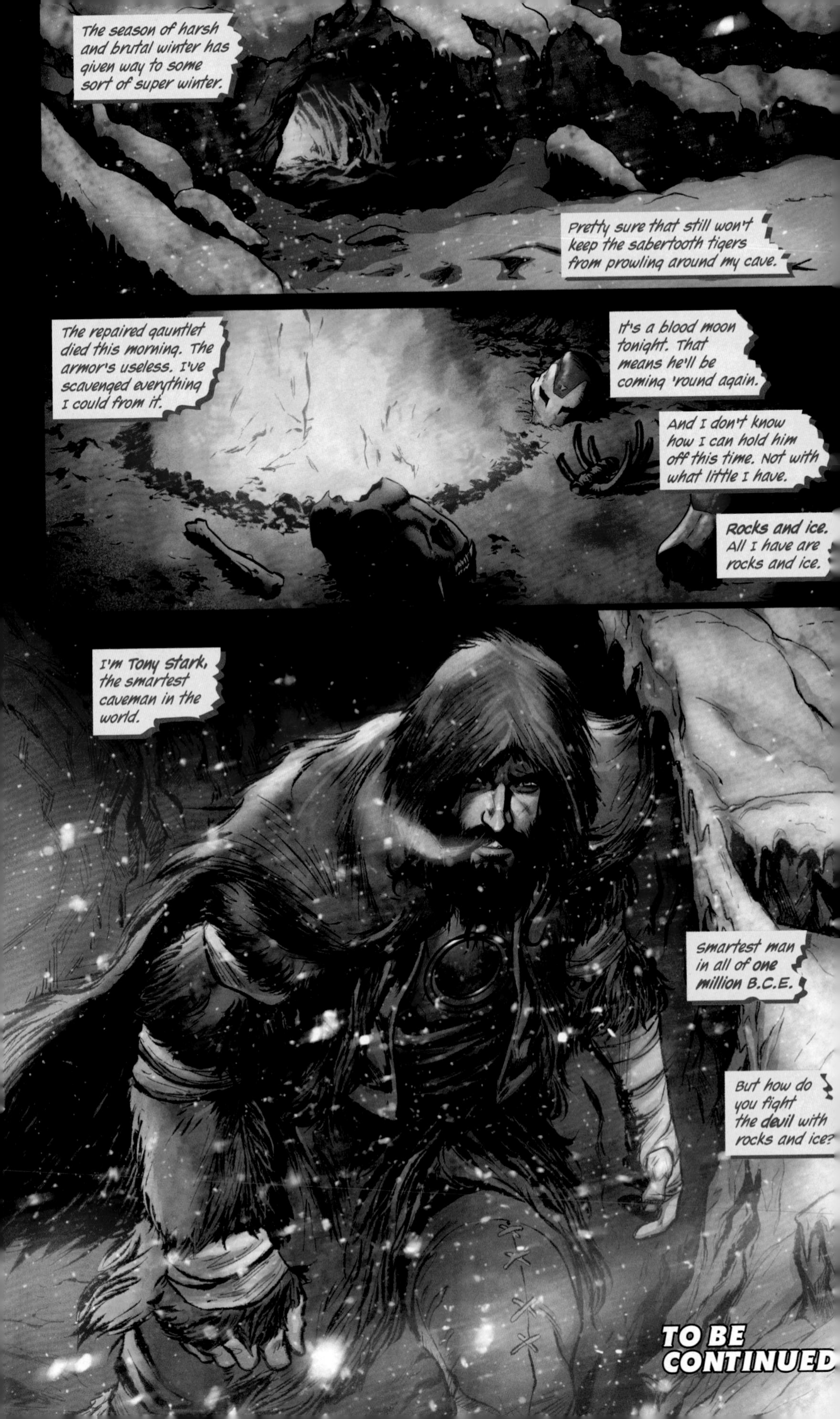
The season of harsh and brutal winter has given way to some sort of super winter.
Pretty sure that still won't keep the sabertooth tigers from prowling around my cave.
The repaired gauntlet died this morning. The armor's useless. I've scavenged everything I could from it.
It's a blood moon tonight. That means he'll be coming 'round again.
And I don't know how I can hold him off this time. Not with what little I have.
Rocks and ice. All I have are rocks and ice.
I'm Tony Stark, the smartest caveman in the world.
Smartest man in all of one million B.C.E.
But how do you fight the devil with rocks and ice?
TO BE CONTINUED

LL-NEW GHOST RIDER 1

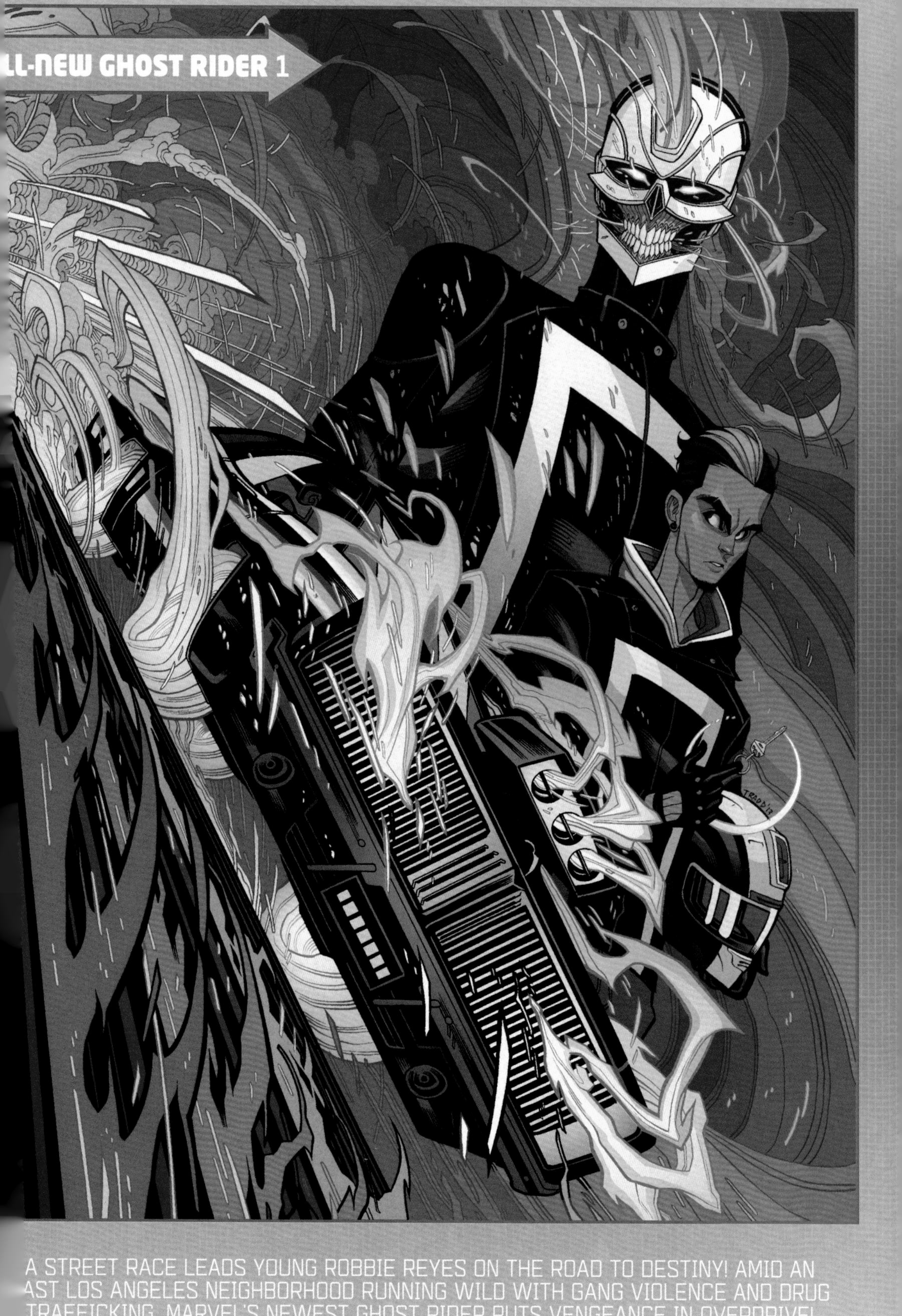

A STREET RACE LEADS YOUNG ROBBIE REYES ON THE ROAD TO DESTINY! AMID AN
AST LOS ANGELES NEIGHBORHOOD RUNNING WILD WITH GANG VIOLENCE AND DRUG
TRAFFICKING, MARVEL'S NEWEST GHOST RIDER PUTS VENGEANCE IN OVERDRIVE!

ALL-NEW

GHOST RIDER

00

« 5.7-LITER OHV « 2600 RPM STALL TORQUE CONVERTER « SMALL-BLOCK V8 CRATE ENGINE « 900-HP
« TURBOHYDRAMATIC 400 THREE-SPEED AUTOMATIC TRANSMISSION « 0-60MPH 4.5 SEC « MOPAR MADNESS

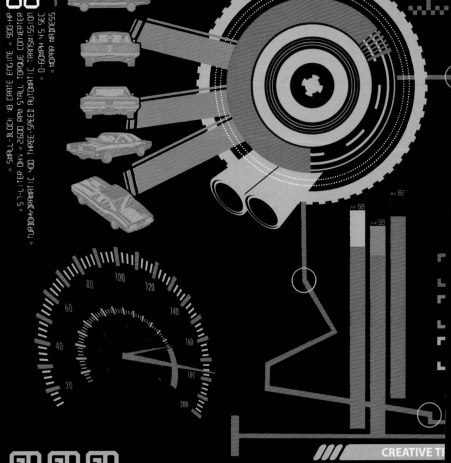

GO. GO. GO.

THE GHOST RIDER.

DEAD OR *ALIVE*?

GOOD OR *EVIL*?

ANGEL OR *DEMON*?

FOR YEARS, A DARK VIGILANTE HAS WALKED THE
LINE BETWEEN TWO WORLDS, HAUNTING THE
DREAMS OF BAD GUYS EVERYWHERE, STARING
INTO THEIR SOULS WITH FLAMING EYES OF
VENGEANCE.

BUT THIS IS NOT THE GHOST RIDER YOU KNOW.

THIS IS THE TALE OF AN ORDINARY KID NAMED
ROBBIE REYES, WHOSE LIFE IS ABOUT TO BECOME
A *HELL* OF A LOT LESS ORDINARY.

GET IN.

LET'S RIDE.

CREATIVE T

WRITER FELIPE S
ARTIST TRADD M(
COLORIST NELSON D/
& VAL STA
LETTERER VC's JOE CARAMA
PRODUCTION MANNY MED
COVER ARTISTS TRADD M(
& LAURA M/
VARIANT COVERS FELIPE S
SCOTTIE YOUNG, MIKE DEL MU
ASSISTANT EDITOR EMILY S
EDITOR MARK PAN
EDITOR IN CHIEF AXEL A
CHIEF CREATIVE OFFICER JOE QU
PUBLISHER DAN BU
EXECUTIVE PRODUCER ALA

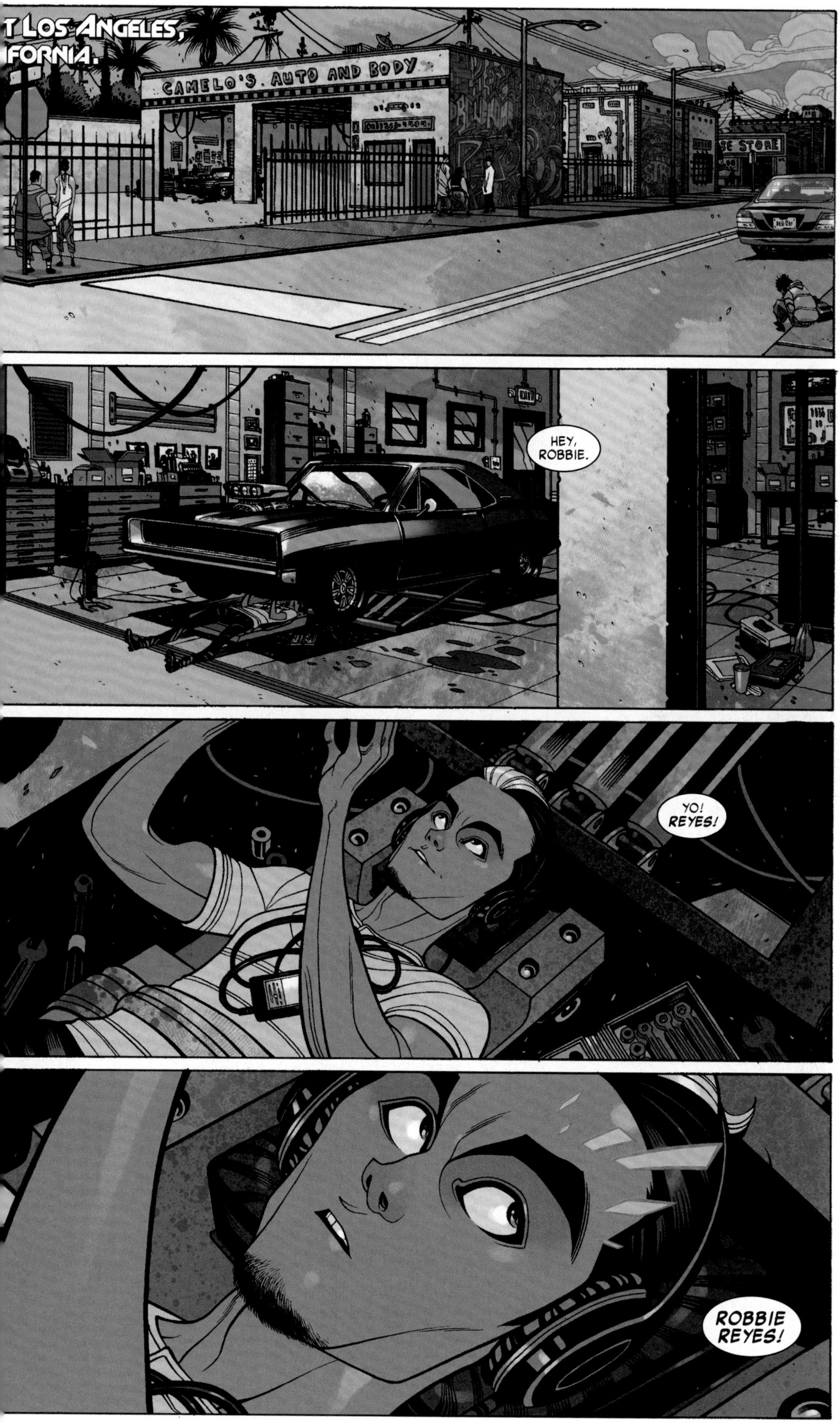
T LOS ANGELES,
FORNIA.
CAMELO'S AUTO AND BODY
SE STORE
HEY, ROBBIE.
YO! REYES!
ROBBIE REYES!

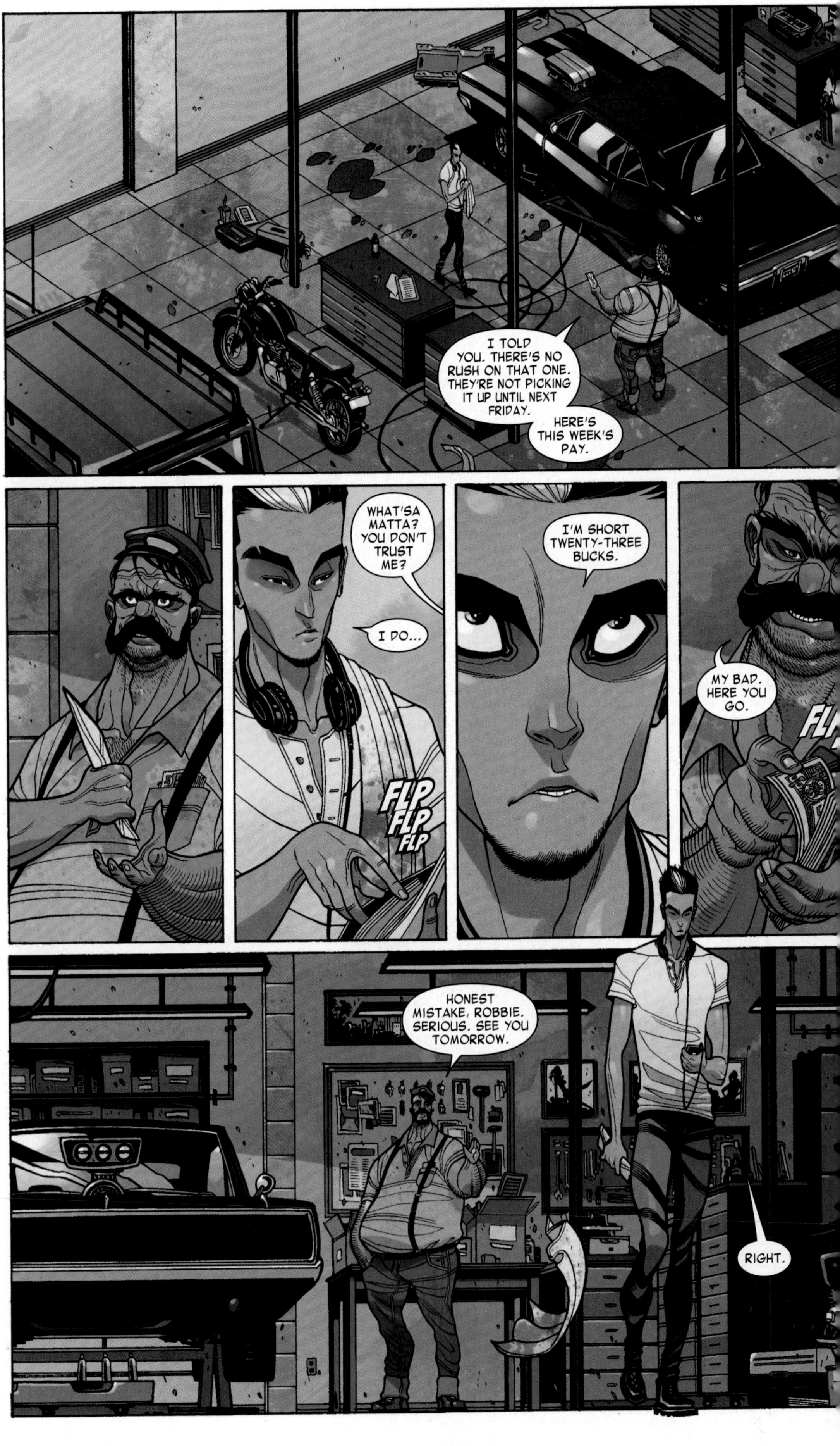

I TOLD YOU. THERE'S NO RUSH ON THAT ONE. THEY'RE NOT PICKING IT UP UNTIL NEXT FRIDAY.
HERE'S THIS WEEK'S PAY.
WHAT'SA MATTA? YOU DON'T TRUST ME?
I DO...
FLP FLP FLP
I'M SHORT TWENTY-THREE BUCKS.
MY BAD. HERE YOU GO.
HONEST MISTAKE, ROBBIE. SERIOUS. SEE YOU TOMORROW.
RIGHT.

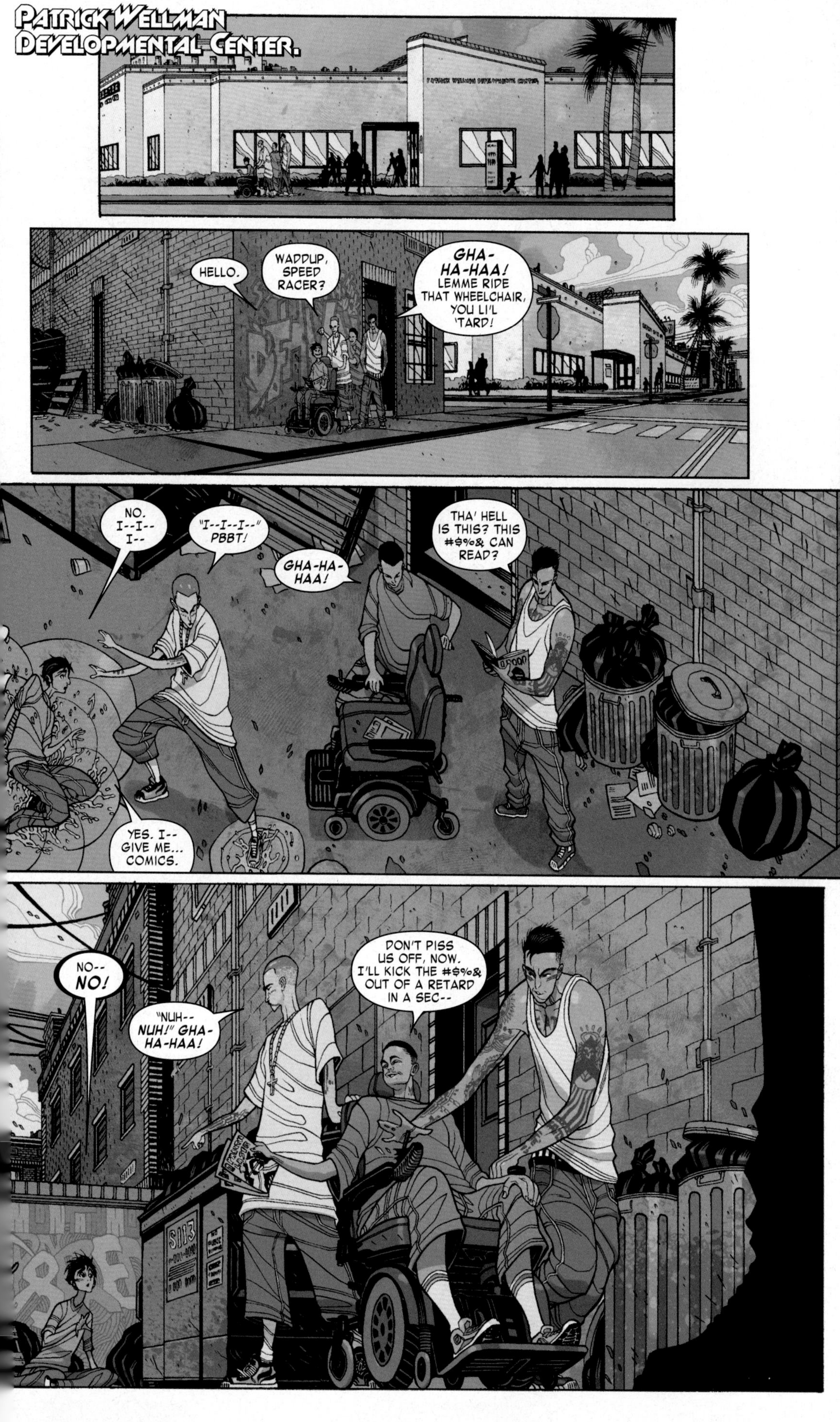
PATRICK WELLMAN DEVELOPMENTAL CENTER.
HELLO.
WADDUP, SPEED RACER?
GHA-HA-HAA! LEMME RIDE THAT WHEELCHAIR, YOU LI'L 'TARD!
NO. I--I-- I--
"I--I--I--" PBBT!
GHA-HA-HAA!
THA' HELL IS THIS? THIS #$%& CAN READ?
YES. I-- GIVE ME... COMICS.
NO-- NO!
"NUH-- NUH!" GHA-HA-HAA!
DON'T PISS US OFF, NOW. I'LL KICK THE #$%& OUT OF A RETARD IN A SEC--

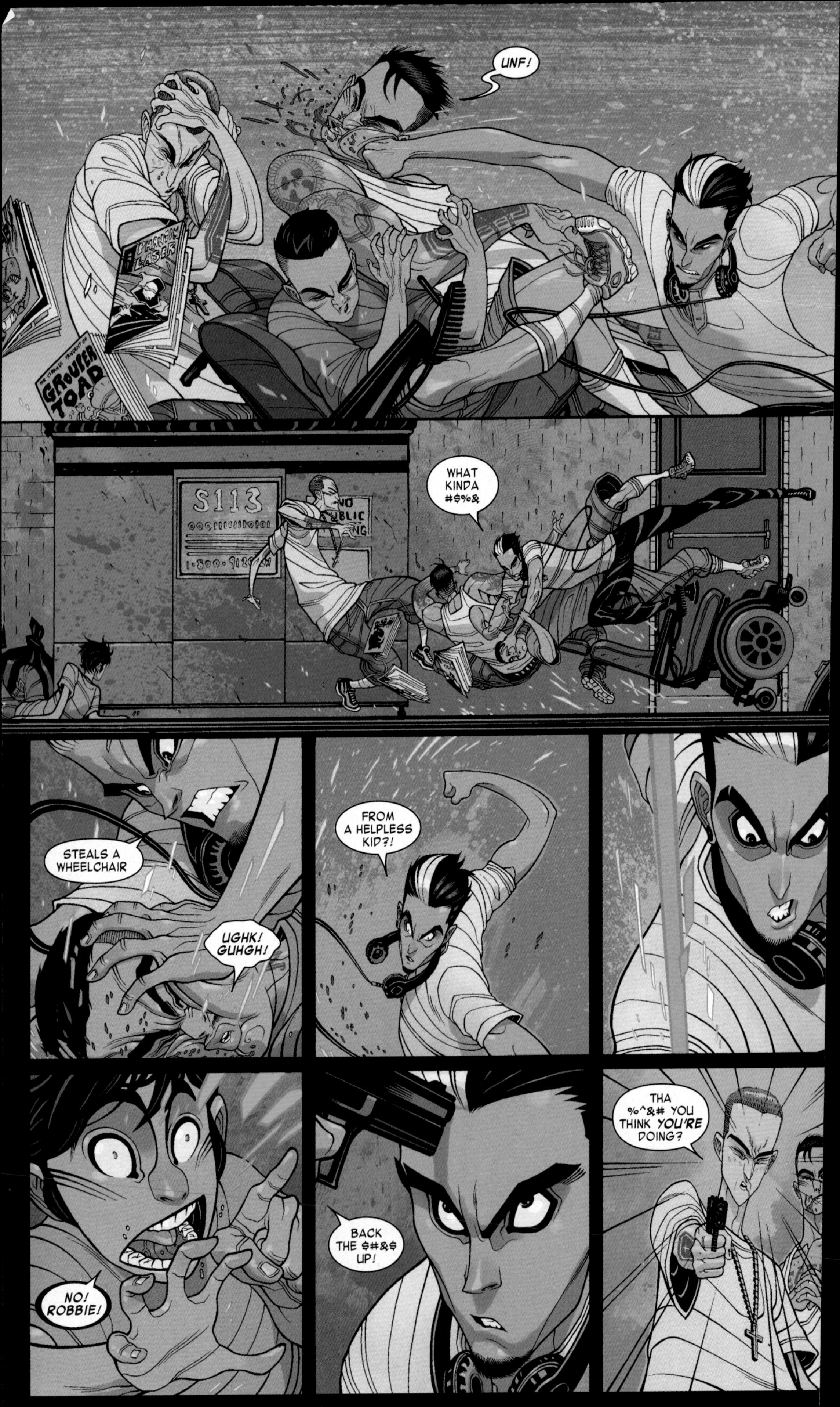
UNF!
WHAT KINDA #$%&
STEALS A WHEELCHAIR
UGHK! GUHGH!
FROM A HELPLESS KID?!
NO! ROBBIE!
BACK THE $#&$ UP!
THA %^&# YOU THINK YOU'RE DOING?

GHA-HA-HA! YOU #&@#& WITH RO YOU GET TOMPED, CUZ!

ROBBIE? *ROBBIE?* YOU OKAY?

UGGGGH. I'M FINE...

DAMMIT.

SORRY, GABE. I'LL GET YOU A NEW WHEELCHAIR. A BETTER ONE. LET'S GO HOME.

YOU ALL RIGHT, THERE, BRO?

YES. I'M OKAY, ROBBIE.

GOOD.

COMICS.

'RE SO YOU'RE MY ROBBIE! SHOWED EM!

YEAH. I SHOWED THEM...

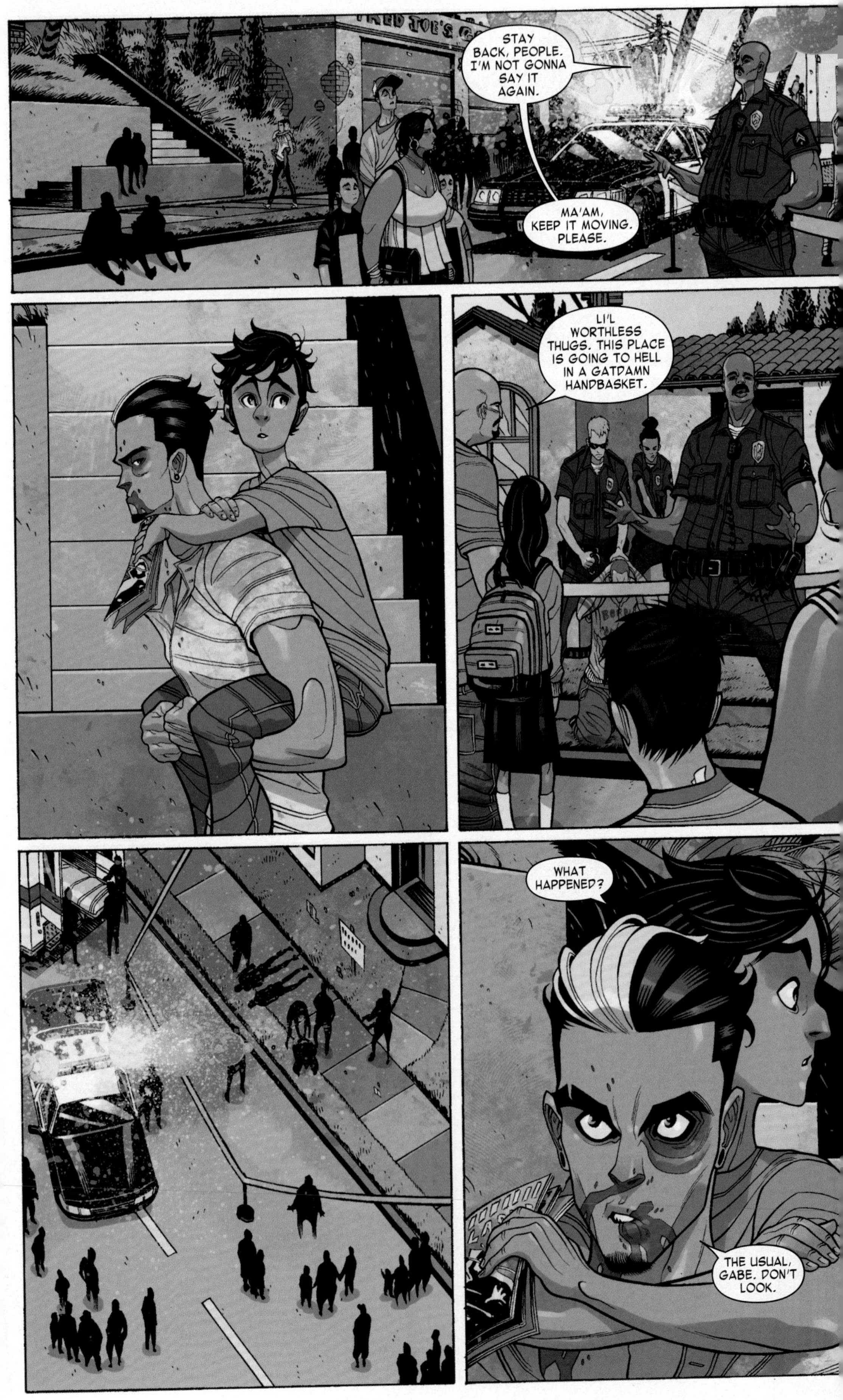
STAY BACK, PEOPLE. I'M NOT GONNA SAY IT AGAIN.
MA'AM, KEEP IT MOVING. PLEASE.
LI'L WORTHLESS THUGS. THIS PLACE IS GOING TO HELL IN A GATDAMN HANDBASKET.
WHAT HAPPENED?
THE USUAL, GABE. DON'T LOOK.

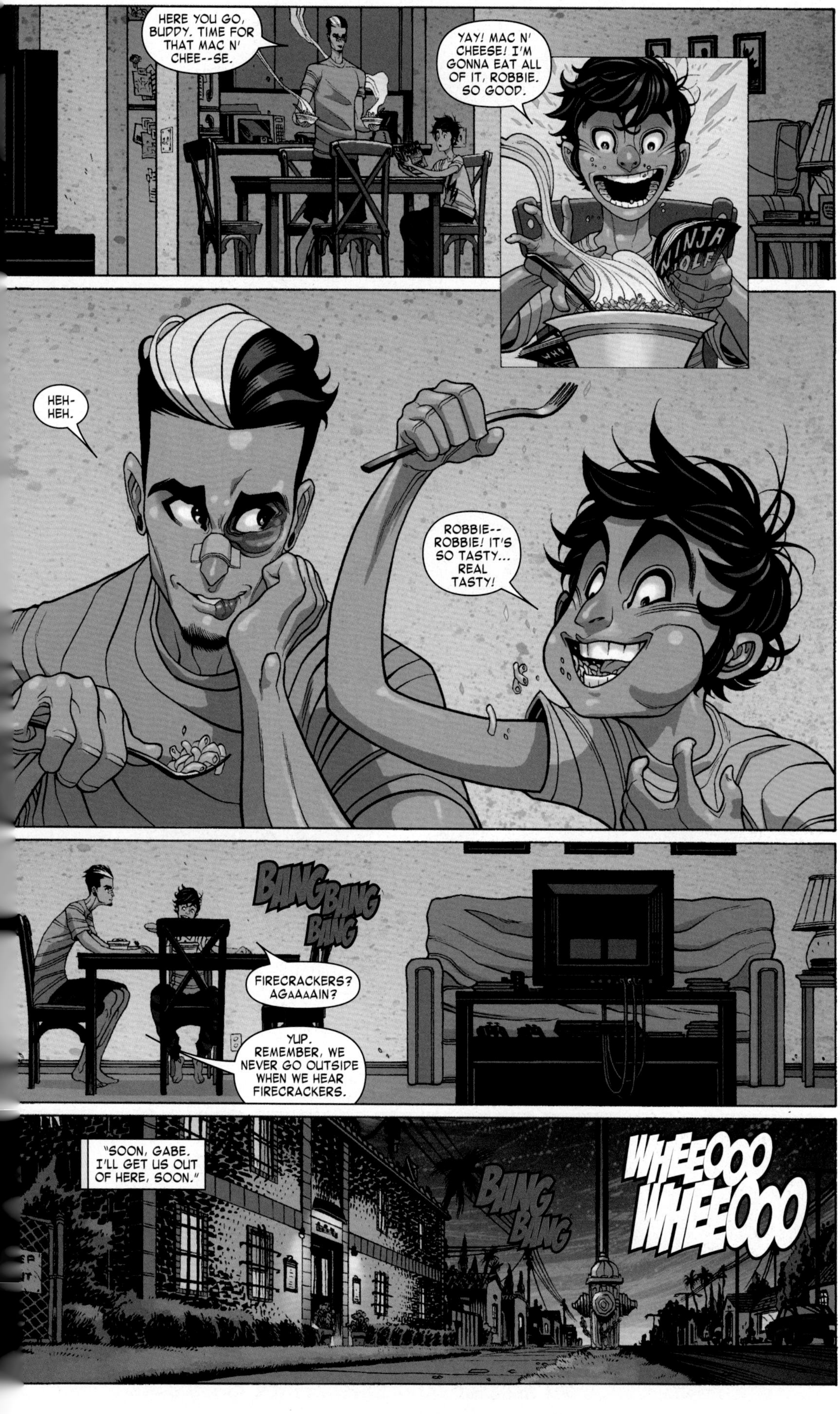
HERE YOU GO, BUDDY. TIME FOR THAT MAC N' CHEE--SE.
YAY! MAC N' CHEESE! I'M GONNA EAT ALL OF IT, ROBBIE. SO GOOD.
NINJA WOLF
HEH-HEH.
ROBBIE--ROBBIE! IT'S SO TASTY... REAL TASTY!
BANG BANG BANG
FIRECRACKERS? AGAAAAIN?
YUP. REMEMBER, WE NEVER GO OUTSIDE WHEN WE HEAR FIRECRACKERS.
"SOON, GABE. I'LL GET US OUT OF HERE, SOON."
BANG BANG
WHEEOOO WHEEOOO

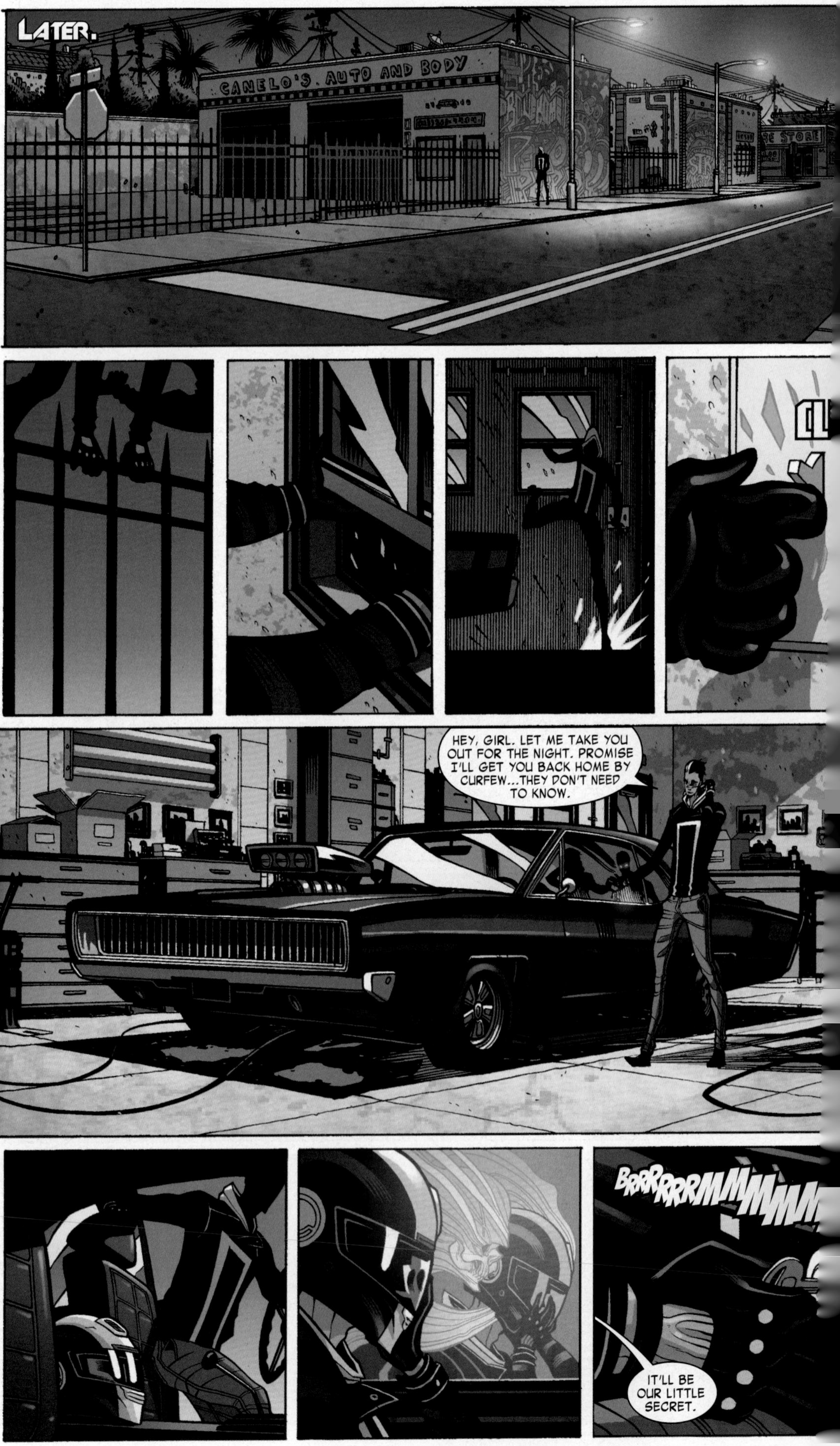
LATER.
CANELO'S AUTO AND BODY
HEY, GIRL. LET ME TAKE YOU OUT FOR THE NIGHT. PROMISE I'LL GET YOU BACK HOME BY CURFEW...THEY DON'T NEED TO KNOW.
BRRRRRRMMMMMM
IT'LL BE OUR LITTLE SECRET.

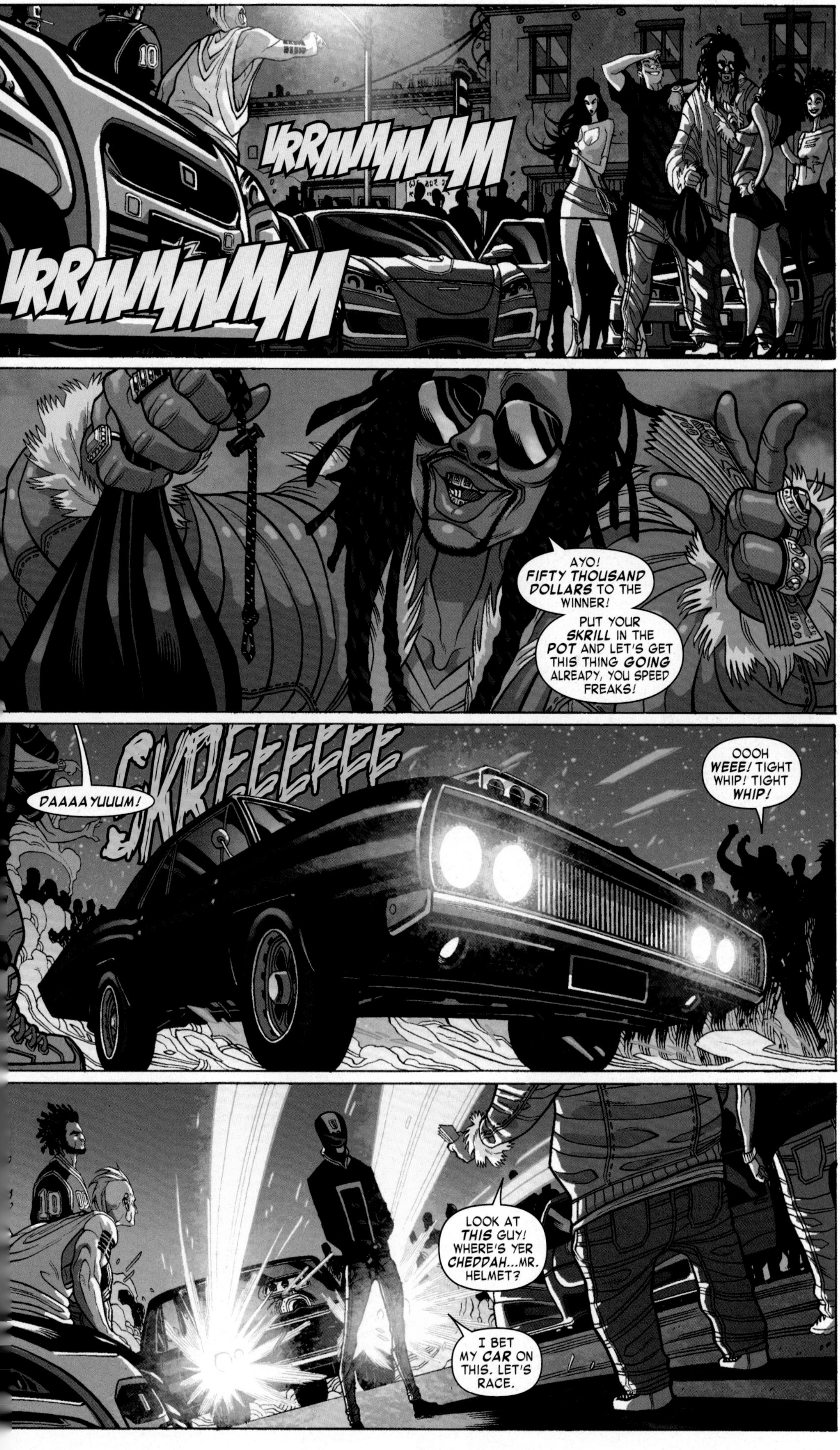
URRMMMMMM
URRMMMMMM
AYO! FIFTY THOUSAND DOLLARS TO THE WINNER!
PUT YOUR SKRILL IN THE POT AND LET'S GET THIS THING GOING ALREADY, YOU SPEED FREAKS!
SKREEEEEE
DAAAAYUUUM!
OOOH WEEE! TIGHT WHIP! TIGHT WHIP!
LOOK AT THIS GUY! WHERE'S YER CHEDDAH...MR. HELMET?
I BET MY CAR ON THIS. LET'S RACE.

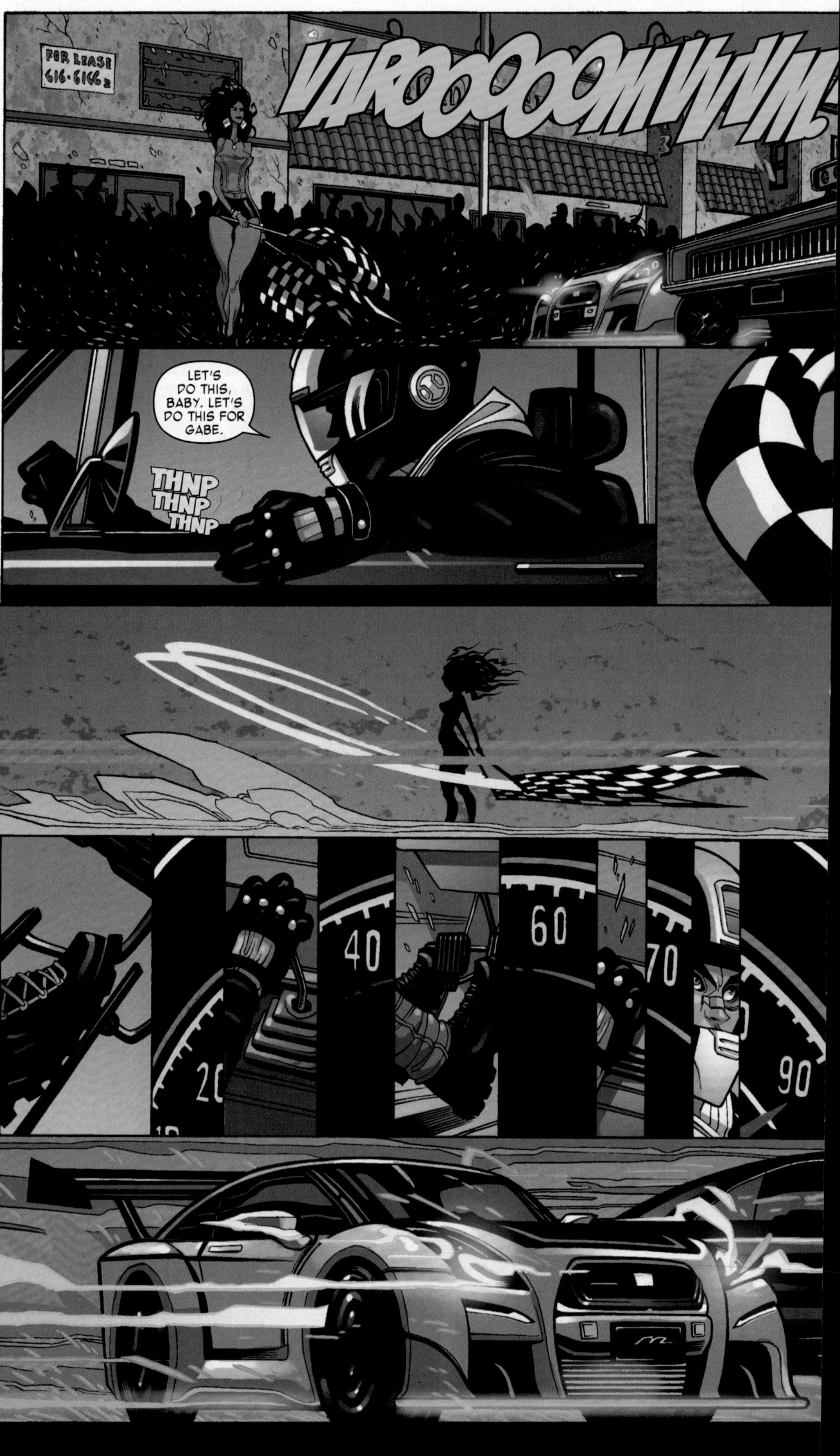
FOR LEASE
616-6166
VAROOOOOMVVVM
LET'S DO THIS, BABY. LET'S DO THIS FOR GABE.
THNP THNP THNP
40
60
70
90

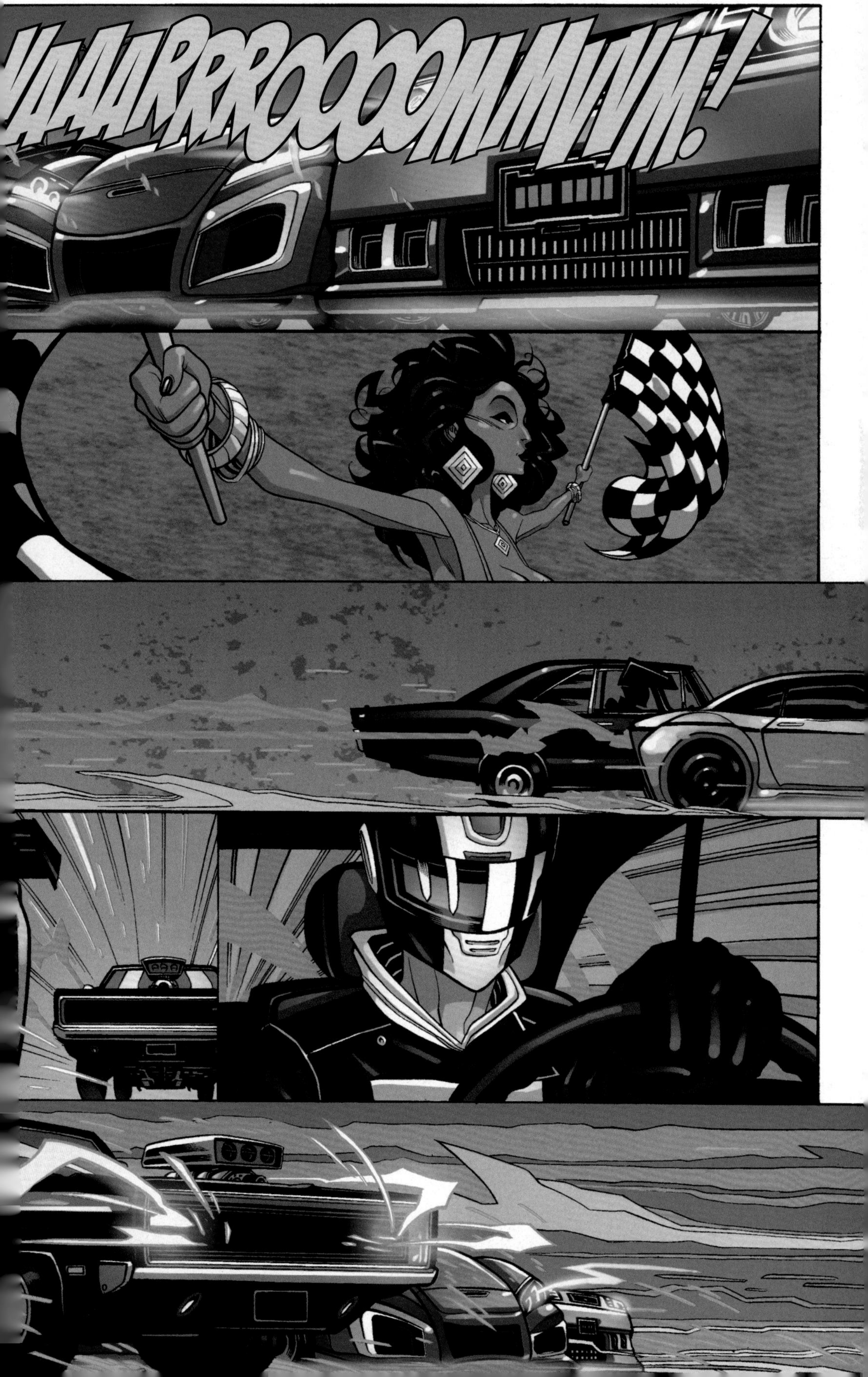
VAARRROOOOOMMVVM!

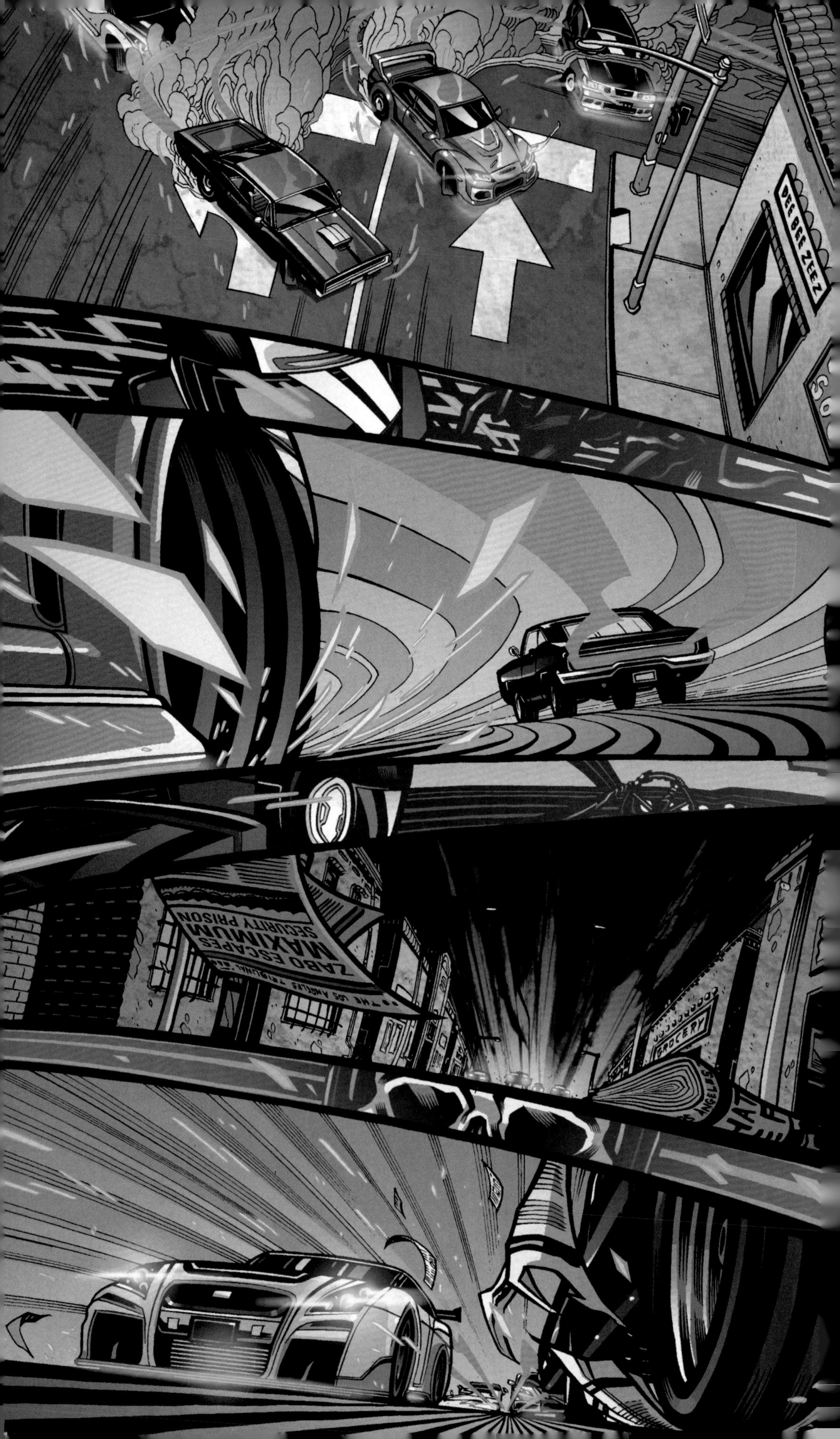
DEE BEE ZEEZ
THE LOS ANGELES TRIBUNE
ZABO ESCAPES MAXIMUM SECURITY PRISON
GROCERY
LOS ANGELES

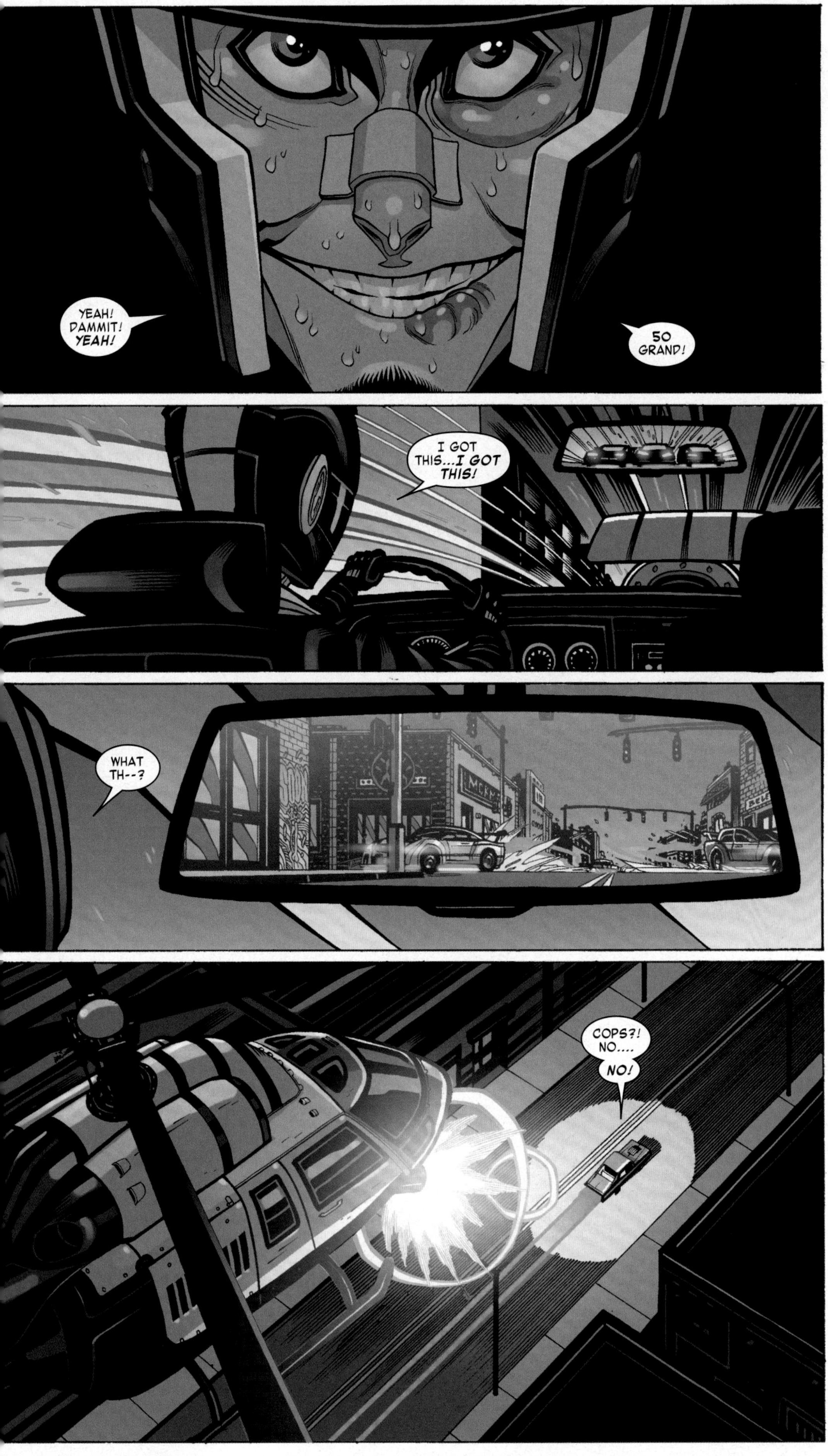
YEAH! DAMMIT! YEAH!
50 GRAND!
I GOT THIS...I GOT THIS!
WHAT TH--?
COPS?! NO.... NO!

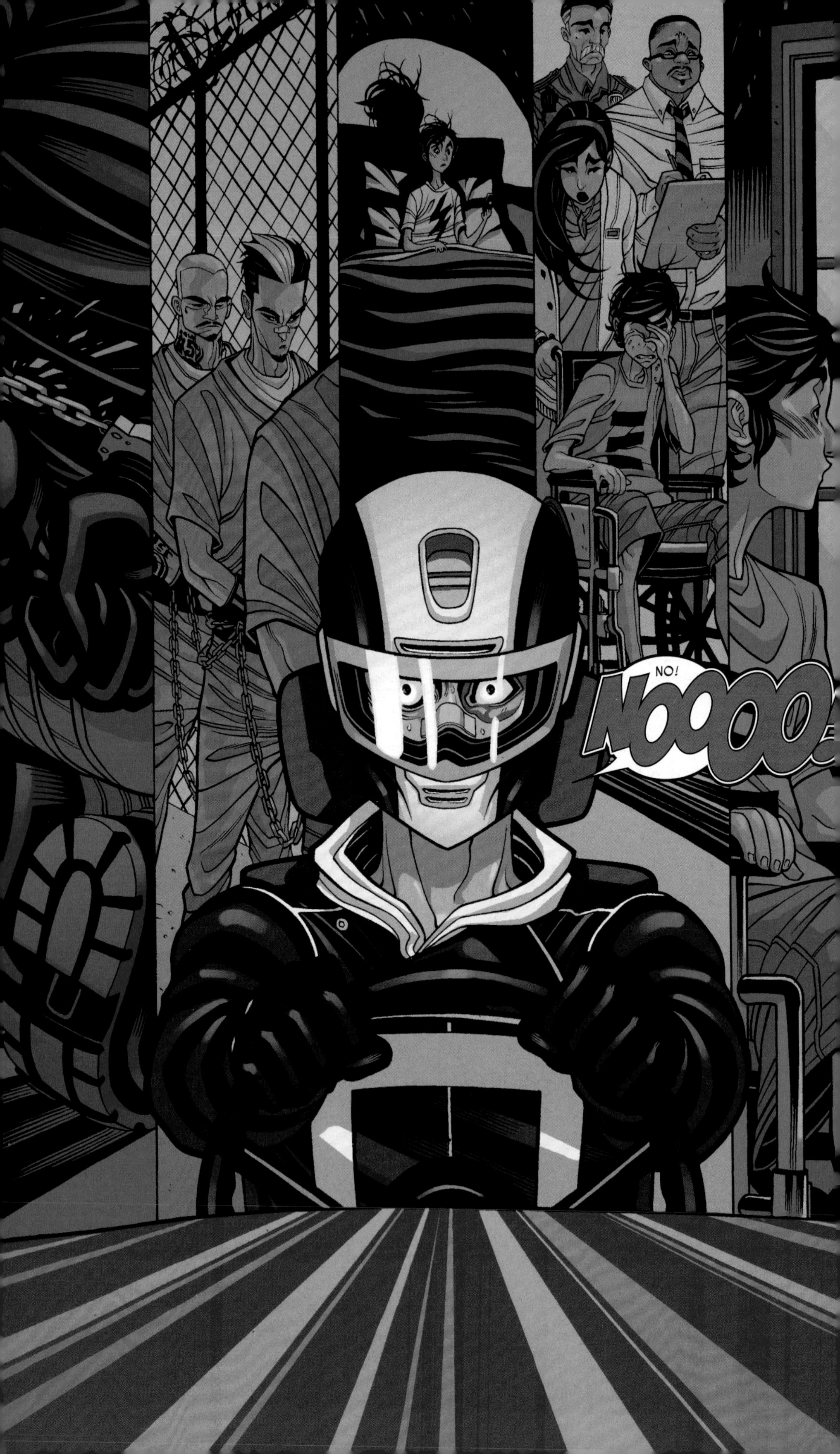
NO!
NOOOO

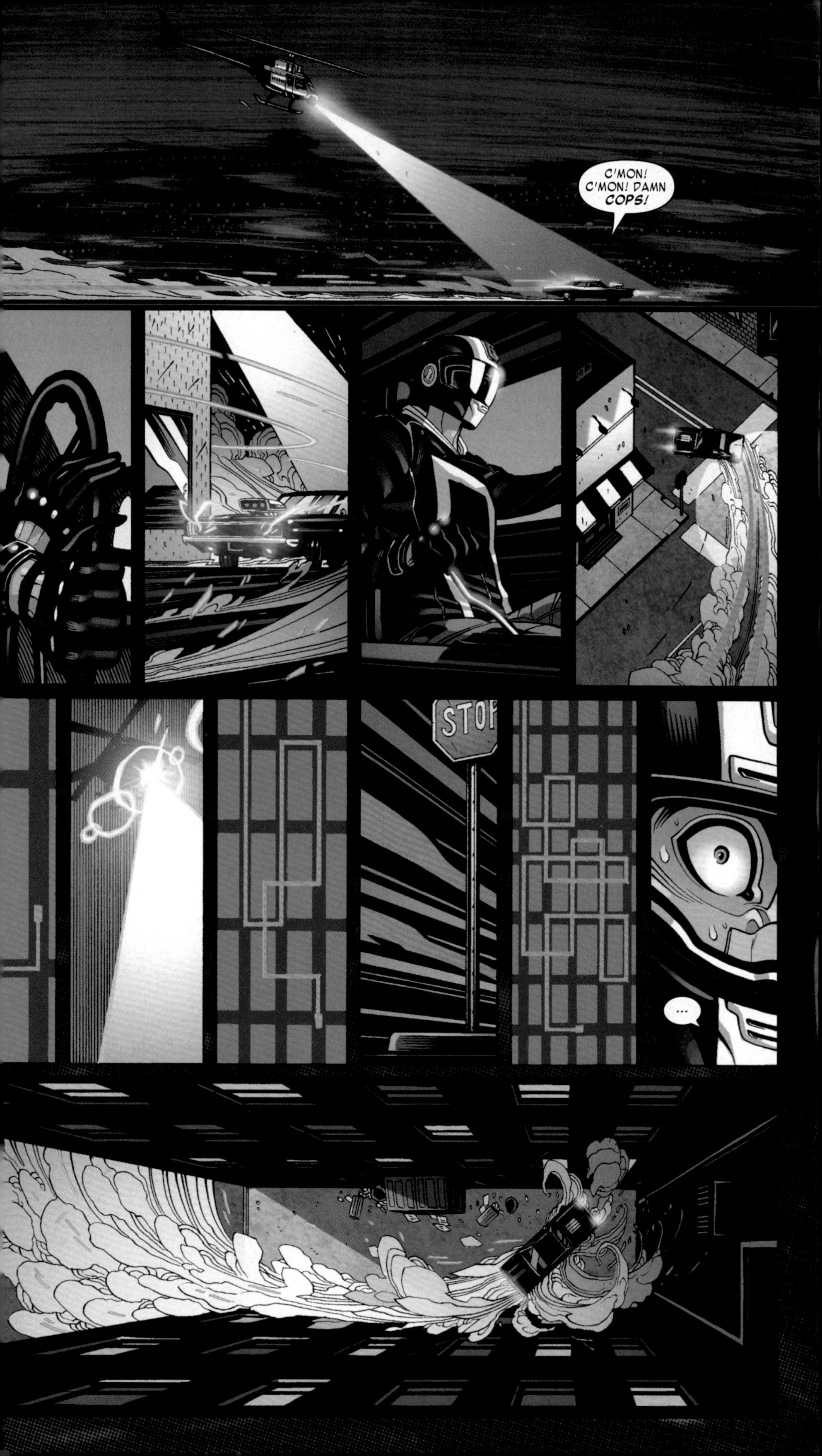
C'MON! C'MON! DAMN COPS!
STOP
...

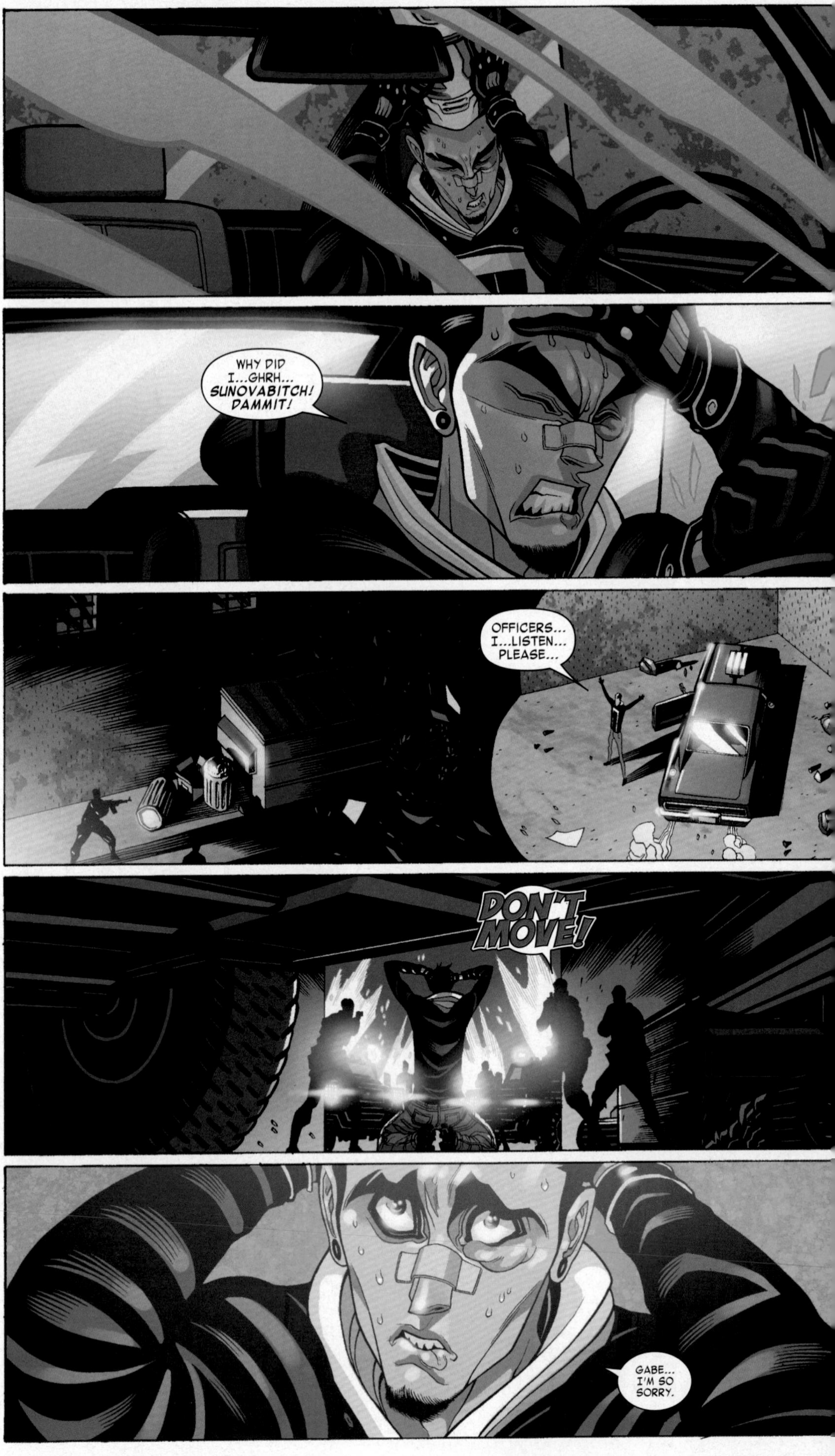
WHY DID I...GHRH... SUNOVABITCH! DAMMIT!
OFFICERS... I...LISTEN... PLEASE...
DON'T MOVE!
GABE... I'M SO SORRY.

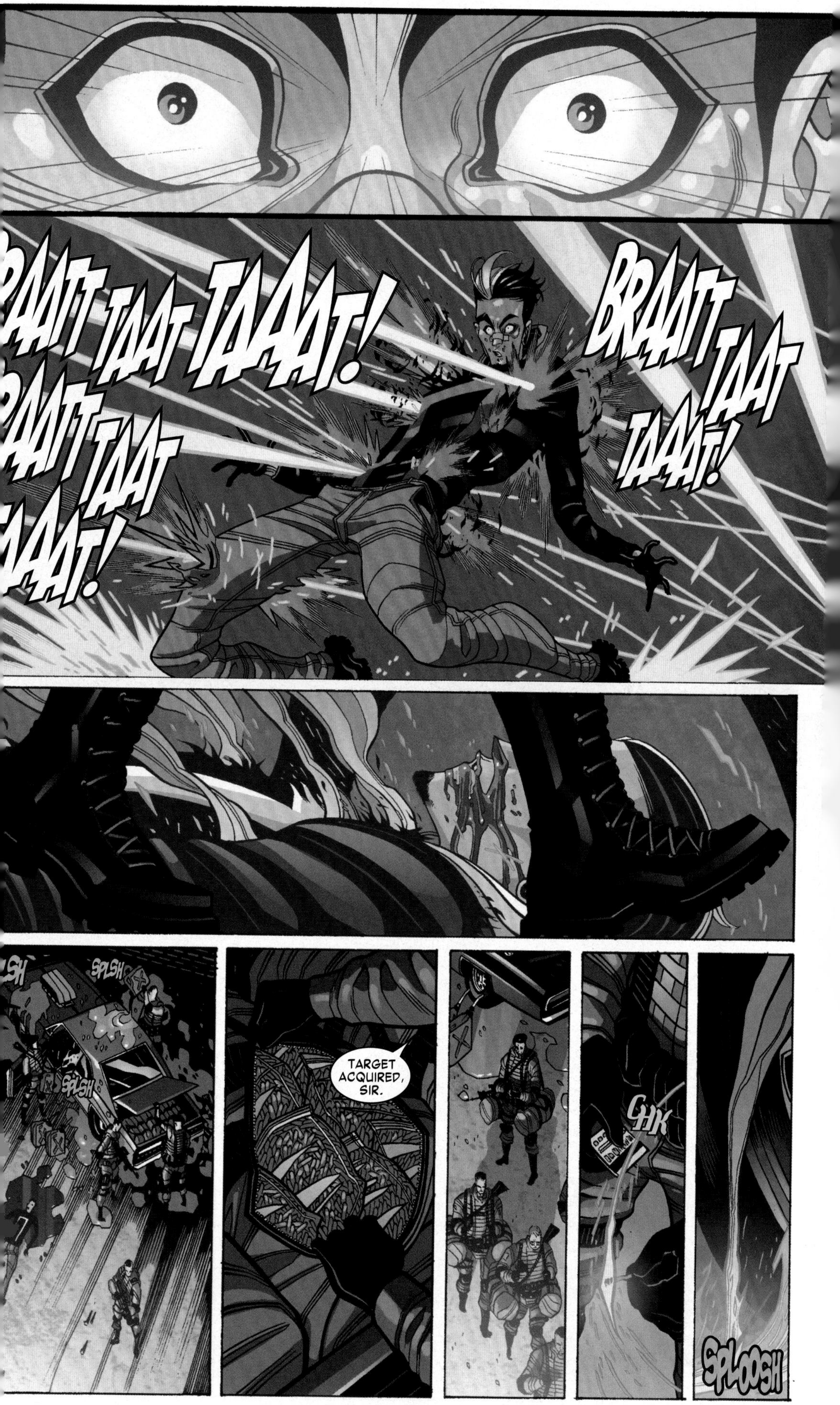
BRAATT TAAT TAAAAT!
BRAATT TAAT TAAAAT!
BRAATT TAAT TAAAT!
SPLSH
SPLSH
SPLSH
TARGET ACQUIRED, SIR.
CHK
SPLOOSH

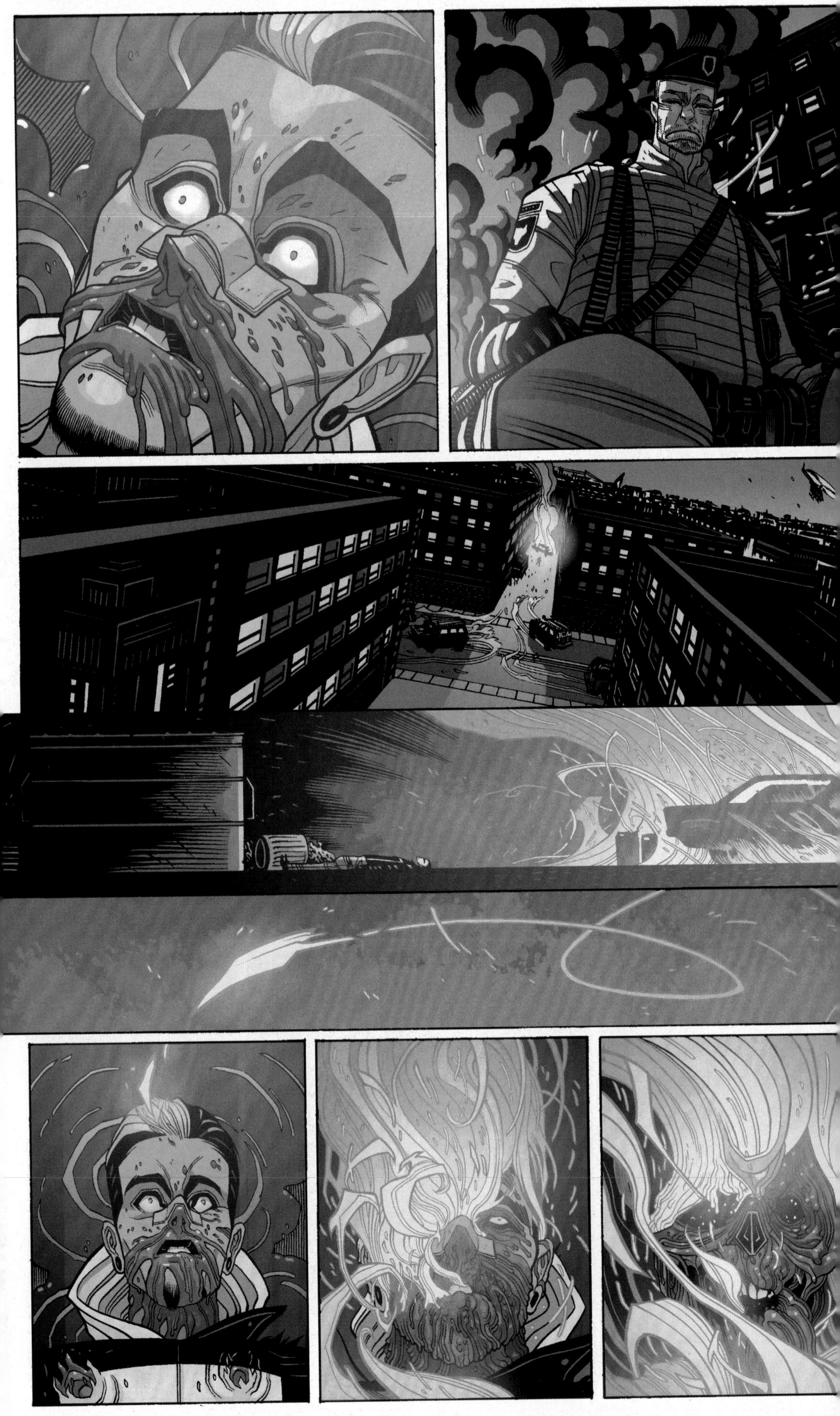

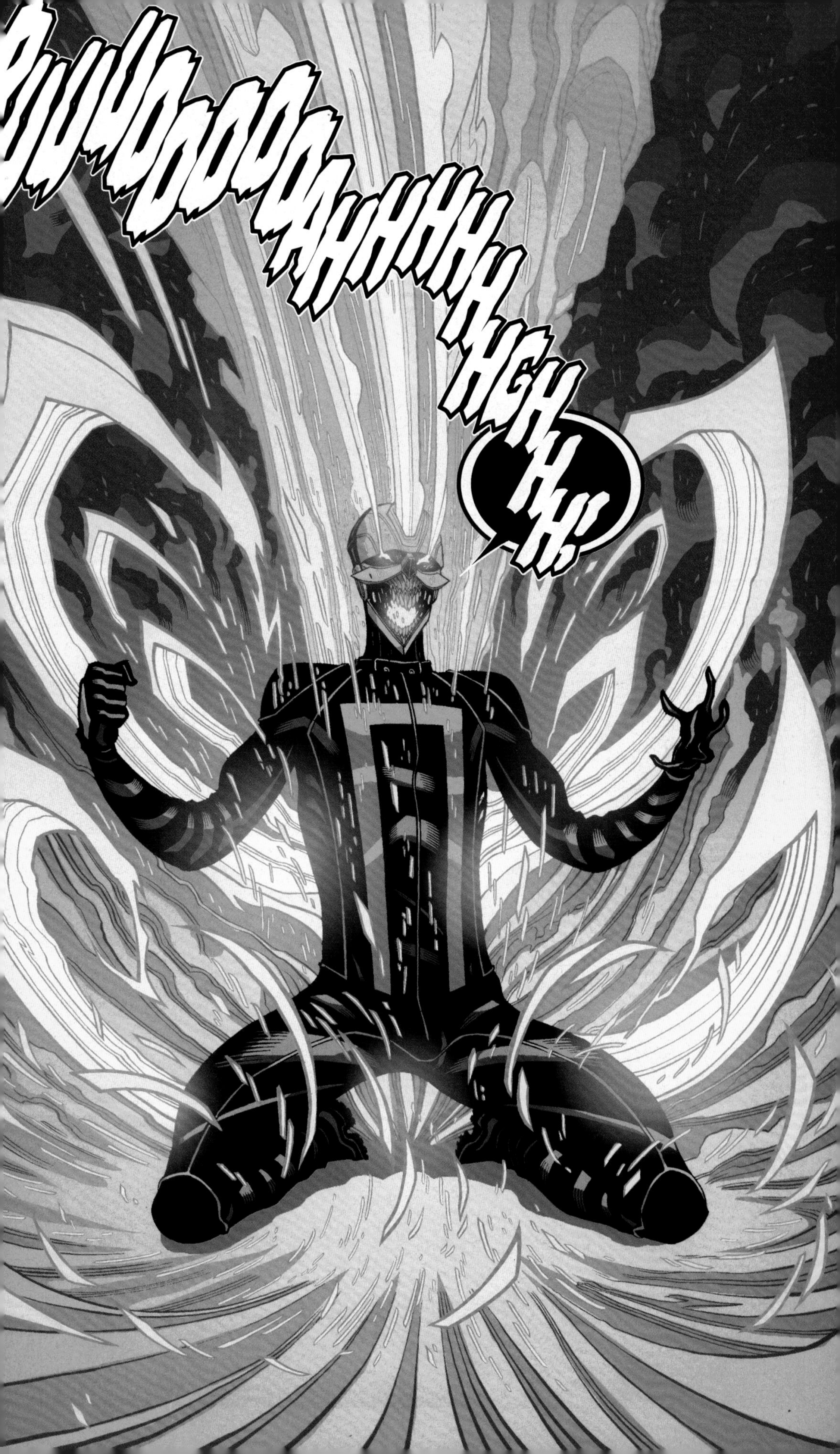

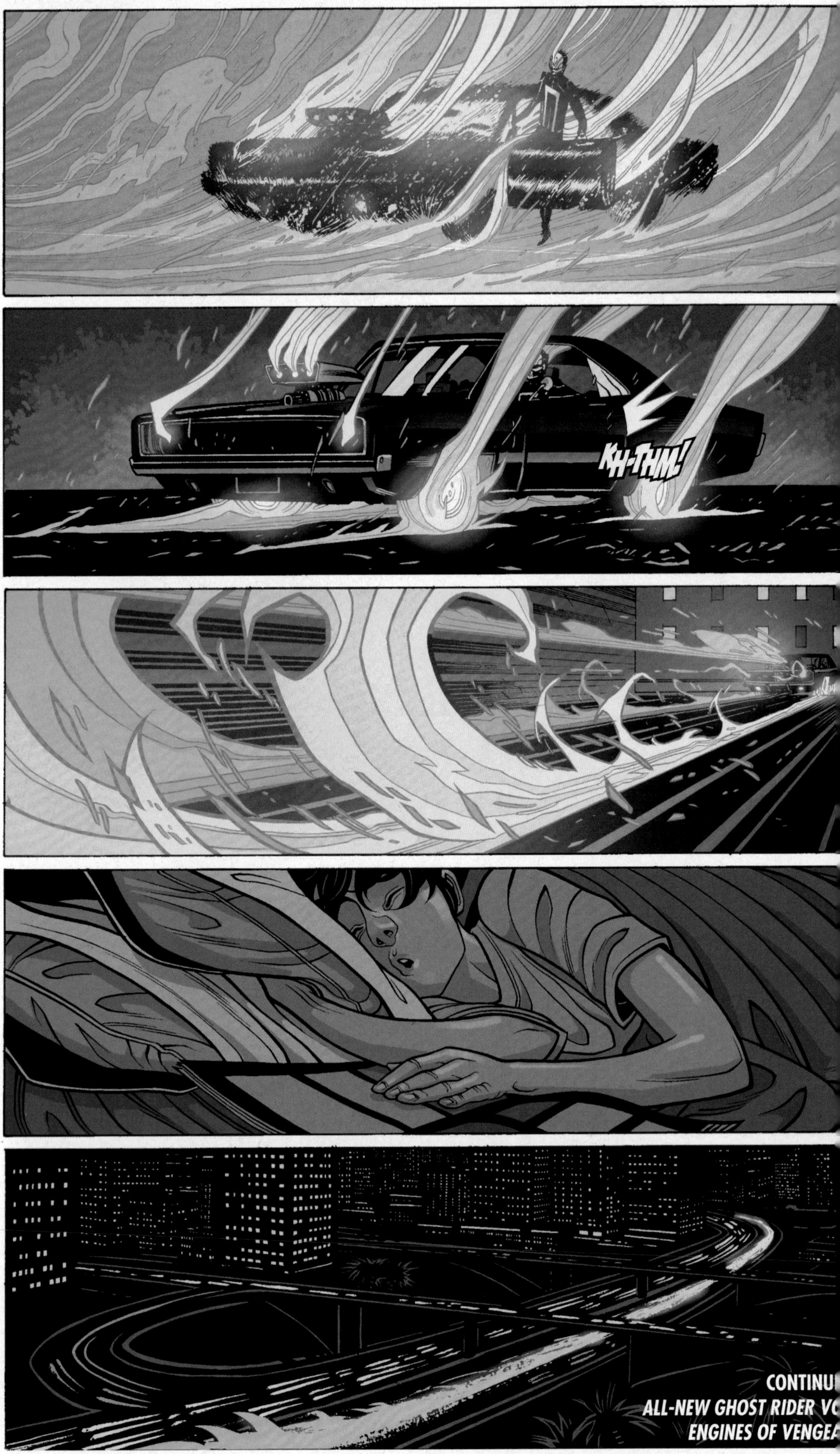
KH-THM!
CONTINU
ALL-NEW GHOST RIDER VO
ENGINES OF VENGEA

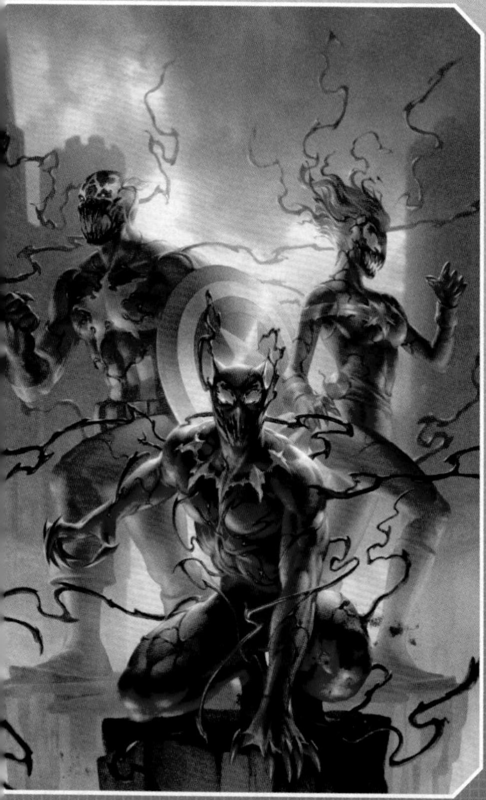

JUNGGEUN YOON
22 CARNAGE-IZED VARIANT

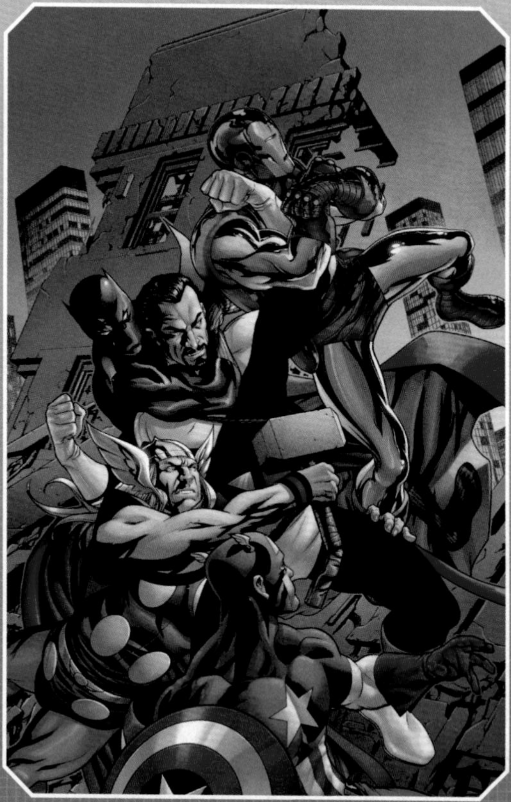

MIKE McKONE & RACHELLE ROSENBERG
23 VILLAIN VARIANT

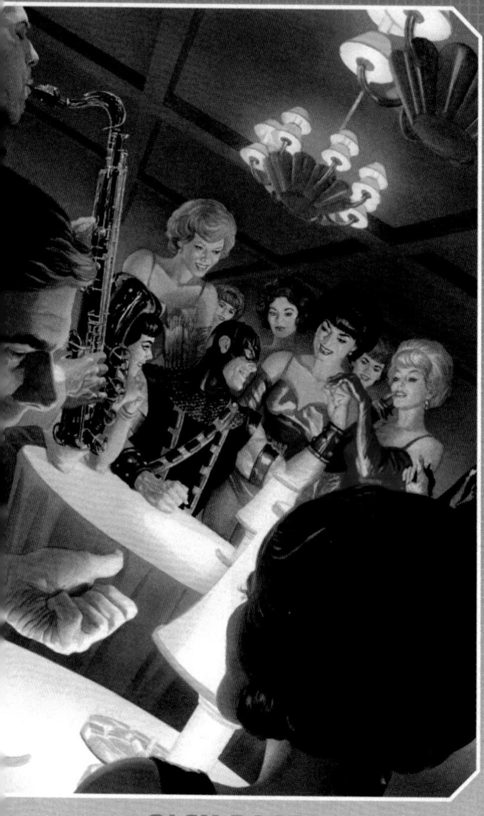

ALEX ROSS
23 MARVELS 25TH ANNIVERSARY VARIANT

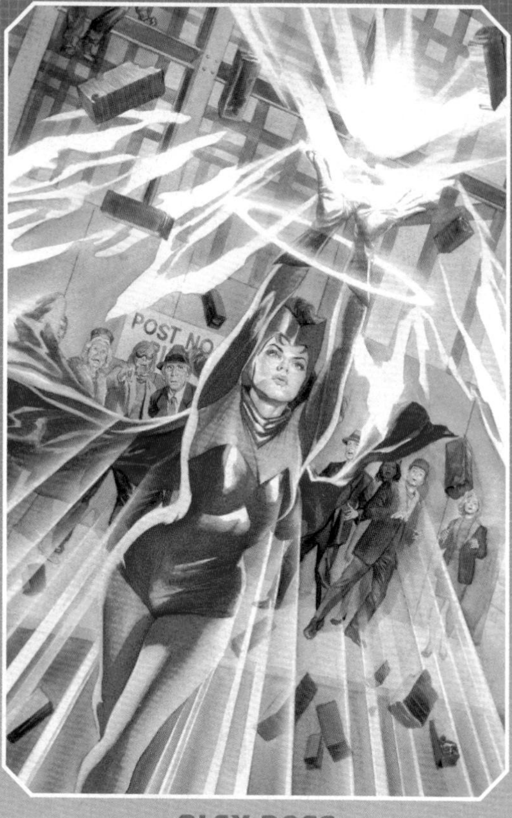
POST NO

ALEX ROSS
25 MARVELS 25TH ANNIVERSARY VARIANT

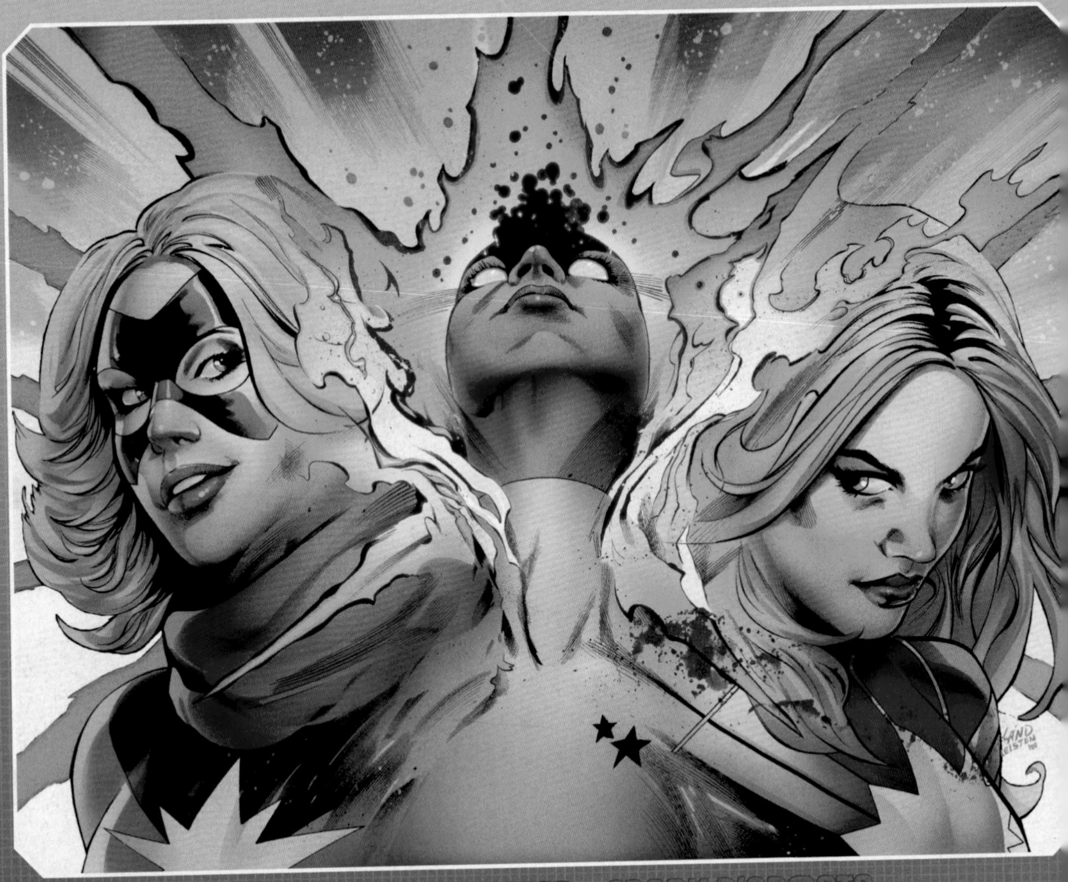

GREG LAND, JAY LEISTEN & FRANK D'ARMATA
24 IMMORTAL VARIANT

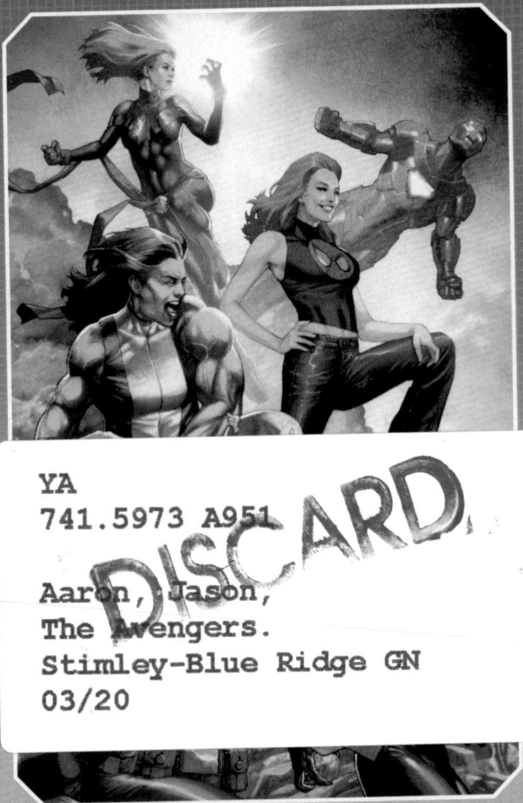

JAY ANACLETO & ROMULO FAJARDO JR.
25 MARY JANE VARIANT